W9-AAC-836

OCT - 2005

EXTRAORDINARY PEOPLE

IN

Jazz

marvin martin

Children's Press®
A Division of Scholastic Inc.
New York   Toronto   London   Auckland   Sydney
Mexico City   New Delhi   Hong Kong
Danbury, Connecticut

This book is dedicated to Duke, Satchmo, Count, Hawk, Pres, Klook, Monk, Diz, Bird, Miles, Trane, Cannonball, and all the rest who have contributed a century's worth of creative energy to jazz, the American art form.

Consultant: Lewis Porter, Professor of Music, Director, M.A. Program in Jazz History and Music, Rutgers University, Newark, NJ

Interior design by Elizabeth Helmetsie

Library of Congress Cataloging-in-Publication Data

Martin, Marvin.
  Extraordinary people in jazz / Marvin Martin.
        p. cm. — (extraordinary people)
Includes bibliographical references, discography, and index.
  ISBN 0–516–22275–9
Jazz musicians—Biography—Juvenile literature. [1. Jazz—Biography.] I. Title. II. Series.
    ML3929.M37 2003
    781.65'092'2—dc21

                                                                 2003007059

©2004 by Scholastic Inc.
All rights reserved. Published simultaneously in Canada.
Printed in the United States of America.

CHILDREN'S PRESS and associated logos are trademarks and or registered trademarks of Scholastic Library Publishing. SCHOLASTIC and associated logos are trademarks and or registered trademarks of Scholastic Inc.
1 2 3 4 5 6 7 8 9 10 R 13 12 11 10 09 08 07 06 05 04

Contents

68

Billie Holiday
1915–1959
Lady Day—Stands Alone
Among Jazz Singers

73

Charlie Christian
1916–1942
Established the Guitar
as a Solo Jazz Instrument

76

Nat King Cole
1917 or 1919–1965
Jazz Trio Leader
Became A Huge Pop Star

80

Ella Fitzgerald
1917 or 1918–1996
First Lady of Song

85

Dizzy Gillespie
1917–1993
Diz—Major Player in
the Bebop Revolution

90

Thelonius Monk
1917–1982
The High Priest
of Bebop

95

Art Blakey
1919–1990
Bu—Innovator
of Hard Bop

99

Anita O'Day
1919–
The Jezebel of Jazz

103

George Shearing
1919–
Pianist Leader Created
a New Jazz Sound

106

Marian McPartland
1920–
Queen of
the Keyboard

109

Charlie "Yardbird" Parker
1920–1955
Bird Lives

115

Billy Taylor
1921–
Ambassador of Jazz

119

Lambert, Hendricks, and Ross
1917–1966, 1921–, 1930–
Group That Popularized
"Vocalese" Singing Style

123

Charles Mingus
1922–1979
Bassist, Composer, Arranger,
and Jazz Innovator

127

Oscar Pettiford
1922–1960
Influential Bassist and
First Prominent Jazz Cellist

Preface

I love jazz and that's why I wrote this book. It was a love affair that started in high school with the big **swing** bands and just kept right on going. At Roosevelt University in Chicago I was a student at the same time as Joe Segal, who became one of Chicago's foremost jazz promoters. He used to gather local musicians to **jam** in one of the halls, charging twenty-five cents admission—the greatest bargain in music history. Through marriage and raising a family the sound of jazz was always there, thanks to the record industry. I started with 78-rpm records that played for three minutes, went on to 33 1/3-rpm **LP**s, then cassette tapes, and finally compact discs. Whatever else happened, jazz was always close by.

The **big bands** went out of style, except for a few: Duke Ellington and Count Basie were among those who managed to hang on. Small groups became more practical from the 1950s on. Bebop came in and spawned **hard bop** and **cool jazz** and **free jazz** and **fusion** and **avant-garde** and whatever else came along. I love it all, but some of the newer modes took a bit more understanding. Ellington, Armstrong, Basie—you didn't have to figure out anything, you just had to listen and tap your foot. Listening to a jazz musician create—quite literally compose—before your very eyes and ears remains one of the great pleasures of life.

So what is jazz anyway? Ask ten different experts and you will most likely get ten different answers. Jazz has been about everywhere and done about everything. It has been presented in symphonic form, as fugues and suites and concertos, it has been composed and played with great discipline, and it has been played free form in small or large groups who improvise simultaneously. In the latter case, some call it noise and some call it great music. Modern classical music sometimes gets the same response, so perhaps it is in the ear of the beholder. Some say jazz must improvise. But Ellington, George Gershwin, Stan Kenton, and many others have composed jazz that is played note for note by large orchestras. Some say jazz must swing. But much **modern jazz** has more to do with modern classical music than it does with a traditional swing band.

In the end jazz is a complex musical form that in its short history has evolved radically, gone off on tangents, and, as often as not, returned to its basic blues, swing, and bebop roots. Jazz is about individual expression as much as anything. Jazz musicians, whether playing someone else's work or improvising on the spot, put their own personal signature on their music, almost as if they were signing a work of art. Jazz grew out of the mixed cultural experience of the American deep South, and found its first expression in the music created by African Americans. It spread throughout the United States, evolved in form, and was exported to all parts of the world. The jazz heard today can show influences from Europe and Latin America, as well as from Japan and other Asian countries. Thus jazz takes many forms and presents itself in many ways. The one thing we know for sure is that the roots of this art form are purely African American.

People argue about jazz and they also argue about jazz musicians. Who is the greatest? It doesn't matter what instrument or composer you're talking about, jazz people will argue through eternity over who is the greatest in any category. That's what made it so difficult to decide on who should be included in the main text of this book. There is only so much space to fill and more great musicians than the space will hold. On certain names there is universal agreement: Ellington, Armstrong, Basie, Holiday, Gillespie, Parker, Davis, and Coltrane among them. For many others, hard decisions had to be made, and many of the great ones could not receive full treatment, although they were just as deserving as ones who did. For that reason, a section was added to the end of the book to provide at least brief mentions of some of them. A list of sources is provided for anyone seeking more information about jazz musicians.

A word about the organization of this book. The main group of jazz profiles are listed chronologically according to birthdate, roughly grouped from the earliest eras to the latest, providing a sense of unfolding jazz history.

Some attempt is made in this book to describe the music played by the musicians in their profiles. This can't really be done with words. There is only one way, and that is to listen. Listen to the beat, the rhythm, and the melody, and enjoy America's music. Jazz lives!

Acknowledgments

A few persons and places deserve special thanks: first, the Chicago Public Library for having an expansive collection of jazz books I could tap, to say nothing of its CD and video tape department, which allowed me to examine my subjects firsthand; the Lincoln Park branch was especially helpful. Then there was my Cincinnati connection, Jerry Schwartz, who made that city's public library jazz tape collection available to me. I would thank my daughter, Jessica, for her patient long-distance assistance in guiding me through one computer glitch after another, and my son, Josh, for putting his more contemporary jazz record collection at my disposal. Help also came from Todd Herbert, New York City tenor saxophone player, who helped me to understand the nuances of the modal scales. And I should express special appreciation to old friend Dick Dell, with whom I have spent decades discussing and listening to jazz. Materials loaned to me by Fred Gorr were useful as well. The Internet proved a handy tool, providing backgound information for each artist and, in some cases, audio samples of their work. Last, I need to express my gratitude to Anne O'Connor, whose support is forever there.

Duke Ellington

Beyond Category
1899–1974

*America's most important composer . . .
the greatest this American society has
produced . . . master musician, master
psychologist, master choreographer.*

—Ralph J. Gleason, jazz critic and historian,
New York Times, May 25, 1974

The highest praise that composer/orchestra leader Duke Ellington could bestow on anyone was to declare that person "beyond category." That phrase, however, perhaps best describes his own talent and contributions to music. Indeed, while the Duke is generally regarded historically as one of the greatest influences in the realm of jazz, he never liked to call the music he created "jazz."

Ellington did not differentiate between kinds of music. "There are just two kinds of music," he often said, "good and bad."

Ellington's work spanned virtually the entire musical spectrum, from popular hit songs, such as "Do Nothin' Till You Hear From Me," "Satin Doll," and "Don't Get Around Much Anymore," to lengthy pieces incorporating both jazz and classical elements such as "Black, Brown and Beige." Ellington was himself a masterful pianist as well as a composer, but as his co-composer, co-arranger, and dear friend Billy Strayhorn would say; "his real instrument is the orchestra."

Edward Kennedy Ellington was born on April 29, 1899, in Washington, D.C. Growing up, he earned the nickname "Duke" in recognition of his classy wardrobe, his refined speech, and his regal bearing—attributes that he carried throughout his life. When he was about seven his mother started his piano lessons. His talent was immediately apparent, but like a typical boy, he yearned for more physically demanding endeavors. His love of baseball led him to his first job, selling peanuts at Washington Senators baseball games.

The **ragtime** pianists of the day first caught the young Ellington's attention, and he began playing local **gigs**, imitating his ragtime idols. Later, from listening to such masters as Fats Waller and James P. Johnson, he would develop the "stride" jazz piano technique popular in Harlem. By the time he was seventeen, while working at an ice cream counter, he had composed his first song, "Soda Fountain Rag." From that modest beginning, Duke Ellington in his lifetime would compose or co-compose more than 1,500 musical pieces.

In 1918 the Duke married Edna Thompson and they had one son, Mercer, who in 1965 joined his father's band as trumpeter and manager. The couple divorced in 1930.

It was not long after his marriage to Edna that the lure of New York City beckoned the Duke. With him went his drummer Sonny Greer, who had joined Ellington in 1919 and would stay until 1950. It began a pattern of highly talented sidemen who would remain with the Duke for extended periods, some for virtually their entire careers. Thus he built an orchestra for which he could create compositions based on the talent of his instrumentalists.

The going was tough at first in New York, but Ellington was encouraged by Fats Waller, and in 1923 the Washingtonians with Ellington were hired by the Hollywood Club (later the Kentucky Club), where they performed for over four years. During that period Ellington began his recording career with his composition "Choo Choo," featuring the hot, growling trumpet of Bubber Miley. That sound would become an Ellington signature.

Ellington thrived at the Kentucky Club, but in 1927 the band had its big break: the Duke was hired to replace King Oliver at the famed Cotton Club. Once the Duke's ten-piece group took the bandstand, it remained for the next four years. The Cotton Club was the top Harlem nightclub in New York, presenting flashy, colorful floor shows backed by the best jazz bands. While all the performers were black, the patronage of the expensive club was almost entirely white, often members of New York's high society.

The Cotton Club gig also included nightly national radio broadcasts, which helped spread the Ellington sound coast to coast. The Duke called his orchestral style African music or jungle music, and musicians of all types came to listen and study his techniques. His band grew to twelve pieces at the Cotton Club and some of the virtuoso musicians closely identified with Ellington came aboard in the late 1920s, including alto saxophonist Johnny Hodges, trumpeter Cootie Williams, clarinetist Barney Bigard, and baritone saxophonist Harry Carney, who joined, among others, trombonist "Tricky Sam" Nanton.

Ellington's recording output also increased as a result of his Cotton Club fame. He recorded "East St. Louis Toodle-oo," "Black and Tan Fantasy," and "Creole Love Call," representing his distinctive style, which was further developed in "The Mooche," "Ring Dem Bells," "Mood Indigo," and "Rockin' in Rhythm." Adding to the Duke's credits was his first movie appearance in 1929, beginning a long association with film that included composing the score for Otto Preminger's classic, *Anatomy of a Murder* (1959).

The band stayed at the Cotton Club until the early 1930s. By then Ellington's reputation was established, and his troupe began playing one-nighters across the country. In 1933 he embarked on a European tour, the first of many overseas trips. In Europe Ellington received high critical acclaim, one London critic comparing his music to that of the respected British composer, Frederick Delius.

Back in the United States the swing movement was building steam, and by the mid-1930s the big name swing bands were taking over the musical firmament. The Duke blended into the new craze, writing and playing ballads and swing dance numbers. It was during this period that he wrote some his most enduring compositions, such as "Sophisticated Lady," "I Let a Song Go Out of My Heart," and the haunting "Caravan." It was also a time when he began to compose longer pieces including *Reminiscing in Tempo* and *Diminuendo and Crescendo in Blue.*

Ellington continued to build the personnel of his orchestra, and between the time he left the Cotton Club and 1940 he added such sidemen as cornetist Rex Stewart, trombonist Lawrence Brown, bassist Jimmy Blanton, and tenor saxophonist Ben Webster. Among the vocalists who would sing with the band were Ivie Anderson, Kay Davis, Herb Jeffries, and Al Hibbler. He was also joined in 1939 by Billy Strayhorn, who became an integral part of the orchestra as Duke's co-composer and co-arranger. It was Strayhorn who composed the Duke's theme song, "Take the 'A' Train."

Ellington led perhaps his most talented ensemble during the 1940s, resulting in an outpouring of musical work. He continued his more serious compositions, which included, in 1941, his musical play *Jump for Joy,* and, in 1943, *Black, Brown and Beige,* a "suite" of related pieces, presented at Carnegie

Hall. He now appeared regularly in concert as well as in clubs. Carnegie Hall became a regular venue for presentation of his works, including *New World a-Comin'*, *The Deep South Suite*, *Blutopia*, and *The Perfume Suite*. In 1947 the African country of Liberia commissioned Ellington to write *The Liberian Suite*.

The early 1950s represented a change in musical styles that spelled the end of the big band era. Ellington managed to hold on as bebop, **rhythm and blues**, rock and roll, and small groups (combos) took over the music scene. Some of the Duke's old guard musicians departed, but the ensemble was replenished by fresh talent, including colorful trumpeter Clark Terry, tenor saxophonist Paul Gonsalves, and drummer Sam Woodyard.

Ellington's fortunes sagged somewhat until 1956 when he played a gig at the country's most prestigious outdoor jazz venue, the Newport Jazz Festival. The band's performance there, recorded live, is legendary. Highlighting the show was an electrifying twenty-seven-chorus solo by Paul Gonsalves that set the audience shouting, stomping, and dancing in the aisles.

The Newport performance propelled Ellington into another era of vigorous accomplishment. In 1957 his musical history of jazz, *A Drum Is a Woman*, was presented as a CBS television special. That same year produced *Such Sweet Thunder*, a musical suite commissioned by the Shakespeare Festival in Stratford, Ontario, and in 1960 the Monterey Jazz Festival commissioned *Suite Thursday*, inspired by the similarly titled John Steinbeck novel. The U.S. State Department sponsored Ellington's overseas tours, one of which, in 1963, inspired a collaborative work with Billy Strayhorn, *The Far East Suite*.

Ellington continued his experimentation with classical forms, recording jazz versions of Tchaikovsky's *The Nutcracker* and Greig's *Peer Gynt*, and in 1963 he presented another tribute to his African American heritage, *My People*. His ballet work, *The River*, produced for the Alvin Ailey company and the American Ballet Theater, appeared in 1970. In 1965 he began his foray into religious music, completing the *Concert of Sacred Music*, which Ellington regarded as his most important work to date. Two more Sacred Concerts followed.

The death of Billy Strayhorn in 1967 was a severe blow to Ellington. Strayhorn had become a virtual extension of Ellington himself, and the Duke grieved at length over his loss. Helping Ellington to rebound in 1969 was a commission from the African country of Togo, resulting in the *Togo Brava Suite.* That same year he was honored on his seventieth birthday by a concert and ceremony at the White House, during which President Richard M. Nixon presented him with the Presidential Medal of Freedom. The music by an all-star group was recorded live, but was not released until 2002.

Ellington kept working to within two months of the end of his life, despite a long struggle with lung cancer. Before his death he managed to complete an autobiographical memoir, aptly called *Music Is My Mistress.* His "mistress," he often said, "plays second fiddle to no one." When he died, on May 24, 1974, he left behind an unfinished opera, *Queenie Pie.*

Some of the more notable honors bestowed on Duke Ellington during his lifetime include, in addition to the Medal of Freedom, the Legion of Honor (France), President's Gold Medal (President Lyndon Johnson), and the Springarn Medal (NAACP). Honorary doctorates in music were awarded by Yale University, Brown University, the University of Wisconsin, and others. He held memberships in such institutions as the Royal Swedish Academy of Music and the American Academy of Arts and Sciences.

When the Pulitzer Prize advisory board rejected Ellington, then sixty-six, for a special prize in 1965 he only commented, "Fate doesn't want me to be famous too young." There was much criticism over that decision, and the award was bestowed posthumously in 1999, at the centennial of his birth.

The Duke had a signature ending to almost all of his performances. He would look reverently into the totally charmed audience and say in his most mellow tone, "And we love you madly." Somehow, you knew he meant it.

Louis Armstrong

Satchmo—A Founding Father of Jazz
1901–1971

What he did, what he played, came from within, and from his mind. . . . It was Louis, what he was, the essence of his being.

—Bassist Arvell Shaw,
in the Ken Burns TV special *Jazz*

So hallowed is Louis Armstrong in the literature of jazz that he would seem to be the very rock upon which the temple of jazz is built. His full-page obituary in the *New York Times,* July 7, 1971, stated, "It was he, more than any other individual, who built Jazz into a unique art form." As a trumpet virtuoso, he was virtually without peer in his prime. Modern trumpeter

Miles Davis has said that no horn player has blown anything that Louis hadn't already played.

Rising from the slum, honky-tonk-filled Storyville district of New Orleans, Louis Armstrong not only led the jazz movement with his brilliant, piercing trumpet solos, but did much the same for jazz singing. Jazz vocalists from Bessie Smith to Billie Holiday to Ella Fitzgerald all paid homage to Louis's singing. This is all the more amazing when one considers that his voice had a raspy, guttural, sandpaper quality. But this only added charm to his skill at delivering a lyric. One of the great pop singers, Bing Crosby, whose early background was jazz, called Armstrong the beginning and end of American music.

In addition to his other talents, Armstrong was a pure entertainer. He loved to please his audience, clowning and displaying his wide-mouth, toothy grin and occasionally singing pop and show tunes. As a result, Armstrong developed a far broader audience than most purist jazz stars. He was sometimes criticized for this. But Louis stated that he didn't need to heed detractors who couldn't tell one note from another telling him how to blow his horn.

Louis Daniel Armstrong was born on August 4, 1901 (earlier sources say July 4, 1900), in New Orleans, Louisiana, in the toughest part of the city. In New Orleans music was everywhere—Negro spirituals and **blues**, dance music, funeral marching bands, classical music, and Creole rhythms, all of which Louis absorbed. He began doing odd jobs at an early age to help support his family, including his mother Mary Ann (called Mayann), the granddaughter of slaves. His father left home when Louis was an infant. During his early boyhood Louis was "adopted" by a Jewish family, the Karnofskys, who put him to work on their junk wagon. The first money he earned in music, however, was from singing in the streets.

A turning point in his life came when he was twelve. On New Year's Eve 1912, Louis was street singing and celebrating. At midnight, all sorts of fireworks went off, and the impulsive Louis, wanting to join the fun, pulled out a blank-loaded pistol belonging to one of his mother's boyfriends and fired shots into the air. That was exciting for Louis but not for the police, who quickly arrested the youth and sent him off to the Colored Waif's Home for Boys.

Years later he reflected that this was the best thing that could have happened to him. It was at the home that Louis bonded with music. Louis soon joined the chorus and band, where he learned bugle and then cornet. When he left the home after eighteen months, he knew that music would be his life.

During his early teen years Louis played whenever he could. A big break came when he was taken under the wing of Joe "King" Oliver, then the featured trumpet with Kid Ory's band. Oliver tutored Louis, and when Oliver decided in 1918 to head for the flourishing Chicago music scene, Louis replaced him in Kid Ory's band. Louis now made a living blowing hot cornet in New Orleans dives, and soon he joined up with Fate Marable and his Jazz Syncopaters, playing aboard Mississippi River steamboats.

It was not long before places like Kansas City, Missouri, and Chicago began clamoring for top jazz talent. King Oliver, in Chicago, remembered his young protégé and tried to convince him that great opportunity awaited him in the big city. Louis was reluctant. He enjoyed the riverboat scene and he was playing with great musicians, such as Warren "Baby" Dodds and Jack Teagarden. He had also married for the first of several times. But the lure of Chicago was tough to resist, and in 1922 Louis packed his cornet and left New Orleans to join Oliver's Creole Jazz Band.

Armstrong was an immediate sensation in prohibition era (when liquor sales were illegal) Chicago. The period called the jazz age, was noted in cities for its speakeasies (illegal clubs), "bathtub" (homemade) gin, bootlegging (illegal liquor sales), and short-skirted, Charleston-crazed flappers (young women devotees of the Charlston dance craze). Oliver and Armstrong shared the stage and the spotlight, playing cornet duets and crowd-pleasing solos. Amstrong **cut** his first records with Oliver in 1923. Before long Armstrong, with his power and speed, his popular vocals, and his magnetic stage presence, was ready to move up. Spurring him on was the band's pianist, Lil Hardin, who became the second Mrs. Armstrong in 1924.

Armstrong had no patience with the business side of music, and he welcomed the management of his educated wife. She urged him to leave Oliver, who she insisted did not allow Armstrong to fully display his skills. When an invitation came to join the Fletcher Henderson orchestra in New York, they accepted. Henderson already had a national jazz reputation.

The dignified, college-educated Henderson and earthy Armstrong were a contrast in styles. Henderson was smooth and sophisticated, and Armstrong loved to clown. Henderson's orchestra was disciplined and played from written **charts**, whereas Armstrong had formerly played mostly by ear. But the young cornetist's talent overcame all. Working in a large group restricted his playing, but Armstrong recorded with other artists, and on those recordings Armstrong blazed through the full range of his instrument.

In November 1925 Lil persuaded Armstrong to return to Chicago and join her in a band at the Dreamland Ballroom. He was also featured in a theater orchestra, and it was during that stint that he switched from cornet to trumpet. Armstrong was soon being billed as the "World's Greatest Trumpet Player," and his ability to play in high registers and to hit sky-scrapping notes became legendary.

During this second Chicago stay Armstrong formed the Hot Five and the Hot Seven, exclusively for recordings during 1926–1928. They cut such Armstrong **classics** as "Cornet Chop Suey," "Potato Head Blues," and "West End Blues." The last of these, distinguished by Armstrong's brilliant opening cadenza, is sometimes considered his masterpiece and a turning point in jazz history. During one recording session, he is said to have dropped the lyric sheet just as he stood to sing. Whether or not he dropped it, he replaced the lyrics with nonword vocal sounds that some consider the beginning of **scat** singing.

Armstrong was back in New York in 1929, playing clubs and also appearing in a Broadway revue, *Hot Chocolates,* in which he performed Fats Waller's "Ain't Misbehavin'," Louis's first really big hit song. In the early 1930s he fronted a number of big bands and traveled extensively, including a triumphant return to New Orleans. In 1932 Lil and Louis were separated. That year, feeling the pressures of both work and domestic problems, Armstrong took off for Europe. During his Palladium appearance in London, one critic referred to him as "Satchmo," a corruption of his nickname "Satchelmouth," and the new nickname stuck. (He was also called "Pops.") At one point a contingent of skeptical British musicians examined his horn, believing it had been rigged to allow him to play with such power and technique.

Armstrong returned for a much longer European tour from 1933–1935, accompanied by a new girlfriend, Alpha Smith, who was his companion for more than ten years and his wife for one. His travels ranged from Italy to Scandinavia, bringing acclaim everywhere he played.

Despite his popularity, Armstrong was in rough financial straits, and when he returned to the United States, he enlisted an old friend, Joe Glaser, as his manager. His finances improved thereafter, especially when he broke attendance records at the Apollo Theater in New York and signed a new recording contract with Decca. Hosting a summer network radio program in 1936 and appearing in numerous high-end supper clubs through the late 1930s, he helped break the barrier for booking black entertainers. He also made the first of several Carnegie Hall appearances and began a movie career, which eventually would include *Pennies from Heaven, The Glen Miller Story,* and *High Society.*

In 1942 Armstrong married for the fourth time. His new wife, former showgirl Lucille (Brown Sugar) Wilson, would remain with him for the rest of his days. By the late 1940s, the big band craze was diminishing and a new interest in modern, **progressive jazz** was growing. But Armstrong frowned on modern jazz, and he formed Louis Armstrong and his All Stars, playing an updated New Orleans style jazz. All Stars was a fitting name, for the group included such artists as clarinetist Barney Bigard, trombonist Jack Teagarden, drummer Big Sid Catlett, and pianist Earl "Fatha" Hines. Armstrong and Velma Middleton shared the vocals.

The All Stars toured Europe and were invited to the first international jazz festival in Nice, France, in 1948. Through the 1950s and 1960s Armstrong toured the Far and Middle East, Latin America, Africa, and Eastern Europe. These trips were sometimes sponsored by the U.S. government, which recognized the goodwill value of the genial entertainer. His 1960 trip to the Congo occurred when that country was fighting a civil war, but a truce was declared for the performance, and Armstrong was carried into the stadium on a makeshift throne.

Armstrong enjoyed his State Department junkets, but in 1957 he spurned a trip to the Soviet Union. It was his reaction to the school integration riots in Little Rock, Arkansas. The sight of little black children being turned away from schools and taunted and attacked by hostile crowds so enraged him that he told reporters that President Dwight David Eisenhower should himself lead the "colored" children into the school. His comment led to many club cancellations.

Armstrong regained his popularity, and in 1960 he appeared in another movie, *Paris Blues,* along with Duke Ellington. He continued to make solo hit records in the 1950s and 1960s, including "Mack the Knife" and "La Vie En Rose," as well as albums with such stars as Ella Fitzgerald, Duke Ellington, and Oscar Peterson. In 1964 he recorded what would be his biggest hit ever,

"Hello Dolly," replacing the Beatles as number one on the charts. He also appeared in the *Hello Dolly* movie. In 1968 he recorded another smash hit, "What a Wonderful World," which became an especially popular classic.

Armstrong did not back away from the rigors of constant travel, minimal sleep, record and movie gigs, and personal appearances. In the late 1960s, although his body weakened, he kept to his grinding schedule. By 1970 he had been to the hospital several times, but kept pushing despite doctors' orders to slow down. He had already given up the trumpet but kept on singing. In March 1971, after an engagement at the Waldorf-Astoria hotel in New York City, he collapsed from a heart attack. After two months in the hospital he returned home, but on July 6, 1971, he died in his sleep. The world mourned his loss, but his spirit remains wherever jazz is being played.

Count Basie

Big Band Leader Noted for His Hard-Swinging Ensembles
1904–1984

Every day I have the blues.

—From the Count Basie and Joe Williams
hit record "Every Day"

It has been said that Count Basie could hit one note on a piano and make it swing. Swing, especially swinging the blues, is the very essence of Count Basie. Basie's band, during its heyday from the late 1930s through the 1940s was often regarded as the country's hardest swinging **big band**. That swinging tradition carried into the 1950s and beyond, lasting to the Count's final days. Even after his death in 1984 the Basie band carried the Count's heritage, under prominent leaders, into the twenty-first century.

What distinguished Basie's music, in addition to his outstanding sidemen and vocalists, was his emphasis on rhythm. In Gary Giddin's *Visions of Jazz* Basie states, "I've always built my band from the rhythm section . . . the living pulse of a band is . . . the rhythm section, a power unit that drives and motivates the entire outfit." The rhythm section that drove the Basie band to national fame, starting in the 1930s, included the Count (piano), Jo Jones (drums), Walter Page (bass), and Freddie Green (guitar).

Other notable band members included at various times, Lester Young (tenor saxophone); Buck Clayton and Clark Terry (trumpets); Dickie Wells and J. J. Johnson (trombones); and Buddy DeFranco (clarinet). Billie Holiday, Helen Humes, Joe Williams, and Jimmy Rushing were among the band's featured singers, and Basie collaborated with an array of other acclaimed singers, including Frank Sinatra, Tony Bennett, and Sammy Davis Jr.

William Basie was born on August 21, 1904, in Red Bank, New Jersey. In music he at first took up drumming but became discouraged. His mother taught him piano, and he was soon influenced by Harlem's stride style pianists, including Fats Waller. He became friends with Waller, who also taught him to play organ. Waller used his influence to land Basie an accompanist job.

Before long he joined the band of a vaudeville touring show called the Gonzel White Big Jazz Jamboree. That unit ran into tough times, and in 1927 the show finally closed. Basie found himself stranded in Kansas City, Missouri, where he encountered Walter Page and the Blue Devils. He had heard that group play jazz in Tulsa, and it was a revelation. "Hearing them that day was probably the most important turning point in my musical career so far as my notions about what kind of music I really wanted to play was concerned," Basie said in his autobiography, *Good Morning Blues*.

After about a year in Kansas City, Walter Page invited Basie to join the Blue Devils, which included such future stars as Oran "Hot Lips" Page and Jimmy Rushing. It was also about that time that Basie began to call himself "Count."

Others were called "King" (Oliver) and "Duke" (Ellington), so Basie decided he would be "Count." Basie toured with the Blue Devils until the band broke up in 1929. He was out of a job, but at least in Kansas City, where jazz thrived.

To make ends meet he took a job in a theater, playing organ to accompany silent movies (common in the 1920s). There were plenty of good bands around, like Andy Kirk and his Twelve Clouds of Joy, although the hottest band on the scene was the Bennie Moten orchestra. Basie was eager to join Moten, but unfortunately there was an obstacle: Moten himself was the group's piano player.

Undaunted, he caught on as Moten's arranger, and sat in occasionally for the leader. Before long he became a permanent band member, traveling extensively with the group and participating in radio broadcasts and recording dates. Basie cowrote one of the band's most popular pieces, the classic "Moten Swing."

After Moten's death in 1935 the band split, and Basie formed his own group that included some Moten personnel. This unit formed the nucleus of what became one of the world's most famous swing bands. Basie landed a long residency at the Reno Club in Kansas City, and the band's reputation grew, partly through regular radio broadcasts. During one broadcast the announcer asked Basie what he was going to play next. The Count had no title ready, so he glanced at the clock, and replied "One O'Clock Jump." His melody became one of the Basie band's signature pieces. Lester Young joined the band in Kansas City, as did Jo Jones. After Jones came aboard, Basie said in his autobiography, "That's when the band really started swinging."

One of the people who heard Basie on the radio was John Hammond, a noted jazz band promoter, who helped the Count secure a gig at the Grand Terrace Ballroom in Chicago. Basie saw ahead the potential of playing the big eastern cities, but he was advised to increase his band from nine to thirteen players. He emphasized, however, that he wanted his larger group to play with the same tight ensemble playing as the smaller band. Going into Chicago, Basie's band played mostly by ear, but with the expanded group written arrangements were needed. Basie was rescued by the prominent arranger Fletcher Henderson, who was in Chicago and loaned Basie some of his charts. They helped establish the Basie big band style.

Despite outstanding personnel, a short stint by Billie Holiday, and Hammond's efforts, that first year on the road (1936–37) was tough. Nevertheless, Basie cut his first records as a leader for Decca and debuted at the Roseland Ballroom in New York City. About a year later the band was booked into the Famous Door on Fifty-second Street (New York City's concentrated block of jazz clubs) and drew rave reviews. The Famous Door was an unlikely place for a big band. It was a long and narrow room that booked mostly small units. The Basie band nearly blew the walls down, but jazz fans loved it and flocked there in droves.

Basie had several long engagements at the Door, cutting some of his most famous swing numbers while there, including "Jumpin' at the Woodside." Basie also played some gigs at Carnegie Hall during those years (about 1938 to 1941), including one as a guest of Benny Goodman at his famous 1938 Carnegie Hall Jazz Concert. The band traveled coast to coast doing one-nighter tours, and by the early 1940s the Basie orchestra, now usually at sixteen pieces, was among the country's top swing bands.

The Count's popularity continued during the World War II years, but by the end of the 1940s the big band craze was waning, and in 1950 he had to disassemble his big band. Undiscouraged, Basie reformed in 1950–51 as a small unit that changed in size according to the gig. He formed a new big band in 1952, and despite the small group trend, it clicked with the public. A long association with the famed Birdland jazz club ensued. Basie now put emphasis on ensemble playing with charts by such outstanding arrangers as Neal Hefti. He de-empasized solos by big name sidemen, but included some stars nonetheless, including Eddie "Lock Jaw" Davis (tenor sax), Thad Jones (trumpet), and blues singer Joe Williams.

One recording that helped bring the band back was a hard swinging 1955 version of "April in Paris." It featured a shattering finishing crescendo, which was repeated twice more on Basie's now famous cues "one more time" and "one more once." Joe Williams also contributed with the best-selling "Every Day I Have the Blues." The bluesy-voiced Williams sings it like a call to prayer to the faithful. Another Basie-Williams hit was "Alright, Okay, You Win."

The band toured Europe in 1954 and again in 1957. During the second tour the Basie band became the first jazz group to play a command perform-ance for the British queen. The band's popularity continued with some hit arrangements by Quincy Jones, and through appearances and recordings with Frank Sinatra in the mid-1960s. Also, Basie's alliance with jazz entrepreneur Norman Granz produced acclaimed small group recordings with all-star players, among them Oscar Peterson.

The Count suffered a heart attack in 1976 and recuperated over the next six months. In the interim, guest conductors replaced Basie. In 1981 Basie was honored with other stars at the Kennedy Center in Washington, D.C., for achievement in the performing arts. A year later the Black Music Association honored the seventy-seven-year old bandleader at a lavish Radio City Music Hall ceremony. By this time Basie had severe arthritis, but he rarely missed a performance, often arriving on a motor scooter that took him to the piano. Despite his determination Basie had to withdraw when he was overcome with cancer. He died on April 26, 1984.

Few leaders were so respected by his band members as Basie. He directed from the piano, and no matter how hard the band was swinging he remained calm and expressionless, directing with a glance, a note, a nod, but getting maximum response from his musicians. Once when asked to explain his music, Basie replied simply, "Tap your foot." And that said it all.

Coleman Hawkins

Hawk—Father of the Tenor Saxophone
1904–1969

Hawkins was the first important jazz tenor saxophone soloist and the most influential figure in the evolution of the instrument.

—Leonard Feather and Ira Gitler, *The Biographical Encyclopedia of Jazz*

In modern music, when an artist renders the ultimate performance of a given piece, he or she is often considered to "own" that composition. In jazz few would disagree that Coleman Hawkins owns "Body and Soul," due to his classic 1939 recording. That rendition launched a whole new concept of the way the tenor saxophone could be played. Virtually every virtuoso of that instrument has acknowledged a debt to Hawkins, among them such masters as Ben Webster and John Coltrane. Other instrumentalists, such as modernists Thelonious Monk (piano) and Miles Davis (trumpet) also recognized the influence of Hawk, as he was called.

Born November 21, 1904, in St. Joseph, Missouri, Coleman Randolph Hawkins grew up an only child in this Missouri River town. His early musical training on the piano was through his mother, who played both organ and piano. He switched to cello at age seven, but somehow became fascinated with the saxophone, then a relatively new instrument in popular music. By age nine he owned his first sax.

Coleman heard the sounds of early jazz, blues, and spirituals that blew up from New Orleans. Although trained in classical music, he was intrigued by the new music. Much of it was being played in another nearby river town, Kansas City, an early jazz mecca. Coleman played his first professional gig at a local dance when he was twelve, and continued his musical development while reportedly attending Washburn College in Topeka, Kansas. Once asked if he could read music, Coleman said, with exageration, that he read music before he could read words.

Young Hawkins found work playing in theaters in Kansas City, and at seventeen he was hired by Mamie Smith, a vaudeville blues singer and leader of the Jazz Hounds. By then he had already developed a different approach to jazz saxophone. Hawkins traveled the Midwest with the Jazz Hounds, playing in Chicago in the early 1920s. From Chicago the group headed east for New York City, where Smith had a recording date with Okeh Records. With Smith, Hawkins made his first record, "Mean Daddy Blues," for Okeh in 1922.

Soon Hawkins was being featured in the Jazz Hounds, but before long he felt the need to move on. About mid-1923 he quit the band and settled in New York. Fletcher Henderson, who was becoming established as the nation's top jazz bandleader, recognized Hawkins's ability and hired him. The Henderson-Hawkins match was near perfect, and Hawkins continued as a featured soloist with the band until 1934. By that time Hawkins was an acknowledged master of jazz saxophone.

During Hawk's tenure with Henderson he heard the pianist Art Tatum whom he considered a major influence. Tatum's incredible dexterity at high speed and his **improvisational** skill dazzled Hawkins. A nonjazz influence was Johann Sebastian Bach, whom Hawkins claimed to listen to every day. The Hawk never forgot his classical roots.

The lure of Europe drew Hawkins away from Henderson after eleven years. His reputation was known in Europe, and he was offered a featured spot with the Jack Hylton orchestra in London. Europe loved Hawkins, and Hawk stayed until 1939, leaving only as war clouds gathered over the continent. Before he left, Hawkins made recordings with numerous jazz legends, including Django Reinhardt (guitar), Stephane Grappelli (violin), and Benny Carter.

When Hawk returned to the United States, he found that he no longer reigned supreme on the tenor saxophone. During his five years absence another tenor, Lester Young, had moved up and was all the rage. Young had developed a style different from Hawk's, and some younger jazz musicians now made Young their model. In 1933 Hawk met Young in Kansas City and a heralded saxophone battle had ensued. They dueled again in New York after Hawk's return. No winner was discerned, but Hawkins showed that he was still at the top of his form.

Hawkins remained in high demand, and he formed a nine-piece band for a gig at Kelly's Stable in Manhattan. A record date with the Bluebird label soon followed on October 11, 1939. It turned out to be a red-letter date in jazz; the day Hawkins recorded "Body and Soul." There were already recordings of the song, which had been written in 1930 by Johnny Green.

According to Hawkins, it was just a melody he liked to play around with, which he did almost every night at the club. He had no thought of recording it at this session until the record producer insisted. Hawkins agreed, but he had no written charts for the music and no idea how he would proceed.

For most of the piece, Hawkins solos with just a rhythm background, weaving a tapestry of richly toned phrases through the song's **chord** structure. The result was a highly melodic and sensuous rendition that became a jazz classic. Of the performance, John Chilton, author of Hawkins's 1990 biography, *The Song of the Hawk*, said that Hawk had created "a solo that remains the most perfectly conceived and executed example of jazz tenor-sax playing ever recorded. . . . It became one of the music's most . . . influential recordings." An almost immediate hit, "Body and Soul" astoundingly found success with the popular audience as well as jazz fans. It was rare for an instrumental jazz improvisation to do well in the popular market.

The 1940s brought a new challenge to Hawkins. Many jazz musicians, particularly the younger ones, were evolving into a new and harmonically complex jazz form called bebop. Older musicians often resisted the new trend, but Hawkins proved amazingly adaptable and was able to change and work with the young progressives. He personally never fully adopted the bebop style, however. In 1944 he made what is considered the first bop record, "Woody 'n' You," which included such emerging modernists as Dizzy Gillespie, Max Roach (drums), Don Byas (saxophone), and Oscar Pettiford (bass and cello). In the late 1940s Hawkins recorded "Picasso," the first unaccompanied jazz tenor saxophone solo, with influences of both Tatum and Bach.

Hawkins played with many of the progressives during 1946–1950 when he toured with Norman Granz's Jazz at the Philharmonic (a series of all-star concerts), and when revisiting Europe during that period. In the 1950s the new bop sound became largely dominant through young giants such as

Gillespie and Charlie "Yardbird" Parker. He joined Roy Eldridge (trumpet) for some dates in the late 1950s, including one at the 1957 Newport Jazz Festival, and from that year through the early 1960s, he recorded with Monk and Coltrane, among others. Hawkins kept up an intense schedule, including record dates with Duke Ellington and Sonny Rollins (saxophone), but by the mid-1960s heavy drinking and his advancing years began to take a toll.

Growing weak and thin, his hair and beard grown out and unruly, Hawkins by the late 1960s played less frequently, and he appeared to be declining. Despite his weakened condition, he agreed to an April 1969 television special in Chicago. Although he made the date, he needed help at the airports and getting to the studio. He played well enough though and managed another gig at Chicago's North Park Hotel the next day. It was his last appearance. He died a month later, on May 19, in New York City.

Hawkins made groundbreaking advancements with his work on tenor sax. Some of his solos, John Chilton states in his biography of Hawk, "are masterpieces by which all jazz tenor-saxophonists will forever be judged." He was, indeed, a musician for all time.

Benny Carter

The King—A Leader in Development of the Jazz Alto Saxophone
1907–2003

People always ask me about the good old days, but my good old days are here and now.

—From the video *Symphony in Riffs*
on the life of Benny Carter

Fellow musicians dubbed Benny Carter the "King," an honorary title that places this multitalented musician in a category with such jazz royalty as bandleaders "Duke" Ellington and "Count" Basie. Carter's main fame, however, came from being a uniquely talented instrumentalist and composer. Along with Johnny Hodges, Carter created the swing style of playing the jazz alto saxophone, an accomplishment similar to that of Coleman Hawkins on the tenor saxophone. But Carter's list of musical accomplishments goes well beyond that. Not only did Carter master other reed instruments, such as clarinet and soprano saxophone, but also instruments outside the reed family, such as trumpet and piano. His work on trumpet is particularly acclaimed.

Carter was also an accomplished composer and arranger, becoming one of the first African Americans to write scores for motion pictures and television. Quincy Jones in a film documentary of Carter's life, *Symphony in Riffs,* credits Carter with breaking down the barrier against blacks in scoring films. "He's a total musician; he was the pioneer, he was the foundation," said Jones.

Bennett Lester Carter was born in New York City on August 8, 1907, and he received piano lessons from his mother when he was ten. His interest soon turned to trumpet, not surprisingly since his cousin, Cuban Bennett, was a respected trumpet player, and his neighbor, Bubber Miley, played trumpet with the Duke Ellington Orchestra. Carter bought his first trumpet when he was about thirteen, but upon discovering that he couldn't play like Cuban and Bubber within a few days, he exchanged the trumpet for a saxophone, thinking, incorrectly, it would be easier. Carter was enormously gifted, however, and by the time he was fifteen he had his first gig, playing in Harlem with pianist Willie "the Lion" Smith.

Playing the Harlem clubs was a great experience, but in 1925 Carter went off to Wilberforce University in Ohio. His pursuit of education was quickly squelched, however, after he joined a band, the Wilberforce Collegians, and went on the road. That group traveled the Midwest and the East and in 1928, when Carter was twenty-one years old, played the Savoy Ballroom in Harlem. During 1927–29 he also played with Charlie Johnson's Orchestra, making his first recording with that group in 1928. Carter had played some gigs with the Fletcher Henderson Orchestra and in 1930 joined that band, also becoming Henderson's principal arranger.

In 1931 Carter left Henderson to assume musical direction of McKinney's Cotton Pickers, based in Detroit. Meanwhile, he had been teaching himself trumpet and clarinet, and now began doubling on those instruments. At the same time, he wrote arrangements for Henderson and for other name bands. Carter returned to New York in 1932 and put together his own band, including all-stars such as Teddy Wilson (piano), Chu Berry (saxophone), Sid Catlett (drums), and Doc Cheatham (trumpet). He felt that Cheatham was his greatest influence on trumpet, which Carter said was his favorite instrument. Unfortunately, the band did not catch on, and in 1934 it broke up.

Carter remained in demand, however, and in 1935 he went to Paris and then to England, where he was hired as an arranger for the British Broadcasting Company (BBC) dance orchestra. Over the next several years Carter toured Europe, helping to popularize jazz on the continent. In 1937 he organized a band that included both black and white musicians, one of the first such integrated jazz groups to play anywhere. With war looming, Carter returned to the United States in 1938, finding the swing craze now full blown. Over the next two years Carter made recordings with the Lionel Hampton orchestra, while a group he led played frequent gigs at the Savoy Ballroom.

By the early 1940s many of the top big bands were using Benny Carter charts. After having cut down briefly to a sextet, Carter reformed his big band in 1942 and headed for Los Angeles, where he made his home. In Los Angeles the Carter big band comprised some of the day's outstanding jazz musicians, including at various times Miles Davis, Max Roach, and Buddy Rich (drums); J. J. Johnson (trombone); Art Pepper (saxophone); and Gerald Wilson (trumpet).

With Hollywood movie studios nearby, it was not long before the film industry beckoned. His first job in films came in the 1943 all-black movie

Stormy Weather, for which he wrote arrangements and played on the soundtrack. Afterward, the demand for his arranging, scoring, and playing in movies and (later) television, grew steadily. Over the next several decades his movie credits would include *As Thousands Cheer, A Man Called Adam, The Snows of Kilimanjaro,* and *An American in Paris.* Television shows he worked on include *M Squad, Chrysler Theater,* and *Alfred Hitchcock Presents.*

The great vocalists of the era also sought out Carter's services, and he provided arrangements for Billie Holiday, Peggy Lee, Ella Fitzgerald, Ray Charles, and Mel Tormé, among others. Carter soon found he was overloaded, and in 1946 he gave up leading his own orchestra, although he continued to accept gigs as a featured soloist. Carter also managed to keep on composing, turning out one of the smash hits of the World War II years, "Cow Cow Boogie." One of his most significant accomplishments in Los Angeles, however, was his participation in negotiating the integration of the local white and black musicians' unions.

Through the 1950s and 1960s arranging took an increasingly larger share of Carter's time. He kept up a vigorous touring schedule, however, including overseas trips to Europe, and, in 1973, a trip to Japan, where he was so revered that he returned almost annually with all-star groups. In 1975 the U.S. State Department sent him on a goodwill tour of the Middle East.

The 1970s also saw Carter turn to another field of interest, music education. He taught as a visiting professor for several semesters at Princeton, receiving an honorary doctorate from that university in 1974. He was a visiting lecturer at Harvard in 1987, where he was also awarded an honorary doctorate. Degrees were conferred by a number of other schools, among them the New England Conservatory and Rutgers.

Benny Carter's unique musicianship was recognized repeatedly in the late 1900s. He was inducted into the Black Film Makers Hall of Fame in 1978 and won the Golden Score award for music arrangers in 1980. He played at the

1984 inaugural of President Ronald Reagan and at the White House for President George H. Bush in 1989. In 1995 Carter inaugurated a multivolume tribute to his work, *The Benny Carter Songbook*. Among his extended pieces are *Harlem Renaissance* and *Echoes of San Juan Hill*. For his compositions, Carter received seven Grammy nominations and two Grammy awards. For his lifetime of achievement, he was presented with the Kennedy Center Honors award in 1996.

Perhaps no other jazz musician stayed at the top of his profession, displaying so many different skills, as long as Benny Carter. His career spanned almost eight decades of the twentieth century and entered the twenty-first. No wonder that the jazz world calls him "King." He died on July 12, 2003, at the age of ninety-five.

Lionel Hampton

Hamp—First Major Jazz Vibraphone Player
1908 –2002

He was an all-around beautiful cat.

—David Ostwald,
leader of the Gully Low Jazz Band,
New York Times, September 6, 2002

Between cuts at a Louis Armstrong 1930 recording session in Los Angeles, Lionel Hampton moseyed over to a vibraphone tucked in a corner, casually picked up the mallets, and played an entire Amstrong solo note for note. Armstrong was so impressed he invited Hampton to play an eight-bar vibe solo at that session on "Memories of You." It was an auspicious moment for jazz. From that recording date, Lionel Hampton went on to become the first significant jazz vibraphone player and the foremost virtuoso of that instrument.

For his accomplishments on jazz vibraphone alone, Hamp, as he was called, secured his place in jazz history. But the vibraphone was not his only talent. He also excelled as a pianist and drummer, and was also a vocalist. He organized and led both large and small jazz ensembles, whose personnel through the decades would read like a who's who of jazz. He was also a composer of note, with some two hundred compositions (some in collaboration), including such jazz classics as "Midnight Sun," "Flying Home," and "Hamp's Boogie Woogie." In addition, Hamp, like Armstrong, loved to put on a show, using rhythmic body language and vocal sounds to accentuate his performance.

Lionel Leo Hampton was born in Louisville, Kentucky, on April 20, 1908. Hamp hardly knew his father, himself a pianist and singer. His first musical influence was through his grandmother, who managed a musical ensemble that played churches in the South. The rocking gospel rhythms he heard certainly influenced his musical direction. Lionel and his mother eventually settled in Chicago, and the boy received his first drum lessons from a Dominican nun at a boarding school in nearby Kenosha, Wisconsin. Later he sold papers for a black newspaper, the *Chicago Defender*, in order to play drums in the company's newsboy band. His first jazz exposure probably came through an uncle, Richard Morgan.

In high school Lionel played in a teenage band led by his saxophonist neighbor Les Hite. So promising was his talent that, when he was only fifteen, he was allowed to go to Los Angeles to play in a jazz band. Hite also had gone to Los Angeles and soon Lionel was playing with him again. When Louis Armstrong went to the east coast, Hite's band backed him at the Cotton Club.

In Los Angeles, Hamp met his wife-to-be, Gladys, a dressmaker with a keen business mind. She became his business manager in 1931, and in 1936 they were married. About that time another up-and-coming bandleader, Benny Goodman, caught Hamp's act and was so impressed that he asked Hampton to join his trio of Goodman (clarinet), Teddy Wilson (piano), and Gene Krupa (drums) as a quartet. Hampton became nationally known as part of the quartet, especially through such recordings as "Moonglow," "Dinah," and "Avalon." Goodman's ensembles were among the earliest to integrate black and white musicians. This caused problems, especially in the South, but Goodman refused to take the stage unless all could play.

In 1940 Goodman broke up his quartet due to ill health. Following this, Hampton formed his own big band, and within a few years it ranked with the nation's top groups. Hamp wanted his band to have a hard swinging **jump** rhythm, and he accomplished this as perhaps no one else of the era. Hamp fronted the band on vibes, emitting audible grunts as he played, rocking in rhythm, clapping hands, and sometimes leaping in the air. He might even dash from vibes to piano to drums on a single piece. His distinctive standing, two-finger piano style, especially on "Central Avenue Breakdown," brought raves. On occasion Hamp exuberantly led his musicians blowing and swinging right into the audience. Playing some of his signature tunes, such as "Flying Home" and "Hamp's Boogie Woogie," he often aroused audiences to dance in the aisles. Hamp also soloed on mood pieces, such as "Stardust" and "Midnight Sun," with exquisite finesse.

Hamp too was insistant on hiring top talent. His 1940s ensemble included (variously) such instrumentalists as Marshall Royal (clarinet and alto sax); Milt Buckner (piano); Dexter Gordon, Illinois Jacquet, Al Sears, and Arnett Cobb (tenor saxophones); Cat Anderson, Clark Terry, Quincy Jones, Clifford Brown (trumpets); Wes Montgomery (guitar); and Charles Mingus (bass). Joe Williams, Betty Carter, and Dinah Washington were among the vocalists. Hamp's big hits (in addition to the above) with this personnel included "Jack the Bellboy," "Hey! Ba-Ba-Re-bop," and "Air Mail Special." He also assembled for special concerts the Just Jazz All-Stars, a small group with such artists as Willie Smith (alto sax); Charlie Shavers (trumpet); Slam Stewart and Ray Brown (bass); Oscar Peterson (piano); and Buddy Rich (drums).

In the 1950s Hampton began touring Europe and in succeeding decades traveled to such far-flung places as Israel, Australia, Japan, Africa, and South America. On some trips he served as a goodwill ambassador for the U.S. State Department, spreading the gospel of American jazz worldwide. In 1949 Hampton led his band at Harry Truman's inauguration, the first African American so honored. Thereafter he played for every president at the White House through President William Clinton, who awarded him the National Medal of Arts in 1996.

Hampton's interests extended into other areas, particularly music education. He received more than fifteen honorary college degrees, and he is virtually enshrined at the University of Idaho, where the music school is named for him. His philanthropic work includes the Lionel Hampton Development Corporation, formed to build affordable housing in the inner city.

The death of his wife, Gladys, in 1971 was a severe blow, but Hamp's love of music sustained him, as it did through several strokes in the 1990s. He remained active almost until his death on August 31, 2002, at the age of ninety-four. His funeral was attended by jazz greats young and old, who lit up the service playing the swinging music Hampton made famous. Former president George H. Bush delivered a eulogy. Recited was the 100th Psalm, Hamp's favorite, which begins, "Make a joyful noise unto the Lord."

Benny Goodman

The King of Swing
1909–1986

He was the Beatles of his day. And he did it with pure, uncompromising music. He never compromised.

—George Wein,
New York Times, June 14, 1986

It had been a long, tough road from New York City to the Palomar Ballroom in Los Angeles. Benny Goodman and his jazz orchestra had not been greeted well during the preceding month-and-a-half–long string of one-nighters. They were playing to half-empty houses or worse. In Denver the ballroom manager wanted their contract cancelled unless they played popular dance music. Goodman had just about decided to give up the band when he arrived at the Palomar on August 21, 1935.

To his surprise the Palomar had a full house. For the first set Goodman played the sweet, popular music that he thought the dancers wanted, but they were unimpressed. Figuring it was the end anyway, he decided to go down swinging. For the second set they jammed on a Fletcher Henderson arrangement of "King Porter Stomp," and to Goodman's amazement the crowd came alive, cheering and applauding. Now the maestro realized: *This is what they came to hear.* The swing era was born.

Some bands were already into swing, but it was Goodman who kicked off the swing craze in the United States. That mania, with its frenzied fans and jitterbug dancing, would last for more than a decade and continue as a viable jazz form into the twenty-first century. It made Benny Goodman a national celebrity, dubbed the "King of Swing."

Benjamin David Goodman was born in Chicago on May 30, 1909, one of twelve children in the family of David and Dora Goodman, immigrant Jews from Eastern Europe. His father, a poor tailor, encouraged his children's education and musical training. Benny's musical education began in 1919 at the local synagogue, which provided him with a clarinet. The next year he joined the marching band of the famed Hull House settlement center and about that time began lessons with Chicago Symphony Orchestra clarinetist Franz Schoepp.

At twelve he won a contest imitating nightclub celebrity clarinetist Ted Lewis, and by fourteen he was playing with a local band. While still in short pants (then the style for children), he started jamming with a teenage group, including members of the "Austin High School Gang," such as Bud Freeman, Jimmy McPartland, and Dave Tough. He was influenced by emerging jazz stars of the day: King Oliver, Louis Armstrong, Bix Beiderbecke, and particularly clarinetist Jimmy Noone.

Ben Pollack, a local drummer, was impressed with Goodman, and when he formed a band and went to Los Angeles, he sent for the "kid in short pants" to join him. It was 1925 and Goodman was only sixteen. In the band were other future stars, including Jimmy McPartland, Glenn Miller, Jack Teagarden, Harry James, Muggsy Spanier, and Bud Freeman. After a few months the Pollack band returned to Chicago, where Goodman cut his first records and became the band's featured soloist.

The band headed for New York City in 1928 and caught on quickly. The next year, however, Pollack and Goodman had a dispute, and Goodman left the band. By then Goodman's reputation as a top sideman was made, and soon he was making from $200 to $400 a week, an astounding sum in the Depression era. Mainly he played radio and recording gigs for top orchestras, including Paul Whiteman, but he also performed in pit bands for Broadway musicals, including the George Gershwin hits, *Strike Up the Band* and *Girl Crazy*. In 1933 Goodman encountered John Hammond, a jazz enthusiast and promoter, and his career took off.

Hammond had been assigned to produce some jazz records, and he hired Goodman to form an orchestra for the date. Goodman assembled an all-star group and the records were released in 1934 with Goodman as leader for the first time. Afterward Goodman, with Hammond's help, formed another group to audition as a house band at Billy Rose's Music Hall. Goodman had an advantage because his was one of the few white jazz bands around, and in those days some venues would not hire black musicians. The Music Hall gig lasted three months, after which Goodman landed a spot on a groundbreaking new radio show, *Let's Dance,* featuring three outstanding dance bands. The program aired coast to coast for three hours on Saturday nights.

Goodman determined that the *Let's Dance* orchestra would reflect his own high and exacting standards of musicianship. Under his direction the band developed into a highly disciplined ensemble. He put up with no sloppiness in rehearsals. If a musician played a wrong note or was in the wrong key he got "The Ray," a dreaded long, icy cold stare from Goodman that froze many a sideman.

Goodman still felt something was missing from the band: a hard swinging drummer. Not just another time-keeping "boom chucka boom" drummer, but someone who could really drive the band. Goodman chose the flamboyant Gene Krupa, also a Chicago native. With Krupa on drums and playing Fletcher Henderson arrangements, Goodman finally had what he wanted.

The *Let's Dance* broadcasts, attended by a large studio audience, dancers, and other sidelights, were a huge success. Unfortunately, the program was cancelled after twenty-six weeks because of a strike in the sponsor's factory. The Goodman orchestra was a critical success, but it was early in the jazz/swing movement, and the orchestra had not yet developed a wide following. After *Let's Dance* the Goodman orchestra followed the sweet Guy Lombardo troupe into New York's Roosevelt Grill. The middle-aged, waltzing crowd rejected Goodman's music, and in two weeks he was out.

The disappointments piled up for Goodman until his hit at the Palomar Ballroom. Goodman's engagement there extended into two months, playing to wildly enthusiastic crowds. Near the end of 1935 Goodman headed for Chicago, his popularity spreading like a brush fire. Playing the Congress Hotel in his hometown, Goodman jammed in the fans, and his stay extended to six months. He also began what are considered among the first jazz concerts when he performed at nondancing sessions with his trio: Goodman, Krupa, and pianist Teddy Wilson. Goodman loved tightknit ensemble playing, in which he strived for the precision of a classical string quartet.

Wilson, who was black, had joined Goodman in 1936 from New York in what was one of the first high-profile integrations of black and white musicians. Later that year Goodman brought in black vibraphonist Lionel

Hampton to form a quartet. Goodman never compromised with club owners who objected to his integrated group.

The demand for Goodman's music was now reaching a frenzied pace, and his personal appearances in the late 1930s acquired a near rock-star hysteria. At the 1937 Paramount Theater appearance, young people lined up around the block at dawn for the first show. During the show and even before and afterward they cheered, clapped, stomped their feet, and danced in the aisles. All attendance records were broken.

In that period Goodman began a three-year radio engagement on the *Camel Caravan* and appeared in two Hollywood movies, *The Big Broadcast of 1937* and *Hollywood Hotel*. His crowning success was a 1938 appearance at Carnegie Hall. For the concert, in addition to his own orchestra, he brought in some of the finest jazz men, including trumpeters Buck Clayton and Cootie Williams; saxophonists Johnny Hodges, Lester Young, and Harry Carney; and pianist/bandleader Count Basie. The climax of the evening was a twelve-minute swinging rendition of "Sing, Sing, Sing," driven throughout by Krupa's drums and topped with outstanding solos.

The Carnegie Hall concert wasn't just about Goodman, it was about jazz coming of age as a respectable art form. It was a huge popular and critical success, whose live recording is a jazz classic that is still selling over sixty years later.

In July 1940 Goodman required surgery and had to disband the orchestra temporarily. Some of the top members, such as Krupa and Harry James (trumpet), had already left, and others, such as Hampton and Ziggy Elman (trumpet), followed before Goodman reformed the band several months later. His new band took on a somewhat different character, with outstanding personnel, including Georgie Auld (saxophone), Dave Tough, (drums), and the legendary Charlie Christian (electric guitar). By the end of the 1940s Goodman briefly assembled a new group to play bebop, although his own style changed little.

From the 1950s Goodman played and recorded mostly in small groups, and began to travel extensively as a roving ambassador for the U.S. State Department. In 1978 he assembled another big band to play for the fortieth anniversary of the Carnegie Hall concert. Goodman never lost his desire to play classical music, and in 1938 he recorded Mozart's Clarinet Quintet with the Budapest String Quintet. Thereafter he played and recorded with leading symphony orchestras, and he commissioned and performed clarinet works by various composers, including Béla Bartók, Aaron Copland, and Paul Hindemith.

Goodman continued to record into the 1980s. He received a Kennedy Center Honors Award in 1982; among his other awards were an honorary doctorate from Yale University and the coveted Peabody Medal. On June 13, 1986, Benny Goodman, the King of Swing, died of a heart attack at age seventy-seven.

Lester Young

Pres—Taking Tenor to a New Level
1909–1959

Every musician should be a stylist. I played like [Frankie] Trumbauer when I was starting out. But then there's a time when you have to go out for yourself and tell your story.

—Lester Young, from a 1956 interview with Nat Hentoff as reprinted in *A Lester Young Reader*, Lewis Porter, editor

Lester Young was amazed when the great Coleman Hawkins, preeminent tenor saxophone player of the day, sought him out in Kansas City and challenged him. Young once sat in for "Hawk" with the visiting Fletcher Henderson orchestra, and the talk was that he could match up with Hawkins. What took place that day in 1933 was a saxophone duel that became a jazz legend. Far into the wee hours the two tenors blew, and other Kansas City tenors joined in as well, Ben Webster and Herschel Evans among them. No quarter was given. At the end Hawkins knew he had been in a battle, and Lester Young, who would be called "Pres," stood on the brink of stardom.

Lester Willis Young was born in Woodville, Mississippi, on August 27, 1909, and began playing drums in the family band at an early age. When he was about eleven, the family moved to Minneapolis, and his father, a Tuskegee Institute–trained musician, led the family on tours throughout the region. Lester added violin and trumpet to his repertoire before he settled on saxophone at the age of thirteen. After some disagreements with his father in 1927, Lester, then eighteen, left the family band.

Over the next few years Young played for several bands, including Walter Page's Blue Devils and groups led by Bennie Moten and King Oliver. In 1934 he joined the Count Basie band, then based in Kansas City. Later in 1934 Hawkins left Henderson, and the famed leader asked Young to replace Hawkins in New York City. Henderson thought that Young, who had a lighter, more relaxed touch, could emulate the deeper-toned Hawkins, but Young refused to change his style, and Henderson fired him. During that New York experience Young made an enduring friendship with an upcoming vocalist, and the two would have a clear impact on each other's lives. Her name was Billie Holiday.

After leaving Henderson, Young performed around the Midwest for some months before reuniting with Count Basie, probably in 1936. Basie knew how to utilize Young's quite remarkable skills, and he quickly became the band's featured soloist. Also in 1936, Basie linked up with jazz impresario John Hammond and the band moved to Chicago where Young cut his first records. His solos on "Lady Be Good" and "Shoe Shine Boy" stemming from that date are classics.

Lester Young remained with Basie for the next three years, during which he established a new style for the tenor saxophone, competitive with that of Coleman Hawkins. Young particularly attracted and influenced younger musicians, Charlie Parker, Dexter Gordon, Illinois Jacquet, Georgie Auld, and Sam Donahue among them. Many of those followers evolved from Young's style into bebop.

In 1936 Young first recorded with Billie Holiday in a small **studio** group led by Teddy Wilson. This began an almost magical, artistic relationship in which Young and Holiday complemented each other as though they shared a single musical wavelength. After she joined the Basie band in 1937, the two played and recorded together often. Holiday nicknamed Young "Pres" (also "Prez") for president of tenors and he called her "Lady Day." Both names stuck. Young also recorded with a small Basie group called the Kansas City Seven, with which he cut what became his signature theme, "Lester Leaps In" in 1939.

By 1940 Young was growing restless with his long relationship with Count Basie. He felt it was time to form his own group, and in 1941 Young and his brother Lee, a drummer, established their own orchestra. They assembled top-notch musicians, and their work was acclaimed. After playing the West Coast, they had a highly successful run at the Café Society Downtown in New York City. Their collaboration ended, however, after their father died in Los Angeles in 1943 and Lee decided to stay on the West Coast.

Young toured USOs (armed forces social centers) for a while, then rejoined Basie briefly before being drafted into the army in September 1944. The army and Lester Young were not a good fit. Young was a very nonconforming person, which did not go over well in the army. He was unusual in his manner and appearance. He was an extremely light-skinned African American, with light eyes, reddish hair, and somewhat Asian facial features. Furthermore, his dialect combined a kind of jazz musician's **jive** talk with a made-up lingo that puzzled some people. He was sort of overrelaxed—some would say cool—another unarmylike trait. Also, unlike other sax players, particularly in his younger years, he held his saxophone diagonally across his body rather than straight up and down.

Not surprisingly, Young's army experience, made worse by racism, was a living nightmare. The army refused to let him play in their band, and he was convicted for marijuana possession and spent most of his army time in detention.

Despite Young's traumatic army experience, some of his finest work came after his release in late 1945. Jazz entrepreneur Norman Granz took Young under his wing, and the two remained in close association for the rest of Young's performing life. Granz had him playing superbly at Jazz at the Philharmonic (JATP) concerts, including appearances at Carnegie Hall in 1946 and 1949, and playing alongside other celebrated saxophonists, such as Coleman Hawkins and Charlie Parker. Granz also included him on some jaunts to Europe. Among his heralded postwar recordings were those he made in a trio with Buddy Rich (drums) and Nat Cole (piano), and with others that included Oscar Peterson, Teddy Wilson, and Jo Jones.

Young could usually handle the ups and downs of a musician's life. What he could not handle was alcohol. He drank heavily and unceasingly, and by the late 1950s that behavior had taken its toll. In 1957 he appeared on a television special with Billie Holiday but had to play sitting down for most of the program. For one short solo, however, he surprisingly stood up and played a hauntingly beautiful piece that seemed to be a personal tribute to Holiday. Young played inconsistently after that, and he died on March 15, 1959. He truly was an original, which is what he most wanted to be.

Django Reinhardt

First Notable European Influence on American Jazzmen
1910–1953

He did more for the guitar than any other man in jazz. . . . Jazz is different because of him.

—Stephane Grappelli,
quoted in *Django* by Michael Dregni
(The Gypsy Jazz Home Page) from a 1954
Melody Maker magazine interview

Possibly there is no more storied and romantic figure in all of jazz than Django Reinhardt. A French-speaking Gypsy, he lived much of his life among his Gypsy "cousins," roaming about France and nearby countries in caravans. His darkly handsome looks were set off by his slicked-back hair, his dark almond-shaped eyes, and a pencil-line moustache. He was an entirely free spirit, whose unpredictability added to his mystique. Rheinhardt attained a stature among guitar players that is said to be equivalent to that of Art Tatum among piano players: an unmatchable original. He was one of the few Europeans to make a name in jazz before World War II.

Jean Baptiste Reinhardt was born on January 23, 1910 in Liverchies, Belgium. His mother nicknamed him "Django." Music was in the family, his parents being part of a traveling troupe of Gypsy entertainers. After World War I broke out in 1914, the family migrated through Spain to North Africa, returning to the Paris region after the war. Django first learned to play the violin and the banjo, but by the time he reached his teens he had taken up the guitar, playing for money in streets and clubs.

Having made music the main part of his young life, Django had little opportunity or interest in formal education. He could not read or write, nor could he read music. When he was thirteen, he accompanied an accordionist who played at the local Parisian clubs, during which time his talent blossomed. That year he won a local talent contest, and over the next couple of years he began to be influenced by American and English popular music. In 1928 Reinhardt made his first recordings, accompanying singers.

In that year the well-known British orchestra leader Jack Hylton heard Reinhardt play and invited him to come to London and play with his ensemble. But Reinhardt never got to London. Returning home one night after playing, he was moving about the caravan with a candle when a fire suddenly broke out and spread so quickly that he could not escape before being badly burned. The little finger of his left hand and the next finger were seared together, and his leg was badly damaged.

Although he recovered, the two fingers of his left hand were rendered useless, and these were regarded as essential to playing the guitar. It seemed he might never play again, but such was Reinhardt's ability and love of music that in eighteen months after the accident he relearned the guitar, using only two fingers of his left hand. He not only learned to play as well as before, he developed a new and unique style using unusual chord structures.

By then Reinhardt had been forgotten, but he began his comeback in 1930. That year he got a job in an orchestra and went on the road, heading south into Basque country. In Toulon Reinhardt had a career-turning experience. There an artist, Émile Savitry, gave him his first real introduction to jazz. Savitry played the records of Armstrong, Ellington, and others for Reinhardt, who was overwhelmed. American jazz became a major influence in his playing, alongside gypsy music and such classical composers as Maurice Ravel and Claude Debussy.

When Reinhardt returned to Paris, he met a jazz violinist, Stéphane Grappelli, with whom he became closely associated. He and Grappelli played in a band together in 1931, and Reinhardt also accompanied the French singer Jean Sablon. The singer, knowing Reinhardt's undisciplined ways, sent his limousine to the guitarist's caravan to assure his arrival. In 1932 the Hot Club of France was formed as a place for jazz musicians and fans to mingle, but it also gave concerts and sponsored its own band. In 1934 Grappelli and Reinhardt formed the Quintet of the Hot Club of France (QHCF), a landmark in the story of jazz.

The quintet developed a swinging style influenced by American jazz. Grappelli and Reinhardt co-led the group, which became internationally famous. The quintet stayed together until the outbreak of World War II in 1939. During this period Reinhardt composed the song for which he is most famous, "Nuages" (Clouds).

After the quintet disbanded, Grappelli went to England, but Reinhardt stayed behind, avoiding the Nazis who were as determined to dispose of Gypsies as they were of Jews. Contact was completely lost with the guitarist at times, but he survived and after the war reassembled the quintet. Grappelli stayed in London, however, and was replaced by a clarinet player, giving the quintet a new sound. Reformed in 1946, the quintet was undoubtedly influenced by Benny Goodman and his electric guitarist, Charlie Christian. Reinhardt had always played the acoustic guitar, but to keep up with the trend, he took up the amplified guitar, losing nothing in the transition. He continued to meet with Grappelli for recording dates.

Reinhardt was invited in 1946 to tour the United States with the Duke Ellington band, then at its peak. The guitarist was thrilled and looked forward to making an impact on U.S. jazz society. The trip, however, was largely disappointing. Reinhardt really expected star treatment in the United States, but his arrival did not cause the big stir he expected. The tour ended with two concerts at Carnegie Hall, the second of which he did not show up for until the very end, leaving the Duke to apologize for his absence. His playing then delighted the audience—but not the critics.

Reinhardt then did two weeks at New York City's Café Society Downtown, before heading back to France. Through the late 1940s Reinhardt was active at first with a big band and then touring with the quintet. He met with Dizzy Gillespie, who influenced him in bebop, and also with Benny Goodman, who failed to persuade Reinhardt to join him in the United States. During an interlude in 1947 Reinhardt hardly picked up his guitar. He instead devoted himself to painting, for which he had a natural talent.

By the early 1950s, Reinhardt was slowing down. He moved with his wife and child to a small house on the Seine River, just outside of Paris. He still played occasionally, recorded frequently, and appeared as a guest in concert with Dizzy Gillespie. But on the whole he devoted more time to his family and fishing. On May 16, 1953, when he was only forty-three years old, he died suddenly of a stroke. His influence continued through the decades that followed, even as his feats on the guitar became legendary.

Art Tatum

Unmatched in the Field of Jazz Piano
1910–1956

I just play the piano, but God is in the house tonight.

—Fats Waller, when Tatum
dropped by to hear Waller play

Probably no other jazz piano player has been so highly acclaimed by his fellow musicians as Art Tatum. Pete Welding, in his liner notes to *Art Tatum, The Complete Capitol Recordings,* said, "In the field of jazz piano one man, Art Tatum, stands alone. Jazz musicians are so amazed at his mastery of the keyboard that some consider his talent superhuman." Welding also quotes Dave Brubeck as saying, "I don't think there's any more chance of another Tatum turning up than another Mozart." When Oscar Peterson heard a Tatum record the first time he thought it was twin pianos.

Tatum's remarkable technique impressed classical as well as jazz musicians. A number of comments have been attributed to the celebrated concert pianist Vladimir Horowitz, who was known to have enjoyed jazz. Reportedly, he stated that he wished he had Tatum's left hand. Andre Previn, another classical pianist, was a staunch admirer of Tatum's piano wizardry, as was George Gershwin.

All that Tatum accomplished musically he did with a handicap: He was almost totally blind. When Arthur Tatum Jr. was born in Toledo, Ohio, on October 13, 1910, it was discovered that he had cataracts on both eyes. Surgery restored a bit of sight in one eye, but his vision was restricted, although it did not hamper him in music. His musical ability was recognized at an early age, first studying violin but soon switching to piano. He had some training at the Toledo School of Music, although he was, in the end, largely self-taught. His teacher, recognizing his phenomenal ability, encouraged him to become a concert pianist. When in his teens, however, Tatum was smitten by the jazz music of James P. Johnson and Fats Waller, and his destiny was sealed.

When he was about eighteen years old, Tatum was hired by a local radio station as a staff pianist. That position led to a contract for his own fifteen-minute radio program, which was broadcast on the national network. Before long he received an offer to go to New York City as accompanist to Adelaide Hall, a club singer. Word of Tatum's artistry spread quickly, and in 1932 and 1933 he made his first solo recordings. He was drawn to New York's "after hours" clubs, where he engaged in "cutting" sessions (in which musicians try to outplay one another). Although still in his twenties, most conceded his supremacy among jazz pianists. His speed, his dazzling runs, his incredible improvisations, and his flawless execution as displayed, for instance, on his 1933 recording of "Tiger Rag," could hardly be challenged.

Tatum recorded with Decca from 1934 to 1941. During those years he played major U.S. cities, and in 1938 made his international debut in London. He was honored in 1944 with the Esquire Magazine Gold Award and an invitation to play at the first jazz concert given at the Metropolitan Opera House in New York. In the early 1940s Tatum formed a trio, consisting of himself, Tiny Grimes (guitar), and Slam Stewart (bass), which performed together on and off over a ten-year period, with Everett Barksdale replacing Grimes in the late 1940s. Tatum's trio produced such recordings as "Melody in F" and "Out of Nowhere." In the late 1940s, Tatum settled in Los Angeles, where he recorded one of his classics, "Aunt Hagar's Blues." In 1953 he signed with Norman Granz, the jazz impresario, to record and perform in concert.

Art Tatum's brilliant career was cut short by illness, which caused his death on November 5, 1956, a month after his forty-sixth birthday. He is remembered for creating unique passages while playing flawlessly. In recording, he seldom did a second take despite the incredible speed at which he sometimes played. His recording of "I Know That You Know" is estimated at times to tear along at about one thousand notes per minute. This is not to say that Tatum did not play with the emotion and sensitivity characteristic of great artists. Tatum is often said to have played his best when performing before friends or at jam sessions. Fortunately, some of those sessions were recorded and continue to be available.

The incomparable Art Tatum was one of the great influences in jazz, and to this day he holds a place of highest reverence in the jazz world.

Gil Evans

Out of the Cool
1912–1988

*Second only to Ellington in the striking
individuality of his work.*

— Leonard Feather and Ira Gitler,
The Biographical Encyclopedia of Jazz

In 1927, when pianist Gil Evans
was fifteen years old, he wasn't
sure of his musical direction. In
that year a friend's father, a jazz
buff, took the boys to San
Francisco to see Duke Ellington.
Afterward Gil Evans knew that his
musical destiny was jazz. Ellington
was among Evans's strongest
influences in his career as a jazz
pianist and as a composer, arranger,
and bandleader. In these various
capacities he established a groundbreaking musical legacy.

Gil Evans is, perhaps, most strongly noted for his creative musical mind, which constantly sought new ways to express modern music. His composing and arranging called for unusual combinations of instruments, including French horns, the tuba, and the synthesizer to create highly individual tonal colors and patterns. He spanned all musical forms, from classical to rock, to create strikingly original works.

Gil Evans's early life was somewhat unsettled. He was born Ian Ernest Gilmore Green in Toronto, Canada, on May 13, 1912, to Margaret Julia MacChonechy. Gil's birth father was not there or disappeared soon thereafter. Later there was a stepfather, and Gil took his name. Gil's mother settled in Berkeley, California, where his formal education and musical life began. He had some piano lessons, but was largely self-taught. In 1928 his family moved to Stockton, California, were Gil found jobs playing piano.

While attending junior college in 1933, Evans started a six-piece band, playing local dates. By 1934 the band had grown to nine pieces, playing from charts that Evans transcribed from records. By 1935 the group was playing top venues in the Los Angeles area, including Balboa Beach's Rendezvous Ballroom, where it stayed for two years.

In 1938 the ensemble was hired as the house band for the Bob Hope radio show, but with a popular singer, Skinnay Ennis, as its leader and Evans as full-time arranger. The show and the band thrived, and in 1939 a second arranger, Claude Thornhill, joined the staff. Before Thornhill left to form his own orchestra, he and Evans found they had a common musical bond. By 1941 Evans had left the show to do arrangements for Thornhill in New York.

Evans' first recorded arrangement was with Thornhill, and his career seemed ready to blossom when World War II erupted. In 1942 Evans headed into military service, where he played in army bands until his 1946 discharge. During service he became intrigued by a new kind of music, later called bebop. Evans rejoined Thornhill and stayed with him until 1948, experimenting with new musical concepts and theories.

Evans's bebop arrangements caught the attention of young modernist jazz musicians. His apartment in Manhattan became a salon for the exchange of musical ideas among New York City jazzmen, among them Gerry Mulligan (baritone saxophone), Miles Davis (trumpet), and John Lewis (piano). From this group evolved the Miles Davis Nonet, a nine-piece group in the bebop idiom that expressed Evans's advanced conceptions.

The nonet marked a turning point in music history. Its innovative repertoire heralded the birth of the "cool" movement in jazz. Included in the nonet recordings were two notable Evans arrangements, "Boplicity" and "Moon Dreams," both models of Evans's blended solo and ensemble playing. The nonet did not record after 1951, but its work was compiled into a landmark 1957 album, *Birth of the Cool.* Evans withdrew into a period of reflection, study, and introspection. Reemerging in 1956, he embarked on what was perhaps the defining period of his career.

Over the next few years Miles Davis and Evans locked into one of the most acclaimed collaborations in jazz. When Davis was contracted to record with a large ensemble, he insisted that Evans be his arranger, and together they produced a trio of classical jazz LPs. The first of these, released in 1957, was "Miles Ahead." Afterward came two even more ambitious pieces, which utilized a nineteen-piece orchestra behind Davis's solo work. George Gershwin's *Porgy and Bess,* also released in 1957, was the first of these extensive works, followed in 1959 by the highly dramatic, plaintive *Sketches of Spain.* These masterworks reflected Evans's influences by such classical modernists as Debussy and Ravel.

Evans received high praise for his work with Davis, but, typically, he sought new ground to break. Evans had begun recording under his own name, demonstrating new directions in such works as *The Individualism of Gil*

Evans, Out of the Cool, and *Svengali.* In the 1960s and 1970s his output became increasingly experimental, incorporating polyphonic rhythms and ensemble improvisation that sometimes seemed just noise. He developed a fascination with electronic instrumentation and rock music, and in 1974 he produced a tribute album to Jimi Hendrix—creating a type of classical rock. He also worked with rock stars Sting and David Bowie.

During the 1970s and 1980s Evans toured extensively in Europe and Japan. In London he provided arrangements for the film *Absolute Beginners,* and in 1986 he scored the soundtrack music for *The Color of Money.* From 1983 Evans had a regular Monday night gig at Sweet Basil's in New York City that took on almost cult proportions—experimentation was the rule.

Gil Evans continued working through 1987, although illness was overtaking him. Finally, on March 20, 1988, he succumbed to pneumonia. Evans spirit lives on in the music he created, which is perpetuated in degree by his son Miles, who took over the sessions at Sweet Basil's and by his avid protégé, composer, and bandleader Maria Schneider.

Kenny Clarke

Klook—Father of Bebop Drumming
1914–1985

He was the first to shift the time-keeping rhythm from the bass drum to the ride cymbal . . . an innovation copied by countless drummers.

—Scott Yanow, from the
Drummerworld Web site

In the early 1940s drummer Kenny Clarke jammed with Dizzy Gillespie (trumpet), Thelonious Monk (piano), Charlie Parker (alto saxophone), and others at Minton's Playhouse in Harlem to create a new jazz style called bebop. Clarke's cohorts called him "Klook," short for "klookmop," which was the sound of the offbeat accent of his bass and snare drums.

Clarke had been seeking a new approach to big band drumming that would depart from the steady four beats to the bar rhythm, the accepted style for swing bands. He wanted to integrate drums more into ensemble playing as well as blend them in with the complex **harmonics** of bebop. Clarke developed these innovations and became known as "the father of bebop drumming."

Kenneth Clarke Spearman was born in Pittsburgh on January 9, 1914, to a pianist mother and a drummer father. Kenny's father left when he was very young, and his mother died a few years later, leaving the young lad and his brother in the custody of a stepfather. The stepfather placed Kenny in a home for boys, where he was able to play drums. After a few years Kenny left the boys' home, living with foster parents until he was sixteen. From that time, he was on his own.

Kenny wanted to study piano, but drums turned out to be a more practical alternative. Before long he struck up a friendship with a girl who danced in a club, and Kenny was able to practice on the club band's drums. Now about seventeen years old, Kenny began listening to jazz at the club and fell in love with the music. He wrangled some drum lessons, and he was soon playing professionally with a trio. After playing gigs around Pittsburgh until 1935, Clarke decided he was ready for New York City.

Clarke had already played with some top musicians, who guided him in New York. In the late 1930s he worked mostly with the Teddy Hill orchestra alongside another promising sideman, Dizzy Gillespie, and it was at the after-hours sessions at Minton's, working with other early modernists, that their theories jelled into bebop. Clarke and Thelonious Monk were in the house band, but other jazz stars popped in to jam into the wee hours.

Musicians referred to Clarke's explosive drumming as "droppin' bombs." It was a prophetic name as it turned out, because it came about the time the United States entered World War II. Clarke was drafted into the military in

1943 and spent part of his three-year service performing with an army band in Paris. European society appealed to Clarke. He realized that he could adapt there easily as an African American and that he earned more respect there as a jazz musician. Europe remained on his mind.

After his discharge, Dizzy Gillespie coaxed him into joining his new big band. Clarke played with Dizzy in 1946 and rejoined him in 1948 for a tour in Europe. After the tour he stayed in Paris for a few months of working and teaching before returning to the United States. But the lure of Paris remained strong. He worked with various groups in New York until 1951 when he became a founding member of the Milt Jackson Quartet (later the Modern Jazz Quartet). Clarke remained the group's drummer until 1955; the next year he moved to Paris.

Clarke had wearied of the pressured New York scene, and a failed marriage to jazz singer Carmen McCrae did not help. He also joined Islam, like many African Americans, adopting the name Liaqat Ali Salaam. In Paris, Clarke worked with Jacques Hélian's big band, but also spent much time recording and playing with touring American jazz artists. He appeared in several French movies in the late 1950s and 1960s, and from 1961 until 1972 he co-led, with pianist-arranger Francy Boland, the Clarke–Boland Octet and Big Band.

Clarke was content in Paris, buying a house in a nearby suburb and marrying a second wife, Daisy, who bore him one son, Laurent. Clarke had one child previously, Toby, with another well-known jazz singer, Annie Ross. Through the 1970s and early 1980s Kenny Clarke remined active, but seldom returned to the United States. He was semiretired when, on January 26, 1985, he died of a heart attack. Decades later jazz drumming continues to bear the influence of Kenny Clarke.

Billie Holiday

Lady Day—Stands Alone Among Jazz Singers
1915–1959

God bless the child that's got his own.

—From the song of that name
immortalized by Billie Holiday

In jazz singing the one name that stands atop the rankings most often is Billie Holiday. Her vocal quality was unique, and while Frank Sinatra would say that she influenced a whole generation of singers, including himself, no one could sound like Holiday. To do that a singer would have had to live the life that Holiday did. One thing most critics agree about is that she expressed, as perhaps no other jazz singer, the pain of her life. And it was a sad and tragic life indeed.

Billie Holiday set a new standard for both the kind of material jazz singers used and the way it was delivered. Before Holiday, blues singers, like Ma Rainey and Bessie Smith, had big shouting deliveries derived from gospel-singing backgrounds. Holiday separated herself from those singers with a new, intimate, and highly personal style, well suited to the microphone. When she sang, she seemed to be delivering a personal message to you. She often sang sad songs, but was not a blues singer. Rather, she sang and created many classic ballads, infusing each with her own emotions. She wanted to sing the way jazz musicians played their instruments.

Billie Holiday was born on April 7, 1915, to teenage parents, Sadie Fagon and Clarence Holiday. Her given name was Eleanora Fagon. Her father, a trumpet player, was gassed during World War I and had to switch to guitar due to breathing problems. His gigs meant heavy traveling, however, and Eleanora and Sadie soon found themselves abandoned. Seeking work, Sadie left Eleanora in the care of relatives, who often abused the little girl. When she was ten years old she was sent to a reform school for allegedly enticing an older man to rape her. Sadie managed to rescue her from reform school, and the two ended up in New York City.

The big city was not kind to Eleanora. Now a teenager, she was put in the care of a kindly woman who turned out to be the madam of a brothel, and before long she was working as a call girl. But the high-spirited young woman was not always cooperative, and an angry customer turned her in to the police. After a few months in jail she was set loose into the 1930s New York street scene. The nation was mired in the Depression and jobs were scarce, but Eleanora refused to do menial labor.

Although underage, she had seen chorus girls dancing in clubs and thought that was the good life. Tall and leggy at about seventeen, she began seeking auditions in Harlem clubs. Finally she got a tryout, but knowing little about dancing, she was promptly rejected. As the saddened young woman prepared to leave, the story goes, the piano player called out something like, "Hey, can you sing?" Not to miss an opportunity, she replied yes, even though she had little experience singing. But she sang one of the few songs she knew and was hired immediately. A jazz legend was born.

Holiday, who now called herself Billie, immersed herself in singing, and her esteem grew quickly. In 1933, when she was only eighteen years old, John Hammond, a jazz impresario, began promoting her and talked Columbia Records into letting her record with Benny Goodman. Hammond helped her get better club dates, and in April 1935 she had a one-week run at the Apollo Theater, where all the top jazz stars appeared. It was her first time before a large audience and she was nervous, but the ovation after she sang "The Man I Love" told her that she was on the right track.

Shortly after her Apollo engagement Hammond had her back in the studio to record with an all-star jazz group led by pianist Teddy Wilson. Although the studio would not let Holiday sing some of the hot tunes of the day (saved for white singers for commercial reasons), at least a few of the tunes became **standards** including "What a Little Moonlight Can Do" and "I Wished on the Moon." About that time she appeared in her first Hollywood film, a short musical with Duke Ellington. In 1937 tenor saxophonist Lester Young joined the recording group backing Holiday, and the two formed an endearing friendship and artistic collaboration that endured throughout their lives.

Soon Holiday and Young were both performing with the Count Basie band. Young eventually moved in with Holiday and her mother, Sadie. During this period Young bestowed Holiday with the nickname "Lady Day," and she, in turn, dubbed Young "Pres" (for president). Both names stuck. Neither Young nor Holiday stayed very long with Basie. They both were mavericks who had an uncanny affinity for each other's artistry, but did not always fit in the jazz **mainstream**.

After Basie, Holiday joined Artie Shaw's all-white band for a short time in 1938, but the racial tensions grew too stressful, and she quit in a huff. Holiday next was invited to sing at a new club in Greenwich Village called Café Society, which was unusual for the times because it had an integrated audience. Holiday became a fixture at the club, and it was there that she introduced the song that took her into a new dimension.

Holiday was not a crusader, and when she realized that the song "Strange Fruit" was about the body of a lynching victim hanging from a tree limb, she balked. But she sang it finally, and it proved an immediate, albeit controversial, hit. Columbia, her record company, had refused to record it, but another label, Commodore, did release it, and the record sold well despite being banned on many radio stations. In 1941 Holiday had another off-beat hit, "God Bless the Child," and in 1944 her hit "Lover Man," written expressly for her, was released.

Holiday, eager for exposure, took a role in the 1947 film *New Orleans* alongside Louis Armstrong, even though she had to play the part of a maid. She recorded for Decca from the mid-1940s until 1950 when she signed with Norman Granz, a jazz entrepreneur and record producer. Through Granz she worked with the finest jazz musicians and recorded a series of hits, including "All or Nothing at All," "Willow Weep for Me," "A Fine Romance," and "Autumn In New York."

Holiday was successful as a singer, but not very good at managing her personal life. Emotionally insecure from childhood, she was inevitably attracted to handsome, sweet-talking men, often musicians, who took advantage of her and gave her little security. She married her first husband, Jimmy Monroe, in 1941 and subsequently married three more times—to Joe Guy, a trumpet player, John Levy, a club owner, and Louis McKay, who became her manager.

Billie Holiday used drugs and alcohol from her early life, but her usage increased, at least partly in reaction to her unhappy romances. No wonder she seemed to be baring her soul in songs like "Lover Man" and "The Man I Love." She toured Europe several times in the 1950s and appeared on a television special with a failing Lester Young in 1957. By 1959 her voice and her body had markedly deteriorated. Lady Day made her last appearance on May 25, 1959, for a mere $300. She barely finished a number and had to be helped home. The suffering vocalist entered the hospital, and briefly rallied, even while police raided her room to confiscate drugs. She relapsed, however, and on July 17, 1959, at age forty-four, death relieved Billie Holiday of her tormented life.

Charlie Christian

Established the Guitar as a Solo Jazz Instrument
1916–1942

He caused the explosion that changed the jazz guitar for once and for all.

—Peter Broadbent,
from the preface to *Charlie Christian*

All too often the stars of jazz glow with a super bright intensity that burns out all too quickly. Among those whose talented lives were cut short, few lit up the jazz scene so briefly with so profound an effect as guitarist Charlie Christian. His life was over at the age of twenty-five, but his telling imprint in jazz and other music remains to this day. It was Charlie Christian who, with his single-note playing technique, brought the electric guitar into prominence as a solo jazz instrument, thus becoming the founding father to generations of jazz, blues, and pop guitarists that followed.

Charlie Christian was born into a highly musical family on July 29, 1916, in Bonham, Texas. Charlie's father, Clarence, played trumpet and guitar and sang as well, while his mother, Willie Mae, played piano and sang. When Charlie was only two, his family moved to Oklahoma City, where the Christian family made some income from playing in the streets. Clarence Christian taught Charlie to play trumpet and guitar, one of his older brothers to play string bass, and another to play mandolin and violin.

While in his teens, Charlie became familiar with a rising tenor saxophone star, Lester Young, who deeply influenced the guitarist. As he developed his skills, he wanted to solo the way horn players did on their instruments. But the low-volume acoustic (nonelectric) guitar Charlie played was used mostly in jazz for rhythm background. Undaunted, Charlie continued to play and study music, learning also the string bass, the instrument he played on his first professional gig in 1934.

Charlie Christian toured with groups in the Southwest at a time when the country-western swing bands were beginning to feature electric guitar. Nearing twenty years of age, Christian must have been influenced by the country-western soloists, and by 1938 he was playing electric guitar. Christian toured as far north as Bismarck, North Dakota, and played some dates in Kansas City, where he jammed with the Jay McShann Band.

In 1939, Christian began a mercurial rise to stardom. His reputation had grown enough that jazz impresario John Hammond, on his way to Los Angeles, made a side trip to Oklahoma City to hear the electric guitar phenomenon. Hammond, who was headed for a Benny Goodman recording date, was so impressed that he persuaded Goodman to give Christian an audition.

When Christian showed up in Los Angeles, Goodman allowed him only a few minutes, without an amplifier, before dismissing him. But later that night Hammond snuck Christian onstage between sets of Goodman's gig and told him to wing it. It wasn't long before Goodman joined Christian and, so the story goes, they ended up jamming on "Rose Room" for some forty minutes. From that point on he was part of the Goodman band.

Charlie Christian became an immediate hit playing and recording with the Goodman orchestra and the Goodman sextet. Over the next several years he was heralded for his solos on such Goodman standards as "I Got Rhythm," "Flying Home," "Stompin' at the Savoy," "Lady be Good," and others. He also freelanced on recordings with the Lionel Hampton Orchestra, the Kansas City Six, the Metronome All-Stars, and others.

Christian played in the swing style that had become the rage. But in New York City in the early 1940s, the winds of change in jazz were stirring. Christian was intrigued by the new sounds he was hearing, and he had his own progressive ideas. Soon he was dropping into Minton's Playhouse in Harlem for sessions with some of the seminal forces in modern jazz, including Thelonious Monk, Dizzy Gillespie, Kenny Clarke, Charlie Parker, and others. Their experimentation evolved into the music known as bebop.

The future seemed unlimited for the twenty-five-year-old guitarist in 1942. He was already world famous playing jazz, and he was in the forefront of a transition of swing music to modern jazz, even recording one piece later called "Swing to Bop." But all of this was to be cut short. The guitar genius had been diagnosed with tuberculosis, which was quite difficult to treat in those days. He was sent to a sanatorium, but the disease progressed, and it took his life on March 2, 1942.

Charlie Christian's legacy is preserved on his Goodman recordings and on such albums as *Solo Flight* and *Charlie Christian: The Genius of the Electric Guitar.* Also, some of his bebop sessions at Minton's are available on *Live at Minton's Playhouse.*

Nat King Cole

Jazz Trio Leader Became A Huge Pop Star
1917 or 1919–1965

The greatest thing you'll ever learn is just to love and be loved in return.

—From the song "Nature Boy,"
one of Cole's biggest hits

Nat King Cole had two successful careers in music. In the first he was a highly ranked jazz pianist and the leader of a popular jazz trio in the 1940s. He sang occasionally with the trio, and, as it turned out, his singing had great appeal for the popular audience. He had a silky smooth voice with a gentle swing and an almost whispering kind of intimacy. This led to his second career as a singer of pop ballads backed by string orchestras. Several of his hits went to the top of the charts.

Pop's gain was a loss to jazz. Cole's piano style grew mostly out of the great players of the 1930s such as Earl Hines, Teddy Wilson, and Art Tatum. But he employed a gentle, relaxed swing and harmonies that sometimes hinted of the early bebop movement. His influence extended to such rising stars as Bud Powell and Tommy Flanagan. The King Cole Trio combination of piano, bass, and guitar was also influential, with a number of trios of the 1940s and 1950s adopting that format. One can only speculate on what Cole might have accomplished in jazz had he not, by some quirk, been blessed with a voice that appealed to pop music fans.

Nathaniel Adams Coles (later changed to Cole) was born in Montgomery, Alabama, on March 17, probably in 1917 or 1919. Sources and Cole himself cite different years. Cole's father, Edward, was a Baptist minister and his mother, Perlina, was a church choir director. In 1921 Edward Coles was offered a ministry in Chicago. At the time, Nat had a brother and two sisters. Two more brothers came along in Chicago. All four brothers became professional musicians.

Nat sang in the church choir and began formal piano lessons at twelve. His progress on piano was influenced by the jazz music he heard in Chicago in the late 1920s and early 1930s. While still attending Wendell Phillips High School, Nat led a big band and a quintet made up of teenagers. At age sixteen he joined his older brother in a sextet called the Solid Swingers. The group was hired by a South Side club, the Panama, and Nat cut his first records with the Solid Swingers in 1936.

By now Nat had dropped out of school and had also taken an interest in girls. At the Panama, he met a dancer named Nadine Robinson, and romance blossomed even though she was ten years his senior. After the Panama, Nat and Nadine hooked up with a touring show called "Shuffle Along," starring jazz pianist Eubie Blake. Nat married Nadine during the show's run, which ended in Los Angeles in 1937. Without a job and with a wife to support, Nat looked for work in Los Angeles, and eventually he got a steady job at the Century Club, a hangout for jazz musicians. Then came a big break. The owner of the Sewanee Inn, a Los Angeles nightclub, asked him to form a quartet and play at his club.

Then what seemed like a disaster actually sparked Nat's career. The drummer did not show up on opening night, and the quartet was suddenly a trio. Drummerless combos were rare in those days, but the threesome made it work, and they were a trio thereafter. During that gig Nat adopted the nickname "King," and the group became the Nat King Cole Trio, which included Oscar Moore (guitar) and Wesley Prince (bass). Over the next couple of years they played top Los Angeles clubs and developed an enthusiastic following. Some record opportunities came up, but sales were pitched to the black "race record" market, which then afforded little recognition.

In 1942 Prince was drafted into the military and was replaced by Johnny Miller. The trio backed some leading jazz vocalists on radio transcriptions, including Anita O'Day, and hit the mainstream record market with some of Cole's signature numbers, including "Sweet Lorraine" and "On the Sunny Side of the Street." Cole also played and recorded with other jazz stars, and some of his finest jazz solos were recorded on albums with Lester Young (saxophone), Red Callender (bass), and Buddy Rich (drums).

A year later the trio was signed by a start-up record company, Capitol, founded by composer Johnny Mercer and others. Until now Cole sang only occasionally to add variety to the trio's repertoire. He had little confidence in his voice, assessing it as weak with little range. But an early record with Capitol, a jivey vocal based on one of Cole's father's sermons, called "Straighten Up and Fly Right," became a big hit.

The demand for the Nat King Cole Trio grew rapidly, and Capitol obliged with more hits over the next several years, including "It's Only a Paper

Moon," "Route 66," and the 1945 smash hit, "For Sentimental Reasons." The latter was an early sign of the trio's move away from its swinging style to the pop ballad mode. The next year Cole recorded Mel Tormé's "The Christmas Song," first with the trio, but later with a large string orchestra, marking a trend away from the trio format. In 1948 Cole divorced Nadine and married singer Maria Ellington (no relation to the Duke).

The Nat King Cole Trio's popularity had grown enough that they were chosen as a summer replacement for Bing Crosby on the Kraft Music Hall radio show. Capitol now pushed for more pop ballads with big orchestral backgrounds. In 1948 the company released "Nature Boy," a tender, sort of whimsical piece that caught on and became a runaway hit. Cole was now essentially a single act and no longer a jazz artist, although he continued to make jazz recordings on rare occasions under assumed names. Hits that followed into the 1950s included "Mona Lisa," "Unforgettable," "Too Young," and "Darling, Je Vous Aime Beaucoup."

In 1956 Cole became the first African American to host his own television show. Although a critical success, the show had trouble getting sponsors and was cancelled after about a year. Cole continued to record and perform, and headed his own tours in the United States and abroad. Hollywood beckoned as well, and Cole appeared in several movies, including *St. Louis Blues, The Nat King Cole Story,* and *Cat Ballou.*

By the early 1960s Cole had lost popularity, so he went for something offbeat and recorded a country-western tune, "Ramblin Rose," that went to the top of the charts. Cole kept working hard, but by 1964 his health began to suffer, and he finally agreed to a medical examination. The news was bad. Cole, a heavy smoker, had lung cancer. He died a few months later, on February 15, 1965. Even in death, Cole went up the charts one more time in 1991 when his daughter Natalie recorded "Unforgettable," **overdubbing** her voice onto the orginal and in effect singing a duet with her father.

Ella Fitzgerald

First Lady of Song
1917 or 1918–1996

I never knew how good our songs were until I heard Ella Fitzgerald sing them.

—Ira Gershwin

She was tall, this seventeen-year-old that stood on the stage of the Apollo Theater on the night of November 21, 1934. It was amateur night, and from the looks of this contestant she was not likely to win a prize. Her clothes were ill fitting and unstylish, and her hair was a fright. This Harlem audience was ready to jeer the ungainly adolescent off the stage. Billed as a dancer, at the last minute she told the announcer she would sing instead. That was a landmark decision in the course of jazz and popular singing in the United States.

On that night Ella Fitzgerald sang the only two songs she knew, "The Object of My Affection" and "Judy," both hit songs of Connee Boswell, the youngster's idol. She sang in Boswell's style, but her voice had a special quality that the audience loved. The singing career of Ella Fitzgerald began at that moment, and before it was over, she would receive the highest accolades in both jazz and popular music. Starting as a swing band singer, she moved easily into bebop, scat, pop ballads, and even novelty numbers. For her accomplishments she was dubbed "The First Lady of Song."

Ella Fitzgerald was born in Newport News, Virginia, on April 25, 1917 (some sources say 1918). Her father, William Fitzgerald, and her mother, Temperance, separated during Ella's first year, and she and her mother moved to Yonkers, a suburb of New York City. There, Ella attended elementary school, but the family was poor, and she earned extra money by dancing and singing in the street.

In 1932 Ella's mother died. The youngster was placed in an orphanage, but later was taken in by an aunt in Harlem. She dreamed of a dance career and had won several dance contests, but during that talent night at the Apollo the dance competition was fierce, so she sang instead. A few months later she won another contest, singing at the Harlem Opera House. Among those taking notice was saxophonist Benny Carter, who arranged an audition with the famous Fletcher Henderson orchestra. Henderson was not impressed, but soon afterward she sang for Chick Webb, the house bandleader at the swing-dancing Savoy Ballroom. Webb at first resisted taking on the teenager, but audience response was great, and he hired her. Because Ella was underage, Webb and his wife became her legal guardians.

Praise came quickly for Ella from jazz critics and reviewers, and by June of 1935 she cut her first records, for Decca. That year she got the idea of doing a swing version of an old nursery rhyme, "A-Tisket, A-Tasket." It went over well, and when she recorded the tune with Webb in 1938 it became her first hit record, selling over a million copies. Ella won a *Down Beat* poll in 1937 and in the three succeeding years, and after Webb died in 1939 she led the band until it disbanded in 1942.

Fitzgerald now became a solo act, while continuing to record for Decca. She had started writing lyrics while still with Webb, including "You Showed Me the Way" and "In a Mellow Tone" for Duke Ellington. Decca began partnering her with other recording stars, and she produced pop hits with The Ink Spots and the Delta Rhythm Boys.

In the early 1940s Fitzgerald was among the first vocalists to incorporate the complex harmonies of bebop into her singing. She had dabbled in scat singing, then in 1945 came out with "Flying Home," which took scat to a new level. In the following years her scat versions of "Lady Be Good" and "How High the Moon" became classics.

In the mid-1940s Fitzgerald worked with Dizzy Gillespie, along with many prominent jazz stars on Norman Granz's Jazz at the Philharmonic (JATP) concert series. Among the musicians was Ray Brown, a famed bassist, whose romance with Fitzgerald resulted in their 1947 marriage.

By the end of the 1940s the big band era was ending. Television now loomed as a new entertainment medium, and in 1949 Fitzgerald made the first of many television appearances. Norman Granz became her manager, and when her contract with Decca expired in 1955, he signed her to record on his new label, Verve.

Granz thought Fitzgerald should sing the ballads written by America's great composers, a concept that resulted in what is now Fitzgerald's "Songbook" series of albums. Throughout that period, from 1956 through the mid-1960s her voice was in full bloom. Her sound was as pure as a bell, she could swing or be sentimental, and her scat was exceptional. In 1956 she applied this incredible vocal instrument to "Ella Fitzgerald Sings the Cole Porter Songbook, " and her career took a new direction. More Songbook albums followed, dedicated to Richard Rodgers and Lorenz Hart, Duke Ellington, Irving Berlin, and others. Perhaps the pinnacle of the series was the tribute to the Gershwins, covering fifty-three songs in five LP records. Some jazz purists complained that Fitzgerald had gone commercial, but her vocal style remained jazz.

Fitzgerald continued to work with big jazz names, including Louis Armstrong, Count Basie, and Duke Ellington. The noted jazz pianist Tommy Flanagan first accompanied Fitzgerald in 1956, beginning a relationship that spanned more than twenty years. In the 1970s she sang with the Boston Pops and appeared with other classical orchestras, and she performed steadily on television specials. Her movie credits by this time included *Pete Kelly's Blues, St. Louis Blues,* and *Let No Man Write My Epitaph.*

Granz started a new record label, Pablo, in the 1970s, and he again went to Fitzgerald. Particularly distinctive was her work with guitarist Joe Pass, and she also recorded with Ray Brown, whom she had divorced years earlier. Fitzgerald worked a heavy schedule through the 1970s despite the beginnings of ill health. Her eyesight began to fail, and her new image included thick-lensed glasses. In 1986 Fitzgerald had open-heart surgery, but she recovered and returned to singing. By the 1990s though, after several years fighting diabetes, her performances grew infrequent.

At one of her last appearances, a benefit for the American Heart Association, the gathering of artists was a virtual who's who of American jazz. On that night Fitzgerald even jammed with classical violinist Itzhak Perlman. In 1993 her diabetes worsened and both her legs were amputated. After that she was seldom seen in public, and on June 15, 1996, at age seventy-nine, she died of complications from various health problems.

Over the decades the honors she amassed are staggering. They include number one awards in polls taken by *Esquire* magazine, *Metronome Magazine,* and *Down Beat* (whose Critics Award she won eighteen successive times); honorary doctorates from Yale and Dartmouth; the Kennedy Center Honors award in 1979; the 1987 National Medal of the Arts; and the French Commandeur Des Artes et Lettres in 1990. She won fourteen Grammys over her career.

Dizzy Gillespie

Diz—Major Player in the Bebop Revolution
1917–1993

One of the most beloved musicians in jazz, and one who irrevocably changed the shape and direction of music.

—The British Broadcasting
Company Web site

The origins of bebop were rooted in the progressive ideas of a number of young jazz musicians who sought to advance jazz out of the swing era. Among that group the dazzling trumpet player Dizzy Gillespie is often recognized not only as one of the chief promoters of the bebop revolution, but someone who was devoted to preserving the art form. Gillespie, in addition to being an outstanding performer, was also a composer and teacher who wrote down his musical concepts to ensure their perpetuation.

While some early bop musicians, like Charlie Parker and Thelonious Monk, tended to be withdrawn and sometimes self-destructive, Gillespie was sparkling and outgoing. He combined his performing-composing genius with humor, amusing the audience as well as entrancing it with his remarkable musicianship. During the late 1940s and early 1950s his flamboyant image came to symbolize the bebop generation. Sporting a beret and goatee and wearing thick-rimmed glasses (dubbed "bop glasses"), he cavorted onstage and, with cheeks pushed out like baseballs, blew his unique trumpet with an up-bent bell. But his clowning detracted nothing from his inspired playing.

John Birks Gillespie was born in Cheraw, South Carolina, on October 21, 1917. His father was a multi-instrumentalist who played bass, mandolin, drums, and piano, and gave young John his first exposure to music. When John was about twelve, he took up the trombone, but gave it up for the trumpet. At about the age of sixteen he entered Laurinburg Institute in North Carolina, an all-black school, where he studied agriculture, played football, and joined the school band. In 1935 he began to find professional work in Philadelphia. During this time he earned the nickname "Dizzy" because of his irrepressible antics.

Gillespie's early idol was Roy Eldridge, a top swing trumpeter. Gillespie imitated Eldridge, and in 1937 replaced him in the Teddy Hill Band in New York City. With Hill, Gillespie played the famed Savoy Ballroom, recorded his first solos, and took his first European tour. By 1939 Gillespie was recording with top jazz stars, and that year he joined the Cab Calloway orchestra, becoming Calloway's featured soloist. But Gillespie's zany behavior did not amuse Calloway, who had his own flashy routine. He also objected to Gillespie's departing from the Eldridge style, which Calloway preferred. By 1941 Calloway had had enough and Gillespie was fired.

Over the next several years Gillespie joined in the jam sessions at Minton's Playhouse in Harlem. There, Gillespie, along with Charlie Parker (saxophone), who became his devoted friend, Thelonious Monk (piano), Kenny Clarke (drums), Charlie Christian (electric guitar), and others, created a modern jazz that became bebop. During the early 1940s Gillespie played with Duke Ellington, Ella Fitzgerald, Earl Hines, and also Les Hite, with whom he recorded what is possibly the first bebop solo on the "Jersey Bounce" in 1942. In that period he wrote what may be his most famous composition, "A Night in Tunisia." In 1944 Gillespie, assisting Coleman Hawkins, recorded his piece "Woody 'n' You," considered the first full expression of bebop. For the next year he played with Billy Eckstine in what has been termed the first bebop orchestra.

From 1945 to 1950 Gillespie and his associates led a musical revolution in which bebop became the dominant jazz form. In addition he set the standard for playing bebop trumpet, just as Charlie Parker did for alto saxophone. Gillespie often played in a remarkably high register, and he improvised brilliantly at incredibly high speeds. Unlike many musicians who concealed their techniques, Gillespie was happy to teach others his theories, spreading the gospel of bop. He even came to be called the "theoretician." The great bebop trumpeters that followed, Fats Navarro, Miles Davis, and Clifford Brown among them, all derived largely from Gillespie.

During this period Gillespie wrote some of his best-known compositions and, with groups that included Charlie Parker, Ray Brown (bass), Bud Powell (piano), and Max Roach (drums). Gillespie, cut such standards as "Salt Peanuts," "Bebop," "Groovin' High," "Hot House," and "Ko Ko." The new sound did not appeal to all jazz lovers, deviating as it did from the traditional swing style.

In the late 1940s Gillespie added another layer to bebop. He met the Cuban conga player Chano Pozo and began a collaboration that produced another new musical form, **Afro–Cuban jazz**. Together they wrote the explosive "Manteca," with its **polyrhythms** and searing trumpet passages. Other Afro-Cuban compositions followed, including "Cubana Be" and "Cubana Bop." Young, progressive jazz musicians were eager to play with Gillespie, and his big band always boasted an array of jazz all-stars. The multitalented Gillespie sang the vocals on some numbers, often spicing his performance with scat singing. Some of his compositions, such as "Ool-Ya-Koo" and "Oo-Pop-a-Da" gave bebop a kind of playful linguistic charm.

By 1950 the big band heyday had ended, and for about the next five years Gillespie played in small ensembles. He took part in the legendary performance of the quintet that played the 1953 Massey Hall concert in Toronto, and included Parker, Powell, Roach, and Mingus. Along with many of his jazz associates he signed on to Norman Granz's Jazz at the Philharmonic tour, continuing with Granz periodically into the late 1950s. At a party in 1953, reportedly, someone fell on Gillespie's trumpet, causing the bell end to bend upward. When Gillespie played the horn, he thought he could hear the sound better and ordered a trumpet with the bell turned up at a 45-degree angle, which he played thereafter.

The U.S. State Department recognized Gillespie's potential as a goodwill ambassador and in 1956 authorized him to form a big band for an oversees tour to Europe and the Middle East. Later, Gillespie made a tour to Latin America. These were the State Department's first uses of jazz orchestras for cultural export. Previously Gillespie had suffered an emotional blow in 1955 when his close friend and artistic alter ego, Charlie Parker, died. Gillespie called Parker the other half of his heartbeat.

In the early 1960s he collaborated with the Argentine piano player Lalo Schifrin in producing several symphonic pieces, including *Gillespiana, Tunisian Fantasy,* and *The New Continent.* Gillespie kept going strong through the balance of the 1960s, and in 1970–71 went on a world tour with the Giants of Jazz.

Pablo Records signed Gillespie to a contract in 1974, and he won Grammys in 1975 and again in 1980. In 1975 the Institute of High Fidelity named him Musician of the Year. Gillespie, ever concerned with communicating his ideas, worked with a collaborator, Al Fraser, to write his 1979 biography, *To Be or Not to Bop*. During the 1980s Gillespie devoted considerable time to teaching workshops and master classes. He received many honorary degrees from universities, Columbia, Tufts, and Rutgers among them. Still, performing was his mainstay, and he celebrated his seventieth birthday by organizing a big band and touring abroad. It featured Jon Faddis on trumpet, who Gillespie personally groomed as his heir apparent.

A year later, in 1988, he formed the United Nations Orchestra, made up of outstanding musicians from various countries. The orchestra embarked on a highly ambitious international schedule through 1991. Gillespie's stamina was remarkable, but at the tour's end he appeared tired and drawn. He was honored for a week in 1992 at a Blue Note nightclub gathering in New York, during which outstanding jazzmen rotated periodically to play one more time with the great "Diz." On January 6, 1993, he died of pancreatic cancer. He had recorded, performed, and taught almost to the end of his life.

Thelonious Monk

The High Priest of Bebop
1917–1982

As complete an original as it is possible to be.

—Randy Weston, pianist, quoted in
New York Times, February 18, 1982

They called him weird, eccentric, idiosyncratic. Some called him mad. In the end, however, he is most often called genius. Different? Yes; offbeat? Yes. But by the measure of most jazz critics, Thelonious Monk was a true genius of jazz piano and composition. Although considered a founder of the bebop school, he did not identify himself with any mode of music. "I like the whole song, melody and chord structure to be different," he once said. "I make up my own chords and melodies." In a musical medium noted for its individualism and creativity, he stood apart.

Monk's playing is distinguished by the original use of melody and themes, often employing unusual harmonies, dissonant chords, and unexpected pauses. He has been compared to Igor Stravinsky and Arnold Schoenberg in the modern classical field. Even some bebop musicians did not understand his music, but few would deny him a place among the elite in jazz.

Thelonious Sphere Monk, named for his father, was born on October 10, 1917, in Rocky Mount, North Carolina. Thelonious was only about four when his mother moved the family to New York City, eventually residing in the tough San Juan Hill area of mid-Manhattan, where he lived for most of his life. Thelonious began piano lessons at about age ten, soon adopting the stride technique, and at seventeen he joined an evangelist troupe that toured the Midwest. When the tour reached Kansas City, Thelonious mingled with jazz musicians there, including the accomplished pianist Mary Lou Williams, who became his mentor.

Years later Williams would comment that the teenaged Monk's playing was already distinctive. Although influenced by Williams, Duke Ellington, and others, Monk developed his own unique style. Even the way he positioned his hands was unusual, holding them flat and almost level with the keys. In the late 1930s Monk returned to New York City, where he formed his first quartet and began composing in earnest. One of his earliest works, "Ruby, My Dear," was dedicated to a West Indian girlfriend whose family rejected him. Afterward, Monk met Nellie Smith, whom he married in 1947. She remained with him throughout the rest of his life.

Monk's first major breakthrough came in 1940 when Minton's Playhouse hired him as its house pianist. It was at Minton's, renowned for its jam sessions, that Monk worked with Charlie Parker, Dizzy Gillespie, Kenny Clarke, Charlie Christian, and others to create the modern jazz called bebop. Monk did not truly join the bebop movement. He incorporated bebop in his own work but continued to develop in his own way. It was the traditional saxophonist Coleman Hawkins who in 1944 invited Monk to cut his first record.

Another break came in 1944 when Cootie Williams recorded Monk's composition "'Round Midnight," which became a jazz standard. Monk got fewer recording jobs than true boppers like Parker and Gillespie, and it wasn't until 1947 that Alfred Lion of Blue Note Records signed Monk to record under his own name. During the Blue Note years, from about 1947 to 1952, Monk recorded some of his finest compositions, including "Evance," "Ruby, My Dear," "Off Minor," and "Straight No Chaser."

Monk's career seemed ready to soar, but in 1951 it suffered a severe blow. He was taken into custody for alleged narcotics possession, and he spent sixty days in jail. When he got out, his cabaret card, which allowed him to work in New York City clubs, was suspended. He could still record and play out of town, but he endured lean times until his card was restored in 1957. During the 1950s the boppers distinguished themselves by their unconventional dress. Berets, goatees, and dark glasses were common. Monk was no exception. Wearing a variety of hats and loose robes, he took on the image of a kind of Middle Eastern mufti. He was dubbed the "high priest of bebop."

Monk switched recording companies in 1952, going over to Prestige, for which he recorded his own works, including "Little Rootie Tootie," "We See," "Reflections," and "Bemsha Swing," the latter becoming a virtual bebop anthem. But Monk was still not getting widespread recognition, and in 1955 he signed with Riverside, where he collaborated with the noted producer Orrin Keepnews.

His first effort, a Duke Ellington songbook album, began a succession of successful albums. Perhaps the crowning achievement of the Riverside years was the album *Brilliant Corners,* embellished by outstanding sidemen such as Sonny Rollins (tenor sax), Clark Terry (trumpet), Oscar Pettiford (bass), and Max Roach (drums). In it he introduced the song "Pannonica," honoring the wealthy Baroness Nica de Koenigswarter, patron of a number of jazz artists, including Monk.

In 1957 Monk began to draw capacity crowds to the Five Spot Café, where he appeared with such stellar jazzmen as John Coltrane and Johnny Griffin (tenor saxophonists). In 1960 Monk played at the Newport Jazz Festival, and the next year toured Europe with his quartet. In 1962 he signed with Columbia Records, which produced his best-selling albums, beginning with *Monk's Dream.* Now at the height of his fame, he made the *Time* magazine cover for February 28, 1964, and in that year performed at New York's Carnegie Hall.

Monk's relationship with Columbia weakened as the 1960s rock and roll craze swept America, hurting record sales in jazz. He made only a few more albums after that. Monk continued to play in New York City, the West Coast, and elsewhere in the country, and in 1971 he went on a world tour with an all-star group called "Giants of Jazz." After the tour Monk seemed unwell and became somewhat reclusive, seldom performing.

By the early 1970s Monk's behavior had become erratic. He had always danced onstage but now acted in other strange ways that some people just thought funny. He seemed to withdraw now to a greater degree. Close friends thought he might be mentally ill, possibly schizophrenic. According to some reports, he was a heavy drug user, which was believed to account for his physical and mental deterioration. Some critics also complained that his playing had suffered. He played his last date at the Newport Jazz Festival in 1976 and was seldom seen thereafter. He spent his final days in the New

Jersey home of the Baroness de Koenigswarter, who cared for him until he died of a stroke on February 17, 1982.

In 1993 the National Academy of Arts and Sciences presented Monk with a posthumous Lifetime Achievement Award, one of many honors he achieved. His name was given to one of the nation's prestigious jazz organizations, the Thelonious Monk Institute. Among others, Monk's work is carried on by his son, T. S. Monk, a jazz drummer.

Art Blakey

Bu—Innovator of Hard Bop
1919–1990

I'm going to stay with the youngsters—
it keeps the mind active.

—Art Blakey,
from the album *A Night at Birdland*

He was the First Messenger, a leader taking his jazz truth to listeners like a biblical prophet. His disciples were the Jazz Messengers, and the truth he delivered was called "hard bop." He was Art Blakey, a bebop drummer whose vision, aided and abetted by pianist Horace Silver, was one of modern jazz with a heavy dose of swinging blues and **funk**. Blakey was, arguably, the chief propagator of this brand of jazz, but he was concerned with more than just playing his message. Preservation of his music was also a priority, and he dedicated himself to teaching his gospel.

The Jazz Messengers became a training ground for young musicians. They acknowledged its toughness, but those who graduated took their place among the jazz elite. Among the stars Blakey helped develop were Clifford Brown, Kenny Dorham, Hank Mobley, Johnny Griffin, Benny Golson, Freddie Hubbard, Keith Jarrett, Chuck Mangione, Jo Anne Brackeen, Wynton Marsalis, and Terence Blanchard. These and others advanced the Art Blakey legacy.

Art Blakey was born in Pittsburgh on October 11, 1919. He first took up piano, and in his early teens organized a big band to play at dances. By the time he was seventeen, he was leading a fourteen-piece group at a local club when, according to Blakey, someone named Erroll Garner (a future great jazz pianist) showed up and replaced him on piano. It was a key career turn for Blakey, who had been teaching himself drums and took over the band's drum kit.

Drummers such as Chick Webb and Sid Catlett became Blakey's idols, and he imitated their driving style. His first big break came in 1942 when Mary Lou Williams hired him to play with her band at Kelly's Stable in New York City. While with Williams, Fletcher Henderson caught his act and signed Blakey to play with his famed orchestra. After touring with Henderson in 1943–44, Blakey was offered a chance to join the new Billy Eckstine big band, an early breeding ground of bebop. The ensemble included, at times, such future modern jazz innovators as Miles Davis, Charlie Parker, Thelonious Monk, and vocalist Sarah Vaughan. Blakey stayed with the band until it broke up in 1947. Afterward he formed a seventeen-member rehearsal group he called the "Messengers," and freelanced with various artists, including the Buddy DeFranco Quartet (1951–53).

It is likely that February 21, 1954, is the date on which hard bop had its true launching. Blakey had formed a new quintet that included Horace Silver (piano), Curly Russell (bass), Lou Donaldson (alto saxophone), and Clifford Brown (trumpet). That group was booked into Birdland on that February day, and Alfred Lion of Blue Note Records was there to record the live performances. The resulting albums, *A Night at Birdland with the Art Blakey Quintet, Volumes 1 and 2,* constitute a landmark in the history of modern jazz. Commentary from Cootie's Jazz Web site states that the music, "raw, urgent and fizzing with energy was to be popularly called 'hard bop,' and was thrust into public consciousness in these records."

Blakey and Silver continued to develop hard bop concepts, with input from others, and in 1955 a cooperative quintet was formed that included Silver and Hank Mobley (tenor saxophone), Kenny Dorham (trumpet), and Doug Watkins (bass) under the name Jazz Messengers. That group stayed together for about a year, then split up, leaving Blakey with the trademark name, "Jazz Messengers." Blakey led various artist combinations under that name for the rest of his career. Through the late 1950s and 1960s Blakey and the Messengers led the way in hard bop.

Blakey did not restrict his work to the Messengers. He was called upon for U.S. and foreign engagements. At one of these, the 1974 Newport Jazz Festival, he participated in a legendary drum battle between himself, Max Roach, Elvin Jones, and Buddy Rich. In 1971–72 he went on a world tour with the Giants of Jazz, which included such premier musicians as Gillespie, Monk, Sonny Stitt, and Kai Winding. Blakey's travels also took him to Africa where he adopted Islam, taking the name Abdullah Ibn Buhaina, from whence came his nickname "Bu."

While in Africa, Blakey learned the techniques of African drumming. He incorporated the practice of using his elbow on the tom-tom and tapping out rhythms on the side of a drum. Blakey saw himself as a hard-driving engine that moved the band, speeding up or slowing down to complement a soloist. He believed in a primal, forceful rhythm, augmented by complex cross-rhythms.

Blakey also worked on film scores, including the French *Les Liaisons Dangereuses*. Always open to new ideas, he performed with African and Afro-Cuban drum groups, and even helped adapt his music to dance. Avant-garde and fusion groups challenged hard bop, but in the 1980s Blakey's music enjoyed a renaissance. Blakey was still delivering jazz through the Messengers in the late 1980s, and he maintained a rigorous schedule, not slowing down until lung cancer took his life on October 16, 1990. His loss to jazz was immeasurable, but his musical tradition lives on in the many artists he trained and influenced.

Among the honors accruing to Blakey in his lifetime were the Down Beat Critics New Star Award (1953), a Grammy Award (1984; for best jazz instrumental group), and the North Sea Festival Charlie Parker Award (1989).

Anita O'Day

The Jezebel of Jazz
1919–

She's a real hot tomato, she's a busted valentine.

—From "And Her Tears Flowed Like Wine," Anita O'Day vocal with the Stan Kenton orchestra

No one quite knew how a record date in 1941 would turn out for the Gene Krupa band and its new, relatively unknown singer, Anita O'Day. Krupa had been mostly recording hits of the day to assure a decent commercial return. But now he wanted to take a chance on a new number, called "Let Me Off Uptown," which required a vocal duet between O'Day and featured trumpet player Roy Eldridge.

Profit-minded record producers were leery of such mingling between black and white musicians in this pre-civil rights movement era. But matching white O'Day's jaunty, swinging, salty-tinged tones to black Eldridge's scorching vocal and cloud-piercing trumpet solo overcame all obstacles. The record became Krupa's biggest hit, and established O'Day as a featured swing vocalist.

In succeeding years O'Day set the standard for big band singers and was emulated by many of the girl singers of the period. O'Day sometimes phrased like Billie Holiday, but she stated that she was more influenced by Martha Raye, a fine singer but better known as a Hollywood comic. O'Day is sometimes called the best of the swinging, big band singers, and few critics do not place her near the top. But she may have surpassed them all in longevity. She was still a headliner at the turn of the twenty-first century. Along the way she had been dubbed "the Jezebel of Jazz."

"Uptown" in the song meant Harlem, but for O'Day it meant the neighborhood of that name where she grew up in Chicago. It was a heavily transient area, replete with bars and musician hangouts. Born Anita Belle Colton on October 18, 1919, she encountered hardships throughout childhood, including an unstable home life. Her father was a chronic gambler and drinker, and her mother was not always supportive of her. In junior high she became a truant.

At fourteen Anita began entering, with a partner, contests called walkathons, a type of endurance dance marathon that was popular in the depression-ridden 1930s. Money could be won at these events. She also began to find work dancing in local northside clubs, and occasionally she sang, although she had little voice training. Anita, not yet sixteen, often had to waitress or play dice games with the customers when not entertaining. Her first break came at seventeen when she was offered a singing job in the Off-Beat club in Chicago's Loop.

The Off-Beat club became a musician's hangout, and one night Gene Krupa dropped in to see the show. Anita knocked him out, and he told her that if his singer ever quit, she had the job. By this time Anita Colton had changed her name to O'Day, which is the pig Latin term (oday) for money (dough). Her success at the Off-Beat club led to other gigs, including a stint with the Raymond Scott band. Finally, in 1941, Krupa called and O'Day joined him on a cross-country tour. Roy Eldridge came aboard about the same time, and together they ignited the band. After "Let Me Off Uptown," Anita cut another hit record with Krupa and Eldridge, "Thanks for the Boogie Ride," and her popularity soared. She won *Down Beat*'s "New Star of the Year" award in 1941 and was named among the top five big band singers in 1942.

O'Day also had ideas about how to present herself. She wanted to be more than just a pretty front for the band; she wanted to be considered one of the musicians. To emphasize that status, O'Day dressed like the musicians, wearing a band member jacket and matching skirt, switching to long gowns for ballroom dates. After the band broke up in 1942, O'Day worked briefly with Woody Herman, then joined Stan Kenton in 1944. Kenton was a serious musician who wanted to play **progressive jazz**. O'Day admired that, but she wanted to swing her vocals. Her stay with Kenton was short, but they recorded at least one solid hit, "And Her Tears Flowed Like Wine."

O'Day rejoined Krupa briefly in 1945, but in 1946 she began a solo career. In 1948 she became a partner in a Chicago club, the High Note. She was one of the club's headliners but also worked other gigs. The High Note experience lasted until about 1951, when O'Day decided to go out on her own again.

Her popularity remained high, and in 1955 she cut an album, *Anita,* that propelled her career. By now swing had gone out of style and pop and jazz were on divergent paths, with pop drawing the big money. O'Day stuck with jazz, however. Bebop had replaced swing in the jazz idiom, and O'Day adapted her style to match. In the process she became one of jazz's premier scat singers. In 1958 O'Day was a sensation at the Newport Jazz Festival, and the 1960 film of that festival, *Jazz on a Summer's Day,* gave her an additonal boost.

Over the next several years O'Day toured extensively. She worked hard and she played hard. O'Day started smoking marijuana when she was a young girl (when it was legal), and hanging out with certain musicians led her to heroin and addiction. In 1966 O'Day almost died from an overdose. Her physical condition had been deteriorating, and after she recovered from the overdose, she had to decide: drugs or a career? With the same will that took her to the top in jazz, she kicked her habit. After rehabilitation she made a triumphal return, keyed by a smashing performance at the 1970 Berlin Jazz Festival, which was recorded live.

Through the 1970s, O'Day toured extensively, particulary in Japan, where she recorded several new albums. In the United States her performances drew rave reviews. She appeared on network telecasts, including the Dick Cavett and Johnny Carson shows, and *60 Minutes* interviewed her in 1980 for its Sunday night telecast. Interviewers invariably probed about her addiction, but she refused to dwell on it. She did confront that problem head on in her 1981 autobiography *High Times Hard Times.*

O'Day celebrated her fiftieth year as a jazz singer in 1985 with a Carnegie Hall Jazz concert, and Los Angeles declared an "Anita O'Day" day. Despite advancing years, she swung into the 1990s, starting with the Grammy-nominated album *In A Mellow Tone.* She had another brush with death (from alcohol). O'Day was honored as a Jazz Masters fellow by the National Endowment for the Arts in 1997. Two years later, at age eighty, she headed the bill at the JVC Jazz Concert in New York. Into the next century, this tough lady from Chicago was still swinging.

George Shearing

Pianist Leader Created a New Jazz Sound
1919 –

If you had to come up with a musical definition of elegant, you would go for that sound (of the George Shearing Quintet).

—Murray Horowitz, vice president,
NPR Cultural Programming

George Shearing was drawing favorable reviews at the Clique Club in New York City. The year was 1949, and Shearing was leading a quartet featuring himself on piano and the acclaimed Buddy DeFranco on clarinet. Then came a shock: DeFranco could not record with the group because he was under contract to another label. Replacing DeFranco would be difficult, so

Shearing went for something else: he expanded to a quintet, adding vibra-phone and guitar. A whole new jazz sound was invented. The quintet's first recording, "September in the Rain," became a runaway hit, and George Shearing soared to jazz stardom.

George Albert Shearing was born in London, England, on August 13, 1919, the youngest of nine children. He was blind at birth but showed an early interest in music and was enrolled at the Linden Lodge School for the Blind, where he received musical training. He was denied further musical education because his family needed support and he was able to work playing in pubs. American jazz was invading England, and the piano techniques of such artists as Fats Waller and Teddy Wilson captivated young George. Then, while playing London's Number 1 Rhythm Club in 1937, he met jazz writer and composer Leonard Feather, who arranged his first record date. It began a great collaboration.

During the late 1930s and early 1940s, Shearing's popularity in England grew. Playing mostly swing, he jammed with visiting American and European jazz artists and delved occasionally into classical music. His recognition in Britain was reflected in the *Melody Maker* magazine music polls, winning the Best British Pianist award seven times running. But despite his success, Shearing knew that the true measure of his jazz artistry could only come in the United States, where jazz originated.

Shearing visited the United States briefly in 1947 and discovered that his fame had not reached America. The next year he moved to New York City, realizing that he virtually had to start over. His break came when a 52nd Street club, the Three Deuces, signed him for an extended run. At first playing solo, he eventually joined small groups, performing with such musicians as Oscar Pettiford (bass) and J. C. Heard (drums). Shearing had become familiar with the modern sounds coming out of the U.S. jazz community. Now, as he associated with jazz modernists, Shearing's own style began to incorporate the complex harmonies of the new jazz called bebop.

In the following year Shearing formed the quintet and, using his locked-hands, or block-chord, piano style to blend with vibraphone and guitar, created a sound that swept the nation. Those three instruments in unison formed a mellow tone that carried melody in an emphatic yet swinging mode. So unified were the players that the quintet came across as a single instrument.

After "September in the Rain," the Shearing quintet produced one hit after another, including, "East of the Sun," "Pick Yourself Up," and "Lullaby of Birdland." The latter of these, a Shearing composition, became a virtual bebop anthem. Through the 1950s Shearing's fame spread worldwide. Everybody, it seemed, loved George Shearing.

Shearing held the quintet together, with periodic personnel changes, for some twenty years. Such notables as Cal Tjader (vibes), Gary Burton (vibes), and Joe Pass (guitar) were at times members of the group. In the 1970s Shearing worked largely in duos and trios. This continued into the 1980s, when his recording career accelerated through collaborations with jazz singer Mel Tormé. The duo won Grammys in both 1982 and 1983. Shearing also sang occasionally, and was particularly engaging on such ballads as "Send In the Clowns." He kept a relentless schedule into the 1990s, returning to the quintet format for a 1994 album *The Shearing Sound*.

Over the years honors were heaped upon George Shearing. In addition to honorary degrees, he was given Britain's Ivor Novello Award for Lifetime Achievement in 1993, and in 1995 he received The Helen Keller Achievement Award. In 1996 he became an Officer of the Order of the British Empire and in 1998 the National Arts Club conferred the American Music Award on him. Perhaps his most gratifying reward, however, was the crowd that still gathered to hear him in the new century.

Marian McPartland

Queen of the Keyboard
1920–

Her playing is sensitive, lyrical, romantic and well-wrought.

—Paul de Barros on the *Down Beat* Web site

What is perhaps most striking about the British-born Marian McPartland's talent is not so much that she is a superb pianist, but that she can adapt to virtually any style of playing. She can go from Chopin to **boogie woogie** or from stride to bebop without losing a note. It is not surprising that McPartland has honed such skills, because she is a true student of music, and especially jazz. She seemingly examines jazz techniques and history from every conceivable angle. It is this curiosity that McPartland demonstrates regularly on her long-running, award-winning radio show, *Piano Jazz,* which explores the talent of each guest jazz artist.

Those same qualities motivated McPartland to become a leading jazz educator. Her work in schools has earned her numerous honorary degrees and awards. McPartland did not enter jazz to make a statement, but in fact, she is one of the few women instrumentalists who broke the barrier to the largely men's world of jazz back in the 1940s, helping pave the way for many others to follow. If her British manner and clipped accent make her seem a little unjazzlike, make no mistake: McPartland swings with the best of them!

Born near London in Slough, England, on March 20, 1920, Margaret Marian Turner began picking out melodies on the piano when she was a little girl. She took some early piano lessons, and in her teens began classical piano studies at the Guildhall School of Music in London. To her parents' dismay, she soon was attracted to modern music, particularly jazz. After about a year, the lure of performing captivated her and she joined a traveling vaudeville troupe. World War II had begun, however, and soon she signed up to entertain the troops.

While on tour in Belgium, she had the opportunity to play with a cornet player, American Jimmy McPartland. They struck up a friendship that blossomed into a romance, and in 1945 they married. The couple went to the United States in 1946, and Jimmy formed a quintet with Marian at piano. Marian, however, did not want to be confined to Jimmy's traditional New Orleans style, and in 1955 she formed her own trio, which played regularly at New York's Hickory House until 1960.

The 1960s brought rough times for the McPartlands. Following separate careers eventually led to divorce, although the two remained close friends. Marian ran into another problem when Benny Goodman signed her to play with his sextet, a great honor, especially (in those days) for a woman.

Somehow, though, the chemistry with Goodman didn't work, and she left the group, suffering an emotional relapse. Goodman was a tough taskmaster, but Marian made no excuses, and she bounced back.

McPartland had recorded for several record labels, but in 1970 she formed her own record company, Halcyon. Among the jazz artists she recorded, in addition to herself, were Earl Hines and Teddy Wilson. In 1979 she contracted to record with Concord, eventually cutting more than fifty albums for them. That was also the year McPartland began her radio program *Piano Jazz,* perhaps the most significant aspect of her career. Featured on a national network, it is said to be the Public Broadcasting System's longest running program.

Marian McPartland is also a composer, whose most famous work is probably "Ambience." Others include "In the Days of Our Love" (with lyrics by Johnny Mercer) and "Twilight World" (with lyrics by Peggy Lee). In 1986 she was inducted into the International Association of Jazz Education Hall of Fame and in 1987 her book *All in Good Time* was published.

Through the years McPartland retained a warm relationship with her former husband, even playing together occasionally. In 1990 Jimmy was diagnosed with lung cancer, and he declined rapidly. Marian cared for him through his illness, and in 1991, just two days before Jimmy's death, they remarried as a gesture of their love. She commented later that their divorce had failed.

Marian kept up a vigorous performance schedule, in addition to her radio show. Her career spanned almost three-quarters of the twentieth century, and in the twenty-first she shows few signs of slowing down.

Charlie "Yardbird" Parker

Bird Lives
1920–1955

[He was] the other side of my heartbeat.
—Dizzy Gillespie, quoted in
New York Times obituary, January 7, 1993

He was fifteen years old and eager to show what he could do on the alto saxophone. One day in 1935 he showed up at a club in Kansas City, Missouri, and asked to join the musicians jamming on-stage. They agreed, and on the downbeat they went into "Body and Soul." Unfortunately, the young alto only knew "Honeysuckle Rose" and eight bars of "Lazy River." Unfazed, he took off on the only tune he knew in the only key he knew. The musicians broke up laughing, and the humiliated teen took his horn and skulked out the door. Those musicians could not have known that in ten years the same alto player would change forever the way jazz would be played, becoming a legend in his own time. His name was Charlie Parker.

Few, if any, authorities in music dispute the genius of Charlie Parker. He, with Dizzy Gillespie and a few others, led the way into the new musical form, bebop. Most of the early experimenters in modern jazz had concepts, but making them work musically was a problem. It was Dizzy Gillespie who said that the man they called Bird showed them how to get from one note to another.

Charlie Parker invented new ways to express **harmony**, melody, and rhythm. His ability to transpose, compose, and improvise at lightning speeds astounded his fellow musicians. His musical ingenuity has been compared to that of Mozart, and his technical skill to Art Tatum. He influenced not only the way the saxophone would be played but also every instrument of the jazz orchestra.

Charles Christopher Parker Jr. was born in Kansas City, Kansas, on August 29, 1920. There was little musical tradition in his family, although his father, Charles Parker Sr. was for a time a dancer and singer in vaudeville. His mother, Addie, was devoted to Charlie and saw to his upbringing and education. Charlie started elementary school in Kansas City, a staid town compared to its rollicking namesake across the river, Kansas City, Missouri.

When he was seven or eight, his parents separated and his mother decided to move across the river, which likely changed the course of Charlie Parker's life. Kansas City, Missouri, was one of the nation's major hubs of the new jazz music. Charlie took up alto saxophone in high school after he was struck by the alto playing of Rudy Vallee, a movie star whose playing was undistinguished. By the time Charlie was fifteen, jazz had become his focus, and he began skipping school and staying out late at jazz clubs.

About that time, Charlie fell in love with Rebecca Ruffin, a classmate, and the two teenagers were married in 1936. Only sixteen years old, Charlie set out to make his living as a musician, although his playing was still raw. He auditioned for Count Basie, but the drummer threw his cymbal at Charlie's feet in disgust. Charlie was still determined to play, but his progress was stymied by an automobile accident. After recovering months later, he landed a gig in Eldon, Missouri, where he honed his skills.

Returning to Kansas City, Charlie found gigs. He really needed to work now because, at age seventeen, he was a father, Rebecca having given birth to a son. He became involved with two older musicians, Jay McShann (piano) and Buster Smith (saxophone). Charlie developed quickly under Smith's tutelage, even then displaying unusual technique. Ben Webster, Chu Berry, Coleman Hawkins, Lester Young, and other saxophonists were playing Kansas City and must have influenced Charlie. He is compared mostly to Young because, like Young, he used less **vibrato** than most others.

Charlie Parker was learning a lot musically, but he was also learning about drugs and alcohol. Later, Parker would say that getting "high" not only did not enhance performance but detracted from it. In the meantime, his domestic life had been deteriorating. Finally, in 1939, with many jazzmen heading eastward and family pressures building, he pawned his saxophone and hopped a freight train to Chicago.

In Chicago, Parker met bandleader-singer Billy Eckstine, whom he impressed playing with a borrowed saxophone. He stayed in Chicago briefly before heading for New York City, where Buster Smith had gone earlier. Parker found Smith, but couldn't land a gig, so for about three months he washed dishes. He associated with musicians, becoming almost an annoyance with his persistent questions about harmonies and rhythm. Finally, he found a collaborator in guitarist Bill "Biddy" Fleet, and the two began working together in the back room of a Harlem chili house. It was there, in 1939, that a new movement in contemporary music began.

On that occasion Parker was fooling around with using different chord **changes** on "Cherokee" when suddenly the music that he had been hearing in his head began coming out of his horn. His experiments would eventually be perfected, with others, as bebop. Progress on his conception was derailed, however, when news came from Kansas City that his father had died. He returned home for the funeral, then soon after joined Jay McShann, whose band was playing there. With McShann in 1940 he cut his first records, including "Hootie Blues." His solos now reflected his new musical concepts, which some musicians and audiences rejected while others praised.

Parker stayed with McShann until 1942, during which time he acquired the name "Yardbird" (later shortened to "Bird"), a reference to an incident in which Parker is said to have salvaged a chicken killed on the road and had it prepared for dinner. It was during this time that Parker divorced Rebecca. Returning to New York, he joined an Earl "Fatha" Hines band, which included Gillespie, Billy Eckstine, and vocalist Sarah Vaughan. Some bebop ideas germinated in the Hines group, but mostly they developed out of jam sessions at Minton's Playhouse and Clark Monroe's Uptown House, where Parker, Gillespie, Monk, Charlie Christian (guitar), Kenny Clarke (drums), and others played after hours. Some early big band bebop came in 1944 when Eckstine formed his own unit, including Parker and Gillespie.

The real breakthrough for bebop, however, came in the Parker and Gillespie small group sessions of 1945–46. Such classics as "Shaw 'Nuff," "Salt Peanuts," "Hot House," "Groovin' High," and "Ko Ko" came out of these sessions, and the two artists became the talk of the jazz world. Also during the 1940s Parker was influenced by such living classical composers as Stravinsky, Hindemith, and Prokofiev.

In late 1945 Parker and Gillespie headed for Los Angeles to introduce bebop to the West Coast. After their engagement Gillespie returned to New York, but Parker remained on the coast. Parker's behavior was now becoming erratic. He began missing dates, arriving late, and disappearing altogether. Nevertheless, he managed some landmark moments, including Jazz at the Philharmonic (JATP) recordings. But by July 1946, his drug use caused him to be confined in a state hospital for six months.

Parker returned to New York in early 1947 and formed what became his classic quintet, made up of himself, Miles Davis, Duke Jordan (piano), Tommy Potter (bass), and Max Roach (drums). That group's performances at the Three Deuces and their recordings are legendary. Later, a gig at the Royal Roost lasted through most of 1949.

The demand for Parker had grown to international proportions, and in 1949 the quintet, minus Miles Davis, was off to the Paris jazz festival. Kenny Dorham replaced Davis, and Dorham later gave way to Red Rodney. Parker loved French culture and made known his intention to return to Paris to study classical music. Later in the year Norman Granz gave Parker an orchestral background for his first "Parker with Strings" album. Shortly thereafter, in December 1949, Parker played the opening of a Manhattan nightclub named in his honor, Birdland, itself a jazz legend. In 1950 the Parker quintet broke up. About this time Parker, who had already married twice more, took up with Chan Richardson, a former dancer, who remained his companion almost to the end of his life.

Parker's recordings with strings were acclaimed, and he formed a string ensemble for a tour of the eastern United States. He followed with a European tour, but upon his return to the United States in 1950 he was arrested for narcotics possession. His drug habit had returned with a vengeance. The arrest meant suspension of his cabaret card, so he could no longer work in New York.

Parker worked outside the city until his cabaret card was restored in 1953. In the meantime, two daughters were born to Parker and Richardson. Parker's physical and mental conditions were deteriorating, and when one of his daughters died in 1954, he went over the edge. After two attempted suicides he was committed to a mental hospital. Upon his release, Parker's behavior became increasingly erratic, and he was banned from Birdland. His break with Chan made matters worse. Remarkably, he rallied to play at New York's Town Hall, and seemed close to his old form. Birdland invited him back on March 5, 1955, but he ended up walking off after a row with pianist Bud Powell.

He took refuge in the home of his friend the Baroness Nica de Koenigswarter, a wealthy patron of jazz artists. A week later, on March 12, 1955, Charlie Parker's heart stopped while he was watching television, the cause of death given as pneumonia. His body had been so ravaged by alcohol and drugs that the attending doctor estimated his age at fifty-three. He was actually thirty-four. In his lifetime a small but growing cult grew up around Parker, and even in the first days after his death a cry went up that resonates to this day: "Bird lives!"

Billy Taylor

Ambassador of Jazz
1921–

[He is] that rare combination of creativity, intelligence, vision, commitment and leadership . . . that make him one of our most cherished national treasures.

—Billy Taylor biography on the Billy Taylor Web site (www.billytaylor.com)

In 1972 Billy Taylor received an honor accorded to few jazz musicians. He was appointed by the president of the United States to serve on the National Council for the Arts, a post he held until 1978. He worked with other council members to promote fine arts in the United States. It was a role entirely befitting Taylor, whose dedication to jazz education is well known. He had already compiled a number of impressive accomplishments: a doctorate in music education, honorary degrees, and appointments to teaching posts at major institutions. But most significant, perhaps, has been his work in broadcasting as a means of promoting jazz to mass audiences.

Billy Taylor has a quite remarkable talent as a jazz pianist, arranger, and composer. He has played with big bands and led his own small groups, and some of the most distinguished of jazz artists count among his musical associates. Taylor has expressed jazz in virtually every artistic medium, and he has taken it abroad as a United States musical ambassador.

Billy Taylor was born on July 24, 1921, into a Greenville, North Carolina family that abounded with musical talent. His father was particularly versatile, being adept in voice, piano, and brass, and he saw to the musical education of his children. Billy began studying piano at seven, but he also embraced drums, saxophone, and guitar. The piano became his chief interest, however, and he studied classical piano with distinguished teachers in Washington, D.C. He played at social occasions through high school and entered Virginia State College in 1938, determined to major in sociology. But his mind was changed by a music professor who urged him to make music his career.

Taylor graduated with his music degree in 1942, and headed for New York City. He had studied classical music, but the music of Art Tatum and Duke Ellington intrigued him, and jazz became his passion. Within a day of his arrival he was jamming at Minton's in Harlem, and a few days later he had his first gig with tenor saxophone titan Ben Webster. On the same bill was the piano wizard Art Tatum, who became Taylor's mentor. Over the next few years he became a fixture in New York's jazz scene, and in 1946 he joined the Don Redman Orchestra for a world tour.

Broadway also beckoned during the 1940s, and he worked in several jazz-related productions, including *The Seven Lively Arts* and *Holiday on Broadway* (with Billie Holiday). Taylor formed his own quintet, playing New

York City clubs during the late 1940s. His prestige soared in 1949 when he was invited to play with Charlie Parker and Strings at Birdland. Taylor then became Birdland's house pianist for the next two years.

Taylor formed a trio in the early 1950s, his standard group when he wasn't soloing. His recordings during the 1950s included such albums as *My Fair Lady Loves Jazz*, *The Billy Taylor Trio with Candido*, and *Taylor Made Jazz*. Taylor's foray into jazz education began about this time, as well. He began writing for publications such as *Down Beat, The Saturday Review of Literature*, and *Esquire*; lectured at various institutions; directed music for a 1958 television series, *The Subject Is Jazz;* and began radio broadcasting.

During the 1960s Taylor cut several more albums, including *Custom Taylored* and *Brazilian Beat with the Billy Taylor Septet*, and perhaps his most significant composition, "I Wish I Knew How It Would Feel to be Free," reflecting the anguish felt by African Americans striving for civil rights. He helped found New York City's Jazzmobile, which has provided free concerts and music clinics to New Yorkers.

Writing, teaching, and producing and hosting radio and television shows occupied Taylor through the 1970s and 1980s. He became musical director of the David Frost Show in the early 1970s and was made program director of a local New York radio station. To further his educational goals, he enrolled at the University of Massachusetts at Amherst, earning his doctorate there in 1975. Taylor went into a period of serious composing then, writing commissioned works, including *Suite for Jazz Piano and Orchestra, Make a Joyful Noise,* and *For Rachel.* Other serious works include *Theme and Variations*, commissioned by the Kennedy Center; a dance piece, *Step Into My Dream,* commissioned by the University of Illinois Krannert Center for Performing Arts; and *Peaceful Warrior,* honoring Martin Luther King Jr.

In the late 1970s Taylor inaugurated his immensely popular *Jazz Alive* program for National Public Radio, one of several significant series he produced for NPR. Television also drew Taylor, who became musical director of the PBS weekly show, *Black Journal Tonight,* and host of the Bravo network's *Jazz Counterpoint.* He also performed with the New York Jazz Repertory Company and the North Carolina Symphony. In 1984 *Down Beat* awarded Taylor its Lifetime Achievement Award.

In the 1990s Taylor became Artistic Adviser for Jazz to the Kennedy Center for the Performing Arts, for which he produced a jazz concert series. The U.S. government saw Taylor's value as an ambassador and sent him on several State Department overseas tours, and in 1992 awarded him the National Medal of Arts, the nation's highest honor in the arts. At the dawn of the twenty-first century Dr. Billy Taylor, despite a stroke in 2002, was still playing and bringing jazz to the people.

Dave Lambert, Jon Hendricks, Annie Ross

Group That Popularized "Vocalese" Singing Style
1917–1966, 1921– , 1930–

I think it was the truth that we created something that is eternal . . . what we did is good and good is good forever.

—Jon Hendricks, from a 1999
NPR radio interview

It swings, we have fun, it's magic!

—Annie Ross, as quoted in the program for
the Northsea Jazz Festival, July 15, 2000

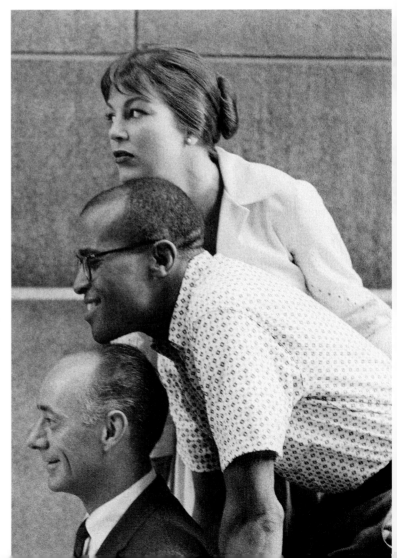

A record contract, a studio, a roomful of singers, and a great idea for an album. But it just wasn't working. Jon Hendricks and Dave Lambert had assembled about a dozen vocalists to sing with them, mostly Count

Basie instrumental numbers for which Hendricks had written lyrics. After a couple of rehearsals with their singers, Lambert and Hendricks knew one thing: this bunch could not swing. Not even if "you hung 'em" Hendricks would tell Billy Taylor in an interview. They had even hired Annie Ross, an esteemed swinging vocalist, to help the singers, but to little avail.

What could they do? A ray of hope came from innovative Dave Lambert. Why not use Lambert, Hendricks, and Ross (LHR) to do *all* of the orchestra parts, which they could accomplish by multitracking? Multitracking is a technique by which one element of a recording is **dubbed** over another element, combining them so it sounds as if they were recorded together. The three vocalists went to work, and the result was quite remarkable. On the hit Basie tune "Every Day," for instance, the two male voices carried the reed section and Annie Ross sang the trumpet parts, even re-creating their high piercing blasts over the ensemble.

It took several months to record *Sing a Song of Basie,* but the gamble paid off. The album was a smash hit and Lambert, Hendricks, and Ross became one of the country's hottest vocal groups. The idea of putting words to and singing instrumental jazz was not new. The technique, called "vocalese," had been employed in previous years by other singers, including Ross, on her popular recordings of "Twisted" and "Farmer's Market," and Lambert and Hendricks, but *Sing a Song of Basie* with its multitracking revolutionized the technique.

Dave Lambert was born on June 19, 1917, in Boston, Massachusetts. His musical education was scant except for drum lessons. After serving in the army during World War II, he landed a job with the vocal group Hi, Lo, Jack and the Dame. During 1944–45 he sang with the Gene Krupa band, teaming with Buddy Stewart to record "What's This," perhaps the first bebop vocal. By the early 1950s Lambert formed the Dave Lambert Singers, who sang behind alto saxophonist Charlie Parker on his recording of "Old

Folks." It was about that time that Lambert met Jon Hendricks.

Jon Hendricks was born in Newark, Ohio, on September 16, 1921, one of seventeen children in his family. At an early age he moved to Toledo, Ohio. He sang in choirs in Toledo and he performed on radio with Toledo-born pianist Art Tatum. After serving in World War II, Hendricks returned to Toledo and began playing drums and singing professionally. Strong academically, Hendricks began studying law, playing music and singing only as sideline. One night he sang in front of Charlie Parker, who had a gig in town. Afterward Parker told him to forget about law and be a jazz singer. Hendricks took his advice, and in 1952 moved to New York to pursue a musical career. He met Dave Lambert, and the two of them recorded a vocalese version of Woody Herman's "Four Brothers," beginning an enduring collaboration.

Annie Ross was born in Mitcham, England, on July 25, 1930. Unlike Lambert and Hendricks, Annie Ross came from a family steeped in musical tradition and theater. Her parents were in vaudeville, and it has been said that Annie could sing before she could walk. She came to the United States when she was about four. Raised in Los Angeles, Annie won a talent contest when she was about eight and awarded a six-month contract with the MGM studios. Subsequently she appeared in several of "The Little Rascals" short film comedies. At eleven she played Judy Garland's sister in *Presenting Lily Mars.*

She returned to Europe in 1947, becoming part of a vocal trio in Paris. While there she sang with such U.S. jazz musicians as Dizzy Gillespie and Kenny Clarke. Ross cut her first record in Paris then returned to the United States when she was twenty to record. Her "Twisted," for which she wrote the vocalese lyrics to an instrumental recording by tenor saxophonist Wardell Gray, drew accolades. In the mid-1950s she went to London to star in a review, *Cranks,* then played the same role in New York. After the show closed, she began her association with Lambert and Hendricks.

After *Sing a Song of Basie,* LHR played to packed houses and racked up impressive record sales. They followed their first hit album with more Basie in *Sing Along With Basie.* In 1959 they cut two more hot sellers, *The Swingers* and *The Hottest New Group in Jazz.* Others included *Lambert, Hendricks & Ross Sing Ellington, High Flying with Lambert, Hendricks & Ross,* and *The Real Ambassadors,* the latter with such stars as Louis Armstrong and Dave Brubeck.

After five almost nonstop years, Annie Ross was exhausted and quit the trio in 1962. The other two members continued the trio, replacing Ross with Yolande Bavan. The new trio was less successful and it broke up in 1964. All three of the LHR group continued their careers, but Lambert's life ended in an automobile accident in 1966. Hendricks applied his talents to other vocalists and formed a vocal group consisting of family members and others. Annie Ross augmented her singing career with roles in movies and theater. In 1999 Ross and Hendricks reunited as a duo. Their performances at the Blue Note in New York and the North Sea Jazz Festival received accolades, just as they had when they revolutionized vocal jazz with Lambert decades earlier.

Charles Mingus

Bassist, Composer, Arranger, and Jazz Innovator
1922–1979

The greatest bass-playing, leader-composer jazz has ever known.

—From "Charles Mingus"
on the All About Jazz Web site

M r. Nice Guy Charles Mingus was not. His reputation as a tough taskmaster who demanded all his musicians could give is well known. Moody and temperamental, he was quick to quash inattentive sidemen or a noisy audience. The large and brawny Mingus even used his size to intimidate. All that being said, Mingus has been heralded as a musical genius, a bandleader and composer who some critics rank alongside Duke Ellington. His irascibility aside, Mingus is remembered for his enduring contributions to music and his influence on the musicians who followed him.

Mingus mastered several instruments, including the piano. As a composer, Mingus produced complex compositions that were difficult to play, which led to some of his conflicts with sidemen. He was even known to write part of a theme and complete it through improvisation during rehearsals. Some of his works became jazz standards. Others include longer, symphonic-like pieces whose recognition has come more slowly. He seemed to weave the entire fabric of his life into his compositions: love, anger, sorrow, and joy, as well as political and social ideas. Much of the direction of **post-bebop, avant-garde jazz** is said to have evolved from Mingus.

Charles Mingus was born on April 22, 1922 on an army base in Nogales, Arizona, where his father was stationed. At an early age his family moved to Los Angeles. He grew up in that city's tough Watts district, a largely African American enclave. Mingus's first musical influence was the gospel singing he heard in church and at home. Other forms of music were shunned at home, but young Charles managed to hear jazz on radio. He studied several instruments during his school years, including piano, violin, trombone, cello, and finally double bass.

Mingus studied with excellent teachers in the region, such as Red Callender, a local jazz musician, and Herman Rheinschagen, a former New York Philharmonic bassist. As a teenager, he began composing, and he played in the high school orchestra, but jazz groups soon recruited the extraordinarily talented young man. He first went with Barney Bigard, in 1942, and then played on the road with Louis Armstrong the following year.

Mingus joined the Lionel Hampton band in 1947, and with that group made a solo on his composition, "Mingus Fingers." He joined a trio in 1950 that included vibraphonist Red Norvo and guitarist Tal Farlow. In 1952 he headed for New York City and enhanced his reputation working with such top jazzmen as Billy Taylor, Stan Getz, Charlie Parker, and Art Tatum. He had a short stint with his idol Duke Ellington, but the Duke fired the headstrong Mingus.

Mingus was familiar with the bebop trends of the 1940s, but it wasn't until he got to New York that he met musicians directly descended from the origins of bop. The hard bop movement was ongoing, which infused more blues and funk into bop lines. Mingus was charged with assembling what many consider the ultimate all-time bebop quintet for a 1953 concert at Massey Hall in Toronto. Joining Mingus onstage were Dizzy Gillespie, Charlie Parker, Bud Powell, and Max Roach. About that time Mingus, Roach, and others had founded Debut Records, which recorded the now legendary Massey Hall concert. Debut achieved some success, but folded in 1957.

By the mid-1950s Mingus had largely left bebop. He was ready to embrace any musical form that suited his work. His *Revelations,* presented in 1955, mixed classical and jazz themes and established him as one of the day's premier composers. He founded the Jazz Workshop to fulfill his need to experiment, and the 1956 release of his album *Pithecanthropus Erectus* proclaimed a new order in jazz.

Through the late 1950s and 1960s Mingus composed and recorded *The Clown, Mingus Ah Um, Mingus Antibes, Money Jungle* (with Roach and Ellington), *Town Hall Concert,* and *The Black Saint and Sinner Lady.* In these Mingus runs a gamut of musical styles and concepts. In *Mingus Ah Um,* for example, he spans gospel, funk, bop, mood pieces, classical touches, avant-garde dissonance, musical tributes, and a civil rights theme.

The pressures and frustrations of several failed commercial ventures, including another crack at a recording company, finally took their toll on Mingus, causing him to leave music for several years. He returned to playing in 1969 and was buoyed in 1971 by a Guggenheim Fellowship in composition and the publication that year of his autobiographical book, *Beneath the Underdog.* Also in 1971 his acclaimed album *Let My Children Hear Music* was released, and he was awarded a chair in music at the State University of New York at Buffalo. A year later the Alvin Ailey ballet company presented a program based on Mingus's music. He also received grants from the Smithsonian Institution and the National Endowment for the Arts, and awards from Brandeis and Yale universities.

Riding a wave of success, Mingus formed a new quintet and traveled extensively, finally slowing in 1977 when his body began to fail. In that year he was diagnosed with a rare degenerative disease, amyotrophic lateral sclerosis (ALS, or Lou Gehrig's disease), which has no cure. By 1978 Mingus was confined to a wheelchair. Nevertheless, he continued to record and was honored at the White House on June 18, 1978. Unable to use his hands, Mingus voiced his last compositions into a tape recorder.

Death took Mingus on January 5, 1979, and his ashes were scattered over the Ganges River in India. Mingus's work and influence kept growing after his death, due at least in part to the efforts of his wife, Sue, and others who promoted his legacy. Through his wife's efforts and a Ford Foundation grant, his most ambitious work, *Epitaph,* was debuted and recorded by a thirty-piece orchestra in 1989. A unit called the Mingus Dynasty, renamed the Mingus Big Band in 1988, was organized to carry on the Mingus musical tradition.

The U.S. government honored Mingus by issuing a postage stamp bearing his image, and the National Endowment for the Arts and the Library of Congress have preserved his scores and other artifacts.

Oscar Pettiford

Influential Bassist and First Prominent Jazz Cellist
1922–1960

The greatest bass player who ever lived.
—Bassist-cellist Buell Neidlinger,
quoted in the *Rough Guide to Jazz*

Sometimes progress comes by accident. Such a case seemingly occurred when one of the foremost bassists of jazz broke his arm playing baseball. While recuperating, Oscar Pettiford experimented with the cello, which had rarely been used as a jazz instrument. Afterward Pettiford began regularly augmenting his bass performances with the cello, becoming the first prominent jazz cellist and the first to play jazz cello like a base, using his fingers to pluck the notes.

Pettiford also made his mark as a composer, some of his compositions having become classics for young bass players to emulate. He played with the top corps of U.S. jazz musicians, including bebop originators Dizzy Gillespie, Charlie Parker, and Kenny Clarke. Pettiford's life was short, but his influence in the art of the bass resonates to the present day.

Oscar Pettiford was born on September 30, 1922, on an Okmulgee, Oklahoma, Indian reservation. He was of mixed Native American and African American descent. His father, Harry "Doc" Pettiford, a veterinarian, and his mother, a music teacher, formed a family band that included the eleven Pettiford children. The family migrated to Minneapolis when Oscar was young, and he was raised mainly in that city. He started on piano, but switched to bass when he was fourteen, and played with the family ensemble until he signed on with the Charlie Barnett band in 1942.

Pettiford left Barnett to seek recognition in New York City. In 1943 he played with trumpeter Roy Eldridge and backed Coleman Hawkins on that saxophonist's classic recording of "The Man I Love." Sessions with Ben Webster, Earl "Fatha" Hines, and the Esquire All-Stars took place about the same time. Pettiford also became involved in the jam sessions at Minton's Playhouse that were the genesis of bebop. In 1944 he co-led a small group at the Onyx Club in what is touted to be bebop's first infiltration of the Fifty-second Street jazz strip. Pettiford joined Hawkins on a West Coast tour the next year, and appeared with him in a film, *The Crimson Canary*.

When Pettiford joined Duke Ellington later in 1945, it confirmed for many that Pettiford was the true successor to Ellington's late bassist Jimmy Blanton, who is credited with setting the standard for modern jazz bass. Pettiford stayed with Ellington for three years, blending his unique style with the Duke's colorful orchestral creations, while continuing to advance bass technique. He left Ellington to lead his own trio, then joined the Woody Herman "Herd" in 1949. It was while with Herman that Pettiford broke his arm and took up cello, subsequently recording on that instrument. He led some small groups over the next several years.

Pettiford formed his own big band in 1956, producing some outstanding work, including the album *Deep Passion,* featuring Art Farmer's trumpet and Lucky Thompson's saxophone. During that period he recorded with Thelonious Monk and the chief proponent of hard bop, Art Blakey. In 1958 Pettiford joined the Jazz from Carnegie Hall tour to Europe, a trip that changed his life. His recognition in Europe was so gratifying that he stayed, settling in Copenhagen, Denmark.

In Europe, Pettiford bore a strong influence on local jazz musicians, and he often linked up with such U.S. jazz artists, as Bud Powell, Stan Getz, and Kenny Clarke. Pettiford's happy life on the continent was cut short when he died suddenly on September 8, 1960. A brilliant soloist and composer, Pettiford's main legacy resides in his role as one of the significant links in the evolution of modern bass playing.

Modern Jazz Quartet: John Lewis, Milt Jackson, Percy Heath, Connie Kay

Jazz Played in the Manner of Classical Chamber Music
1920–2001, 1923–1999, 1923– , 1927–1994

What these four gentlemen brought to jazz and the
world of music . . . was the sound of elegance.
                              —Bob Mariani, All About Jazz Web site

In the early 1950s, when many people thought jazz could not possibly go off in yet another new direction, along came the Modern Jazz Quartet (MJQ). **New Orleans jazz** begat swing in the 1930s, and swing begat bebop in the 1940s. From bebop, the stirrings of cool jazz and hard bop were already audible in the 1950s, but John Lewis and the quartet had their own ideas. MJQ would reflect the dignity and refinement of a classical quartet, and the music would be similarly distinguished. The four members dressed in three-piece suits with white shirts and neckties or in tuxedos, depending on the occasion.

The music, much of it written by Lewis, was inspired as much by classical composers as it was by jazz predecessors. They did not play the **riffs** usual in jazz, but followed more of a classical structure, while retaining jazz modes. One of Lewis's favorite forms was the fugue, commonly employed by J.S. Bach. Each of the quartet members had some classical background, but their main experience was jazz and allowed for improvisation. Beginning in the early 1950s, the group was composed of piano, vibraphone, bass, and drums. That format remained until the quartet disbanded for the last time in 1999. Their seldom-broken run of almost fifty years could be a record for any small group in any kind of music.

John Aaron Lewis was born in La Grange, Illinois, on May 3, 1920, but moved with his mother to Albuquerque, New Mexico. An aunt gave him piano lessons, and while in high school he began earning money playing in local clubs. After graduation Lewis enrolled at the University of New Mexico, where he studied music and anthropology. Before John could determine his career path, World War II intervened and he went into military service. In the army he was assigned to an army band and sent to Europe, where he met drummer Kenny Clarke, a fateful encounter.

After service Lewis earned his degree in New Mexico before heading for New York City, now assured that music, and jazz in particular, was his future. In New York he found Clarke, who introduced Lewis to Dizzy Gillespie. Lewis then became part of Gillespie's rhythm section, which evolved into the Modern Jazz Quartet.

Milton "Bags" Jackson was born in Detroit, Michigan, on January 1, 1923, and before his fifth birthday he was singing gospel music. Music consumed the youth as he explored several instruments, including the guitar and the piano. In high school he learned to play vibraphone, his preferred instrument. The influence of jazz was strong in Detroit, the center of rhythm and blues, but Jackson, like Lewis, had intellectual interests and pursued musical studies at Michigan State University. In the early 1940s he toured with a gospel group and played in a Detroit combo before moving to New York in 1945 to join the Dizzy Gillespie band. He stayed with Gillespie until 1947, then freelanced with groups led by Howard McGhee, Thelonious Monk, Tadd Dameron, and others. After a stint with Woody Herman in 1949–50, he rejoined Gillespie, staying with him until 1951 when he formed his own quartet.

Percy Heath was born on April 30, 1923, in Wilmington, North Carolina, but had most of his upbringing in Philadelphia. He and his two brothers, Jimmy and Albert (Tootie), were exposed to music from birth, their father playing clarinet and their mother and grandmother both choir singers. All three boys grew up to become professional musicians. Percy first studied violin and sang but did not begin serious music training until after World War II military service, when he took up bass. By the late 1940s he was working with top New York City jazzmen. In 1950 Dizzy Gillespie hired Heath, who joined Milt Jackson in the rhythm section. He stayed with Gillespie until 1952.

Connie Kay was born on April 27, 1927, in Tuckahoe, New York, and began studying piano when he was six and drums when he was ten. By the mid-1940s he was in New York City playing with leading jazz figures, including Miles Davis, and, by the end of the decade, Lester Young. Between 1950 and 1953 he played with Charlie Parker and Coleman Hawkins and had gigs at Birdland. He also made recordings, including some hits such as "Shake, Rattle, and Roll," featuring singer Joe Turner. He played again with Lester Young before joining the Modern Jazz Quartet in 1955.

In 1951 Milt Jackson and John Lewis formed the Milt Jackson Quartet with two other former Gillespie band members, Ray Brown (bass), and Kenny Clarke (drums). That group recorded together until 1952 when Brown left and was replaced by Percy Heath. The quartet recorded and played together as the Modern Jazz Quartet over the next several years, developing musical concepts mainly conceived by John Lewis.

Lewis, who became the group's musical director, wanted the quartet playing together as though it were a single organism, similar to what is found in classical chamber music. The group recorded Lewis's compositions "Django," "Milano," "La Ronde" (four parts), "Vendome" and "Delauney's Dilemma," all of which became standard quartet repertoire. Kenny Clarke left in 1955, and Connie Kay replaced him. Kay, a highly innovative drummer whose skills with the symbols, triangle, chimes, and timpani were a perfect match for the group. This group played together over some four decades.

At first the group mainly played standards, but as time went on, original works, mostly by Lewis, became dominant. They adapted classically oriented themes such as the fugue treatments of Sigmund Romberg's "Softly, As in a Morning Sunrise" and Lewis's "Concorde." Initially the U.S. jazz crowd seemed puzzled by MJQ's dignified approach. After the group won accolades on its 1956 European tour, however, it returned to a warm U.S. reception. Its acclaimed 1956 album *Fontessa* introduced two more Lewis classics, "Versailles" and the eleven-minute-long "Fontessa," as well as Jackson's "Bluesology."

In the following years MJQ toured constantly, performing mostly in concert and at festivals. Testimony to their success was the demand for their presence year after year in the recording studio, at major jazz festivals, and in rarified classical settings, such as the Salzburg Mozarteum. The quartet produced dozens of albums up to its first breakup in 1974, among them *Modern Jazz Quartet and Oscar Peterson at the Opera, Blues at Carnegie Hall, Under the Jasmine Tree, Blues on Bach,* and their farewell piece, *The Last Concert.*

After twenty-two years of playing together, the quartet split and went off in different directions. Lewis gravitated to education. He had already acquired his master's degree in music. He taught at the City College of New York and the Manhattan School of Music. The group reunited in 1981 for a tour of Japan. They stayed together after that, taking more and longer breaks while trying to hold to a less grueling schedule. The MJQ played into the 1990s, the fifth decade in which the same musicians had shared a stage, changing only after Connie Kay died in 1994.

The first replacement to the quartet since the 1950s was Percy Heath's brother, Albert "Tootie" Heath. The new group carried on, but when Milt Jackson died in 1999, the Modern Jazz Quartet was silenced at last. John Lewis then directed his work toward the "**third stream**," the merging of jazz and classical music, believing to the end it would become an acceptable musical form. He died in 2001. The remaining member of the classic Modern Jazz Quartet, Percy Heath, received a Jazz Masters award in 2002 from the National Endowment for the Arts.

Buddy DeFranco

Clarinetist Famed in Both Swing and Bebop
1923–

*Buddy was the first bebop clarinetist—
the style he played was for me the
swingingest and probably the best.*

—Terry Gibbs on *Jazz Profiles* from NPR

In 1944 Tommy Dorsey, leading one of the headliner big bands of the swing era, hired a young Buddy DeFranco to be his lead clarinetist. It was a dream come true for DeFranco. His skills were already being compared to those of clarinet virtuosos Benny Goodman and Artie Shaw. In 1948, with new jazz styles emerging, the clarinetist began experimenting on some of his solos. Dorsey wanted the solos always played exactly as they were on his popular records. When DeFranco kept innovating, Dorsey told him to take his new ideas elsewhere.

DeFranco was becoming one of the great swing clarinetists when bebop-powered modern jazz began to supplant swing. Big bands shrunk to small groups that seldom included the clarinet. Buddy DeFranco was not about to give up music or the clarinet because of this new trend. The problem was, it was extremely difficult to adapt the clarinet to bebop. But DeFranco made the transition, becoming generally recognized as the first, and one of the few, to successfully do so on clarinet.

It is easy to understand why DeFranco adopted his nickname, "Buddy." His given name was Boniface Ferdinand Leonard DeFranco. Born in Camden, New Jersey, on February 17, 1923, Buddy began clarinet lessons at age nine. His father, a blind musician and piano tuner, sacrificed rent money to purchase his son's first clarinet. The youth studied at the Mastbaum School and quickly mastered the instrument, playing classical music. His musical direction changed, however, when he heard the playing of jazz clarinetist Johnny Mintz, and then was smitten by Shaw and Goodman. As an eager fourteen-year-old, he won the Tommy Dorsey National Swing Contest, bringing him to the attention of swing bandleaders nationwide. At sixteen he began his professional career with the Johnny "Scat" Davis big band.

Through the 1940s De Franco played with name big bands led by Gene Krupa, Charlie Barnet, Tommy Dorsey, Boyd Raeburn, and others. In 1950 he joined a septet led by the legendary Count Basie, staying about a year. Afterward DeFranco decided to take a crack at leading his own group and formed a big band, writing many of his own arrangements. Although critically successful, the big band stumbled financially, and DeFranco moved on, leading a quartet over the next few years.

DeFranco had been hearing the sounds of bebop since the middle 1940s, and its influence grew on him. He especially admired alto saxophonist

Charlie Parker. DeFranco's 1949 recordings, particularly "A Bird in Igor's Yard," reflected his musical progress. In that year DeFranco was selected as one of the Metronome All-Stars. His quartet of the early to mid-1950s featured such bebop practitioners as Art Blakey (drums) and Kenny Drew (piano). But the clarinet remained unpopular in bebop, and DeFranco had some difficult times through the 1950s and early 1960s.

During the 1950s DeFranco managed some tours, including a European trip with Billie Holiday, and he toured and recorded with Norman Granz's Jazz at the Philharmonic. Granz had him playing alongside such jazz stars as Art Tatum, Lionel Hampton, and Oscar Peterson. In the 1960s DeFranco co-led a small group with Tommy Gumina, an accordionist (rare in jazz), and from 1966 to 1974 he led the popular Glenn Miller Orchestra. During this period DeFranco taught the art and techniques of jazz through clinics at various universities and organizations.

The late 1970s and 1980s brought a kind of DeFranco revival. In those years, he produced such albums as *Gone With the Wind* (with pianist Willie Pickens), *Like Someone in Love, Holiday for Swing* (with vibraphonist Terry Gibbs), and *Chip off the Old Bop.* DeFranco also began a collaboration with Terry Gibbs, usually in a quintet, which continued through the 1990s. In 2001 DeFranco played the Benny Goodman parts in a rendering of Goodman's classic 1938 Carnegie Hall Concert, as presented by William Russo's Chicago Jazz Ensemble.

Probably there is no more accurate assessment of DeFranco's abilities than the judgment of the jazz community. Through his long career, going back to the heyday of Goodman and Shaw, the major jazz polls voted him number one jazz clarinetist in the world some forty-five times. A rather convincing score.

The Jones Brothers: Hank, Thad, Elvin

From One Family, Three Acclaimed Jazz Musicians
1918– , 1923–1986, 1927–2004

Hank Jones

> *There were not many instruments around. Hank had his piano. Thad had his trumpet. It took me a little while before I was able to get some drums. We grew up during the Depression. Money was very scarce. . . . We enjoyed each other's company more than anything else.*
>
> —Elvin Jones, quoted in an
> interview on All About Jazz Web site

The history of jazz is replete with outstanding musicians named Jones—Jo, Philly Joe, and Quincy among them. Most of these Joneses are not related. Not so with Hank, Thad, and Elvin, the three brothers who registered a major contribution to jazz. Hank has played piano with most of the major jazz artists through the swing and bebop eras, has been prominent in film, broadcasting, and theater, and is a renowned accompanist. Thad, the second oldest, started as a trumpet, cornet, and flügelhorn player, but he is perhaps better known as an arranger and bandleader. Elvin, the youngest, is possibly the most famous, occupying a revered place in the annals of jazz because of his revolutionary work with hallowed saxophonist John Coltrane. The brothers played together at times, but generally followed separate musical paths.

The Jones boys were raised in Pontiac, Michigan, but only the two youngest were born there. Henry (Hank) Jones was born on July 31, 1918, in Vicksburg, Mississippi, soon migrating with his family to Pontiac. Thaddeus Joseph (Thad) came along a few years later, on March 28, 1923, and Elvin Ray entered the world on September 9, 1927. There were ten Jones children altogether, which made it tough during the Depression, but father Jones held a job at General Motors and was a deacon in the local Baptist church. The Jones parents encouraged their children's musical ambitions, and nearby Detroit, with its rich tradition in music, particularly jazz, influenced the brothers.

Hank's earliest influences included such founding fathers of stride piano as Fats Waller, Earl "Fatha" Hines, and Teddy Wilson. But it was the incredible Art Tatum from nearby Dayton, Ohio, who had the greatest impact on his playing. Hank took piano lessons, but it was from these masters that he developed his jazz technique. From the age of thirteen he played in local bands, and he became a leader in Detroit's talented field of jazz pianists. Hank finally left Detroit to take a gig in Buffalo, and then in 1944 he headed for New York City.

Hank first found work on Fifty-second Street with Hot Lips Page, then bounced around, playing with the likes of Andy Kirk, John Kirby, Billy Eckstine, and Coleman Hawkins through the mid-1940s. He came into contact with modern piano stylists such as Bud Powell, who was adapting to bebop. In 1947 he toured with Norman Granz and his Jazz at the Philharmonic all stars, the first of several engagements with Granz. From 1948 to 1953 Hank accompanied Ella Fitzgerald, then freelanced with various ensembles, including those led by Benny Goodman, Lester Young, and Cannonball Adderley.

Hank joined brother Thad in 1966 in the Thad Jones–Mel Lewis Orchestra, and he teamed up with Stan Getz in the early 1970s. While carrying on his jazz career, Hank supplemented his income through a deal with CBS from 1959 to 1975, working on musical aspects of various programs. In 1976 he led the Great Jazz Trio and in the late 1970s signed on as pianist and conductor for the Broadway show *Ain't Misbehavin'*. Hank traveled to Japan during the 1970s, producing the album *Live in Japan*. His piano skills continued to evolve as seen in his 1989 album *The Oracle*. In his eighties Hank began a study of West African music, his work resulting in a recording session with musicians of the Mandingo people from Mali. At the turn of the century Hank Jones's creative surge continued to lead him into new musical realms.

Thad Jones followed a path similar to that of his older brother. He had little formal training on the trumpet, picking it up mostly on his own. While an early teenager, he played some local gigs, and when he was sixteen, took his first professional job alongside brother Hank and saxophonist Sonny Stitt. During World War II he played in army bands overseas. In the early 1950s he joined a quintet in Detroit that included his brother Elvin and Tommy Flanagan. In New York City Thad worked with the great bassist Charles Mingus, and in 1954 he joined the Count Basie Orchestra for a nine-year run. During that stay, Thad established himself as a soloist, composer, and arranger. He left Basie in 1963, and in 1964 toured Europe with the George Russell group.

In late 1965 Thad joined with drummer Mel Lewis to form the Thad Jones–Mel Lewis Orchestra, which initially included brother Hank on piano. Under the Jones–Lewis leadership the orchestra had a successful run of some thirteen years, including a regular Monday night gig at New York's Village Vanguard. The zest of the Vanguard performances is captured on the album *Thad Jones & Mel Lewis Live at the Village Vanguard*. The orchestra gave Thad an outlet for composing, resulting in several standards, includ-

Thad Jones

ing his noted "A Child Is Born." In 1975 and 1977 Thad and Mel Lewis made trips to Sweden where they recorded with a radio jazz orchestra.

The trips to Scandinavia had a profound effect on Thad, who in 1978 suddenly quit the Jones-Lewis organization and moved to Copenhagen, Denmark. There he became resident conductor of the Danish Radio Big Band. He also freelanced, sometimes with touring American musicians. After Count Basie's death in 1984 Thad returned to the United States in 1985 to lead Basie's orchestra, but his tenure with that group was brief. The following year his health began to deteriorate, and he returned to Copenhagen, where cancer took his life on August 20, 1986.

Elvin Jones can't remember wanting to do anything else but play drums. He claims that his desire for drumming had already begun when he was two years old. Elvin had some music training in school, but mostly he drove himself relentlessly to master the drums. He was practicing eight to ten hours a day by the time he was thirteen and dreaming about performing. His drumsticks were with him at all times, and he tattooed rhythms on any surface available. Elvin performed with the school band, and he played gigs for fun with his brothers and other local musicians. His career was interrupted by World War II, during which he gained playing experience while in the air force. He had many idols by then, including Chick Webb, Max Roach, Art Blakey, and Kenny Clarke. But a major inspiration was when he heard Sid Catlett on the Parker-Gillespie 1945 rendition of "Salt Peanuts." Afterward he knew that's how he wanted to play.

After his discharge Elvin received his first real professional experience playing with local Detroit groups. Elvin also played with such well-known touring artists as Miles Davis, Charlie Parker, and Dizzy Gillespie. One night, while playing in a club, Elvin got a stunning phone call: it was Benny Goodman asking him to come to New York to audition. Goodman's call was prompted by Elvin's brother Hank, then working with Goodman. The audition did not go well, but Elvin was able to immerse himself in the city's dynamic jazz scene. Elvin played with many local jazz stars, and eventually landed a job with Charles Mingus, who was organizing a band.

When the Thelonious Monk group took a gig at the Five Spot Café in 1957, Elvin began dropping by often. Eventually he met all the members of that group, including John Coltrane, who would make a huge impact on his life. When he filled in for a week with Miles Davis, he firmed up his relationship with Coltrane and Davis. In 1960 Coltrane asked Elvin to join what became his classic quartet, which also included Jimmy Garrison on bass and McCoy Tyner on piano. The quartet stayed intact until 1965, creating a virtual revolution in jazz and bringing Elvin into the limelight as part of one of the most highly acclaimed jazz groups of all time. Elvin left Coltrane, as had Tyner, early in 1966 when the leader's experimentation went to a more extreme level.

Among the Coltrane albums on which Elvin appears are two all-time classics, *My Favorite Things* and *A Love Supreme.* The latter reflects the religious background that influenced both Coltrane and Elvin. While with Coltrane, Elvin's drumming evolved into a style distinguished by its continuous high level sound with little emphasis on an obvious beat, yet with a rythmic force that drove and inspired the other players. He was now a major influence on

Elvin Jones

young drummers. After Coltrane, Elvin formed his own group, which in the 1990s became known as Elvin Jones Jazz Machine. Elvin's travels included trips to Japan in 1978, where he recorded *Live in Japan,* and Europe in 1992, where he recorded *The Elvin Jones Jazz Machine in Europe.* His career showed no signs of abating as the twenty-first century dawned. However, his health began to fail by 2004, and he died on May 18 of that year.

In the jazz world it is not unusual for family members to follow each other as players of this uniquely American music. What distinguishes the Jones brothers is that all three members achieved such a high level of accomplishment in jazz. They have left a permanent and valued legacy in the annals of American music.

Tito Puente

The Mambo King
1923–2000

I must dance in the studio while the whole band is playing to see if it works. I want to feel the beat.

—Tito Puente in an interview
with Alan Feuerstein as reproduced on
the Planet Salsa Web site

Lucky for **Latin jazz** that young Tito Puente broke his ankle in time to halt his dancing career and divert his explosive, rhythmic energy into instrumental music. As a result, Puente became a main force behind the rise of Latin music in the United States. Puente was a multi-instrumentalist, but it was his expertise as a percussionist that spurred his success. Dressed in colorful costumes, onstage he became a dynamo of rhythm, his drumsticks flying at blurring speeds as he pounded the timbales (tom-toms) and an array of other percussive instruments. Puente is said to be the first to bring his drums to the front of the band and play them standing up, dancing as he drummed. His explosive **polyrhythmic** beats fueled the mambo craze in the 1940s and 1950s, earning him the title of The Mambo King.

Puente also mastered other forms of Latin music, including the cha-cha, of which he was a chief popularizer. He provided much of the thrust that fused Latin rhythms and jazz to create the hybrid Latin jazz. Puente would eventually collaborate with outstanding jazz artists, including Woody Herman, Cal Tjader, George Shearing, Terry Gibbs, and Arturo Sandoval. Puente also made inroads into the pop field, Broadway musicals, and films. He mastered the piano, vibraphone, and saxophone, becoming an adept composer and arranger as well. With all of that, whether or not he may have missed a dancing career is probably beside the point.

Ernesto Antonio Puente Jr. was born on April 20, 1923, of Puerto Rican parents who had recently arrived in New York City. Raised in the East Side neighborhood called Spanish Harlem, he was the oldest of three children. Young "Tito" displayed musical talent early, and his mother encouraged his training in music and dance. He studied piano at the New York School of Music, but hearing Gene Krupa's solos on the Benny Goodman jazz classic "Sing, Sing, Sing," triggered his passion for drums.

Puente quit school when he was sixteen, driven by an overwhelming desire to perform. He had grown up listening to all kinds of music, but his first regular musician's job was with a Latin band. On that gig Puente met pianist, José Curbelo, who was knocked out by Puente's drumming and arranged for Puente to go with him to a gig in Miami. After Puente returned to New York, he played with Noro Morales and Curbelo, building his reputation. In 1941 he recorded and appeared in film shorts with Morales, then in 1942 came a major break. He was hired by the popular bandleader Machito, with whom he made hot-selling records and played top Latin dance halls. With Machito he first displayed his exciting showmanship in front of the band.

World War II was gripping the country, and Puente was drafted into the navy in 1942. He made good use of his time, however. While at sea he played drums and saxophone in the ship's band and wrote arrangements, but it was not just a musical romp. Puente served in combat in both the Atlantic and Pacific theaters and received a presidential commendation. After his discharge in 1945 he took advantage of the GI Bill, enrolling in the prestigious Juilliard School, where he studied orchestration, conducting, composition, and theory.

In 1949 Puente formed the Picadilly Boys, which became one of the regular groups at the famous Palladium Ballroom. Groups led by Puente, Perez Prado, and Tito Rodriguez brought in droves of fans eager to dance to the new Afro-Cuban based mambo. Puente's popularity soared. His recordings of "Ran Kan Kan" and "Picadillo" sold briskly, and "Abaniquito" was a solid hit. A 1956 poll conducted by the Spanish language newspaper *La Prensa* voted Puente the "King of Latin Music."

Puente also performed at such jazz clubs as Birdland and The Royal Roost, and recorded Latin jazz albums, including *Puente Goes Jazz* and *Night Beat.* But his biggest hits were his Afro-Cuban-mambo discs, such as *Cuban Carnival* and *Dance Mania,* the latter becoming his all time top-seller. In 1961 Puente cut *Puente Now!,* produced by jazz promoter Norman Granz. A year later he toured Japan, popularizing Latin music in that country, subsequently returning to Japan several more times.

Puente's popularity remained high in the 1960s despite new Latin dance trends, such as the boogaloo and disco. Helping to spice Puente's music during the period were several female singers, including the fiery La Lupe. In 1970 he went to a new level when rock guitarist Carlos Santana took an old

Puente song, "Oye Como Va," and turned it into a smash hit. In 1979 Puente won the first of his five Grammy awards for *Homenaje a Beny,* dedicated to Cuban musical legend Beny Moré.

Puente made a major commitment to jazz in the 1980s, fueled by a recording contract with Concord Records. He formed a new jazz-oriented unit called the Tito Puente Latin Ensemble, with whom he made a series of recordings, including *On Broadway,* featuring the music of Duke Ellington and jazz trumpeter Freddie Hubbard. A subsequent album, *El Rey,* offered works by John Coltrane, and another, *Salsa Meets Jazz,* the alto saxophone of Phil Woods. In 1987 he received *Down Beat*'s Best-Percussionist Award.

Puente ranks among the most prolific record makers, and the release of his one hundredth album in 1991 brought a surge of hoopla. Called *The Mambo King: 100th Album,* it coincided with his appearance as actor and bandleader in a film, *The Mambo Kings.* In the 1990s Puente cut several more albums featuring compositions by jazz artists, including Fats Waller, Billy Strayhorn, and Dizzy Gillespie. In 1997 Puente performed on his son Tito Puente Jr.'s debut album.

Puente maintained an intense travel schedule through the 1990s, but in the waning years of the century he began to slow down, professing the need for the new generation to step up. Finally the Mambo King's heart weakened, and on May 31, 2000, at age seventy-seven, he died due to complications from heart surgery.

Puente was hugely honored in his lifetime. He performed at the White House for all the presidents from Carter through Clinton. He was a recipient of the ASCAP Founder's Award, *Billboard*'s Lifetime Achievement Award, and the National Medal of Honor. Puente composed more than 450 songs in his career.

Bud Powell

Among the Seminal Artists Who Created Bebop
1924–1966

If I had to choose a single musician for his artistic integrity, for the incomparable originality of his creativity . . . it would be Bud Powell. No one comes anywhere near him.

—Bill Evans, pianist and composer

On a night in 1945 a Philadelphia jazz club was getting ready to close when a squad of police suddenly burst into the room on a raid. They arrested the piano player, Thelonious Monk, when he refused to show his ID. As they led him away, Monk's friend, a young, upcoming pianist named Bud Powell, tried to intercede. For his trouble, Powell received a crushing blow to the head and was arrested. Monk was released rather quickly, but Powell was first treated in a hospital and then returned to prison until released into the custody of his mother. Shortly thereafter he was treated for psychiatric problems.

Jazz authorities have debated the extent to which Powell's mental and physical problems and his playing ability were related to the incident. From the time of the beating, Powell developed severe, recurring headaches, and he also suffered periodic episodes of mental illness, some of them quite long lasting. But there is some evidence of instability prior to the incident. The effect on his playing is more difficult to assess, however, because he produced a body of brilliant work afterward. Whatever his mental and physical condition or the reason for it, there remains little argument that Bud Powell, one of the originators of bebop, was a musical genius.

Earl Rudolph Powell was born in New York City on September 27, 1924, into a family endowed with musical talent. Bud's father and his father's father were both accomplished musicians. His grandfather was a flamenco guitarist, and his father, William Sr., was himself a jazz piano player, who encouraged his sons in music. Older brother William Jr. studied violin and trumpet, while younger brother Richie took up piano and eventually played with the Clifford Brown-Max Roach quintet. Richie died in the 1956 automobile crash that also took trumpeter Clifford Brown's life.

Bud began piano lessons at six and continued until thirteen, studying the classics and winning awards for his Bach recitals. The jazz influence was strong in New York, however, and the music intrigued the teenager. Bud dropped out of school when he was fifteen and played briefly with his brother William's band before picking up gigs in New York. Over the next years he came under the influence of Art Tatum and drew attention from the New York jazz scene. Like Tatum, Powell could play with lyrical softness or explode with a lightening-fast right hand.

One of the musicians impressed by the precocious pianist was Thelonious Monk, who introduced him to the Harlem haunts where early modernists spawned the new jazz called bebop. He sat in with seminal boppers, such as Dizzy Gillespie, Charlie Parker, and Kenny Clarke, and before long he was transposing what Gillespie and Parker did on their horns to the piano and adding his own unique ideas. Monk passed many of his compositions on to Powell, believing he was the only other pianist skilled enough to play them.

Powell played with the Cootie Williams band during 1943–44, cutting his first records with that group, including the now classic Monk composition, "'Round Midnight." Powell also arranged for Williams's band despite his young age. After Williams, Powell became a fixture on New York's Fifty-second Street jazz row. Then in 1945 he had his run-in with the police, followed by his first psychiatric confinement. Although headaches brought on increased drinking, Powell bounced back, recording with Dexter Gordon in 1946 and Charlie Parker in 1947. He then recorded another Monk tune, "Off Minor," which also became a classic. Unfortunately, Powell was confined again in 1947, receiving electroshock therapy for the first time.

After almost a year's confinement Powell went through a period of exceptional accomplishment. From 1947 to 1951 he composed and recorded many of his outstanding compositions, including, "Bouncing with Bud," "Dance of the Infidels," "Hallucinations," "Un Poco Loco," and the incredibly high-speed "Tempus Fugue-it." About that time Powell recorded with a trio including bassist Ray Brown and drummer Buddy Rich, with whom he cut "Tea for Two" and "Hallelujah." Around that time he also recorded his own "Parisian Thoroughfare." In 1951 Powell underwent further treatment and was released in the care of Oscar Goodstein, owner of New York's Birdland jazz club. Goodstein saw to Powell's needs, but to be sure he showed up for gigs, Powell was largely confined to his hotel room. His composition "Glass Enclosure" is said to reflect his experience with confinement.

On May 15, 1953, Bud Powell took part in a jazz concert at Massey Hall in Toronto, Canada, that reunited him with associates in the conception of bebop—Charlie Parker, Dizzy Gillespie, Charles Mingus, and Max Roach. The performance was recorded, resulting in the classic *The Quintet: Jazz at Massey Hall*.

Out of that same session Powell also recorded *Bud Powell Trio: Jazz at Massey Hall*. He continued to play under Goodstein's supervision, and reunited again with the bopper originals at Birdland in 1955. During the performance, however, Powell became angry at the erratic Charlie Parker, yelled and pounded the piano. Parker died a few days later. Afterward, Powell played in a trio with Mingus and drummer Elvin Jones. In 1956 he was released from Goodstein's guardianship.

Now unrestricted, Powell signed up for a European tour, and while in France he performed with a trio at the St. Germain, returning for an extended engagement in 1957. In Paris, Powell made the acquaintance of graphic artist and jazz aficionado Francis Paudras, who became his close friend and lifelong supporter. The death of Powell's brother Richie in 1956 aggravated his mental condition, and his increased drinking and reported drug use complicated matters. Powell returned to the United States for about a year, but returned to Paris to live in 1959.

At the Blue Note in Paris, Powell became part of a trio that included Kenny Clarke, another expatriate, and Pierre Michelot. The influx of acclaimed American jazz stars was making Paris a world jazz center. Powell also toured other European countries, playing with American jazzmen and top European talent. While Powell was uplifted by the respect he received in Europe, his physical and mental condition deteriorated. Paudras, however, cared for his friend and helped him return to relatively good health. From their relationship Paudras produced a book of memoirs, *Dance of the Infidels,* which insightfully describes Powell's Paris experience. A 1986 movie, *'Round*

Midnight is based on Paudras's writing. Although a tenor saxophonist, Dexter Gordon played the lead.

Powell remained in Europe until 1964, producing a bounty of recordings, including *Cookin' at the Saint Germain, Groovin' at the Blue Note, The Complete Essen Jazz Festival Concert,* and *Bouncing With Bud.* By the time Powell returned to the United States he was suffering from tuberculosis, but he managed an extensive gig at Birdland in 1965. His skills, however, began to diminish, and on July 31, 1966, at age forty-two, he died from multiple causes. Bud Powell lived a tragic, pain-filled life, but he forged a new path in jazz that influenced generations of musicians.

In his liner notes to the Verve album *The Best of Bud Powell,* Max Harrison wrote, "Powell in his most inspired moments improvised like one possessed, reaching what must be described, no matter how paradoxically, as a lucid expression of delirium. Through the unforgiving intensity attained at such heights he, even more than Parker, conveyed the romantic agony of modern jazz."

Max Roach

Drummer, Composer, Arranger Delved in Multiple Musical Forms
1924–

He refuses to be bound and secured into some tight little niche of history—and that makes him a rare, unclassifiable, treasurable breed of cat.

—Richard S. Ginell,
from the *All Music Guide to Jazz*

Max Roach certainly ranks among the most accomplished, diverse, and honored artists of jazz. Fortunately, this innovative drummer has had time on his side. His career began in the early 1940s, spanned the rest of the 1900s, and plunged into the new century. Roach has never been stuck in a single style, starting in swing, evolving as a seminal player in bebop, and riding in on the cutting edge of hard bop, cool jazz, and free jazz. Beyond that he has explored forms that sometimes stretched into uncharted musical waters. Even hip-hop found a place on his musical palette. As a composer and arranger, he has dabbled in theater, television, film, dance, and classical music. Roach has involved himself in education and in African American issues, and he has been honored at home and abroad for his contributions to music.

Maxwell Roach was born in New Land, North Carolina, on January 10, 1924, but when he was just four his family moved to Brooklyn. Although he lived in a black ghetto, music was part of the school curriculum, and he could take instruments home to practice. One of Max's earliest musical experiences was in the church, where his mother sang gospel and he played drums in the gospel band. By twelve he had his own drum kit, and in his teens studied theory and composition at the Manhattan School of Music. By the time he was eighteen, he was sitting in at the cradles of bebop, Minton's Playhouse and Monroe's Uptown House, where he became house drummer. In those clubs he consorted with future jazz stars Charlie Parker, Dizzy Gillespie, and the bebop drummer Kenny Clarke, who inspired young Roach.

In 1943 Roach made his record debut with Coleman Hawkins, then regarded as king of tenor saxophone. In the next year Roach played with Gillespie, toured in California with Benny Carter, and sat in with the Duke Ellington Orchestra. Between 1945 and 1950 he skipped from one elite group to the next, performing and recording primarily with Charlie Parker, but also with Stan Getz, Coleman Hawkins, and Miles Davis. The Davis group included J. J. Johnson (trombone), Lee Konitz (alto sax), Gerry Mulligan (baritone sax), and Clarke alternating on drums with Roach. The music they played became the foundation of **cool jazz**. Roach played and recorded intermittently with Parker again from 1950 until 1953.

In 1952 Roach joined the Norman Granz Jazz at the Philharmonic tour. That same year he and Charles Mingus established Debut Records, which was dedicated to improving the lot of recording jazz artists. Among the albums that the company produced was the great bebop classic *The Quintet: Jazz at Massey Hall,* which featured Parker, Gillespie, Bud Powell (piano), Mingus (bass), and Roach. After recording on the West Coast with the Lighthouse All-Stars in 1954, Roach formed a quintet that was co-led by the blazing young trumpet star Clifford Brown. The hard-bop–playing quintet caused a sensation wherever it toured. Among its highly rated albums are *Brown and Roach, Inc.* and *Study in Brown.*

In 1956 tragedy struck: Clifford Brown was killed in an automobile accident. Roach was devastated, but he bounced back and assembled a new quintet, comprised of Kenny Dorham (trumpet), Ray Bryant (piano), and, from the previous group, Sonny Rollins (tenor saxophone) and George Morrow (bass). That bunch continued the tradition of the earlier band, cutting some outstanding recordings, including *Max Roach Plus Four.* Playing to capacity houses, the quintet kept going until the end of the 1950s.

In the 1960s Roach expressed his support for Martin Luther King Jr. and the civil rights movement through his music. His first major political offering, *We Insist! Freedom Now Suite,* was a collaboration with singer-activist Oscar Brown Jr. The seven-part album stimulated emotions through such pieces as "Tears for Johannesburg," "Driva' Man" (with simulated whip-lashing), and "Protest," featuring acclaimed singer Abbey Lincoln, whom Roach married in 1962. Later, in a film, he performed a drum solo backing to King's "I Have a Dream" speech. Roach and Lincoln's marriage ended in 1970.

The 1970s saw Roach take a new direction in jazz that was often highly experimental. He began doing drum solo performances and led a ten piece percussion orchestra called M'Boom that included various exotic drums, steel pans, and vibraphone. By the end of the 1970s Roach was gravitating into avant-garde jazz, and he performed as a duo with such extremely progressive artists as Cecil Taylor, Archie Shepp, and Abdullah Ibrahim. Still seeking new ground, in the 1980s he performed with his daughter Maxine's African American, all female, string quartet, and he led a **double quartet**, consisting of his daughter's and his own quartets. In 1994 he presented a multimedia performance entitled "JuJu," which included M'Boom, a dance group, and a video artist. Reaching out even further, he dabbled in hip-hop.

Roach has extended himself into education as well, having become a frequent lecturer on jazz and, since 1972, a professor of music at the University of Massachusetts, Amherst. His honorary degrees include one from Columbia University and another from the New England Conservatory of Music. In 1988 he was awarded a MacArthur Foundation Fellowship for his distinguished contributions to American cultural life. He is the recipient of an OBIE award for his score to playwright Sam Shepard's *Shepard Sets,* and in 1989 the French government presented him with its highest award, Commander of the Order of Arts and Letters. In 1992 Roach completed the musical score for an opera, *The Life and Life of Bumpy Johnson,* which premiered in San Diego. He entered the Grammy Hall of Fame in 1995. The list of his accomplishments, like the jazz master himself, goes on and on.

Sarah Vaughan

The Divine One
1924–1990

The world's greatest singing talent.

Ella Fitzgerald

Sarah Vaughan could have been any kind of vocalist she wanted to be. She could have been an opera diva, so strong and controlled was her voice. Betty Carter, a renowned jazz singer, said Vaughan could reach the level of operatic star Leontyne Price, with whom, coincidentally, Vaughan was good friends. Vaughan was a jazz singer, and she was a successful pop singer as well, having cut dozens of pop sides to bring in extra cash and satisfy the record producers. The single humongous hit of her career was a pop tune called "Broken Hearted Melody." That song and the rest of her pop output have been largely forgotten, however. What remains for posterity is Sarah Vaughan the jazz singer.

Critics have long marveled at the qualities and sheer versatility of Vaughan's vocal instrument. Her four-octave range alone was stunning. She could sing with equal facility in the soprano or contralto (lowest female) range, and she could at will (and for fun) imitate the baritone range of her friend Billy Eckstine. She went up and down the scale with astounding vocal dexterity, and her vocal gymnastics sometimes astounded other singers. Jazz writers generally place her on a par with Ella Fitzgerald in scat singing (but she did it less often), and she could sing with emotion reminiscent of Billie Holiday. The ultimate characteristic of her voice was a sensuous, silken tone that she could extend with unwavering control. It is not surprising that in the mid 1940s Dave Garroway, then a local late-night Chicago disc jockey, dubbed her "The Divine One."

Sarah Lois Vaughan was born in Newark, New Jersey, on March 27, 1924, to musically inclined parents. Her father was a guitar-playing carpenter, and her mother sang and played organ at Mount Zion Baptist church. Before she was eight, Sarah was studying piano and organ and singing in the church choir, and in her preteens she was subbing for her mother on the church organ. She wanted to sing, but was compelled to be the accompanist. While in her mid-teens, she began playing piano and singing in local clubs. Whenever she could, she traveled across the river into New York City's Harlem district, where she could hear such jazz stars as Fitzgerald and bandleader-drummer Chick Webb rehearse.

Vaughan might have done well on piano talent alone, but she opted to sing. Like Fitzgerald, her career got a kick-start in 1942 when she won the famed Apollo Theater's weekly amateur night contest. The vocalist Billy Eckstine heard Sarah and offered her a tryout with the Earl "Fatha" Hines band, for which Eckstine was the male singer. Hines hired the eighteen-year old to be the girl singer for his band, which was composed largely of such all-star jazz musicians as bebop inventors Dizzy Gillespie and Charlie Parker.

Vaughan's career was stymied somewhat by the recording ban in effect because of World War II when she was with Hines in 1943–44. Her reputation grew nevertheless, and when Eckstine formed his own band, he asked Vaughan to join him. Some of her specialty numbers while with Eckstine were "Body and Soul," "Lover Man," "East of the Sun," and "Mean to Me." Vaughan's contact with Gillespie, Parker, and others led her to become one of the first singers to adopt bebop phrasing to her vocals. After about a year with Eckstine, she decided to be a solo act, which she remained for most of her career.

Vaughan had a superb voice, but her appearance and stage presence in those days required some upgrading, and to facilitate matters she hired a personal manager, who became her husband (the first of four). Changing her appearance and improving her stagecraft helped move Vaughan's career along, but it was her recording of "Tenderly" in the late 1940s that rocketed her into national prominence. That song made the charts, and the record company Columbia, seeing dollar signs, quickly made her an offer. She recorded for that company from 1949 to 1953. The tradeoff was that she had to do pop tunes to satisfy Columbia executives; her jazz output during those years was sparse.

During the 1950s Vaughan was in demand for television appearances, concerts, and international tours. After she left Columbia, she split her record production between pop and jazz. Especially significant in jazz was her 1954 recording collaboration with the acclaimed bebop trumpeter Clifford Brown, and in 1958 her big pop hit, "Broken Hearted Melody," was released. The mid to late 1950s were particularly productive for Vaughan, including releases of songbook albums of works by Irving Berlin (with Billy Eckstine),

Rogers and Hart, and George Gershwin, and two live albums from Chicago clubs, *At Mr. Kelly's* and *After Hours at the London House.* In the same period Vaughan recorded "Misty," which became one of her trademark numbers.

By the 1960s Vaughan was traveling almost constantly and recording with backings that ranged from trios to big bands to symphony orchestras. During that time she produced some of her best jazz recordings with a new company, Roulette. One of the highlights of the Roulette years was her work with Count Basie, in which she cut outstanding versions of "Perdido," "I Cried for You," and "Lover Man." From 1963 to 1967 she worked for Mercury, producing some string-backed pop material, but also making one of her top-rated jazz albums, *Sassy Swings the Tivoli,* recorded live in Copenhagen, Denmark. After she left Mercury in 1967 she quit recording completely until the early 1970s.

Vaughan was in demand worldwide, and in the early 1970s she traveled to Japan, where she appeared in concert before adoring fans in Tokyo. Back in the United States Vaughan made one of her most satisfying moves in jazz. She signed with impresario Norman Granz to record for his Pablo label. With Granz she worked with some of the finest jazz backing in the industry, including Oscar Peterson (piano), Joe Pass (guitar), Ray Brown (bass), and Louie Bellson (drums). By this time her voice had deepened, but her range and tone were still awesome. Her album *How Long Has This Been Going On?* is a career highlight, as are her Duke Ellington songbook albums. For a change of pace, Granz worked in a Latin Jazz idiom, represented by *I Love Brazil.*

Vaughan's health began to suffer during the 1980s. By her own admission she loved to smoke and drink and "hang out." She never slowed up, however, touring and performing in the United States and other countries, and despite occasional labored breathing, she showed no signs of illness while performing. She continued to record for Granz, cutting one of her most moving and emotional numbers, Stephen Sondheim's "Send in the Clowns." In 1982 she won an Emmy for her rendition of "The Man I Love." One of her most unusual record dates came in 1984, when she recorded *The Mystery of Man,* in which she sang the philosophical poems of Pope John Paul II as translated by jazz writer Gene Lees.

She continued to work until the end of the 1980s, even attempting a recording of Beatles' tunes, but by 1990 her body gave out, succumbing to lung cancer on April 3 of that year. A year earlier she had been honored with a Lifetime Achievement Grammy award.

Oscar Peterson

Pianist Sometimes Compared to Art Tatum
1925–

The piano is like an extension of his own physical being . . . I'm speaking of times when you find him under optimum conditions of creativity. His mind can move as quickly as his fingers and that is what is so astounding.

—Phil Nimmons, orchestrator, as quoted in Gene Lees's article in *McLean's,* July 1975

From a very early age Oscar Peterson astonished audiences with his technical and artistic skills as a classical and jazz pianist. Eventually the young Peterson concentrated on jazz, but unlike most jazz musicians, he spent little of his early career as a sideman. A Canadian by birth, Peterson's name was little known in the United States before he went there to play jazz piano while in his mid-twenties. But he started at the top. Peterson began his U.S. jazz experience playing at Carnegie Hall on the same bill with world-renowned jazz musicians. His fame spread like a brush fire across the United States and the world.

Few jazz musicians can match the number of honors and awards that have been accorded Oscar Peterson. He had piled up at least seventeen honorary degrees by the early 2000s, and the count goes on. The recording industry has honored him with seven Grammy awards and he has won the *Down Beat* and *Playboy* polls for best jazz pianist a combined twenty-four times. The official Oscar Peterson Web site offered a list of an additional forty-seven awards and honors. Not all of these were solely for music. In 2001, for instance, the U.S. House of Representatives awarded him a commendation for his contributions to society.

Oscar's brilliance on the piano is often compared to that of Art Tatum. He idolized Tatum, but was so intimidated by the master that after first hearing him he wanted to give up piano. Peterson's dexterity and speed on the keyboard eventually could be matched to Tatum's, and both improvised at blinding speeds. Peterson, like Tatum, had roots in the older stride style, but he learned to play just as skillfully in modern jazz genres. He can swing hard or play the sensitive ballad with equal facility. Other jazz influences include Nat "King" Cole, Bill Evans, James P. Johnson, Audrey Morris, Charlie Parker, and George Shearing. Some authorities suggest a classical influence by Liszt, as well as Bach, Chopin, and Debussy.

Oscar Emmanuel Peterson was born in Montreal, Quebec, Canada, on August 15, 1925, the fourth of five siblings. His parents were immigrants from the West Indies. His father, Daniel, came to Canada in 1917 and eventually moved to Montreal, where he became a railroad porter and met Oscar's mother, Kathleen. Daniel played piano and determined that all of his children would learn music. Oscar began piano lessons when he was five, and took up trumpet at the same time. However, he contracted tuberculosis when he was seven, causing him to give up trumpet. An older sister, Daisy, also became an accomplished pianist and was one of Oscar's early teachers. In high school he was tutored by a noted Hungarian pianist, Paul de Marky.

Oscar learned Franz Liszt and other classicists under de Marky, but he was irresistibly drawn to American jazz. Despite an early onset of arthritis, which affected him throughout his career, the teenage Peterson astounded his peers and teachers with his keyboard talent. When he was fourteen, Oscar won a Canadian Broadcasting Corporation amateur piano contest, which gave him a $250 first prize and also landed him a spot performing on a weekly radio program.

During high school Oscar played with the Montreal High School Victory Serenaders, which included future jazz star Maynard Ferguson on trumpet. Oscar left high school, over his father's objections, to seek a musical career. In 1942 he joined the Johnny Holmes Orchestra, in which Peterson was the first black member. Oscar had some of his early run-ins with racial prejudice with the group. He made his first recordings with Holmes, including such numbers as "The Sheik of Araby," "I Got Rhythm," and "Oscar's Boogie." Boogie woogie was Oscar's specialty at the time.

Peterson met Lillie Fraser in 1946, and they married a year later. The next year their first child was born and four more followed. In 1947 Peterson also began leading a trio at Montreal's Alberta Lounge, where his perfomances first gained widespread attention. American jazz stars visiting Montreal carried word of the mythic Canadian jazzman back to the States. Finally jazz impresario Norman Granz came to town, and after hearing Peterson, persuaded him to come to the United States. Granz chose a Carnegie Hall Jazz at the Philharmonic (JATP) concert to introduce him. Peterson was called onstage as a surprise guest to play a duo set with esteemed bassist Ray

Brown. The audience and critics gave Peterson rousing approval, effectively kick-starting his career.

Peterson stayed mostly with the duo format for a couple of years before forming a trio, eventually settling on a piano-bass-guitar format. One of the early groupings to receive high acclaim included Peterson and Brown, with Barney Kessel on the guitar. Herb Ellis later replaced Kessel, and that group stuck together through most of the 1950s, touring with JATP, playing clubs and concerts, and recording for Granz. With Granz, Peterson traveled to such far-flung places as Japan, Hong Kong, and Australia. When Ellis decided to leave in 1958, observers assumed that Peterson would bring in another guitarist, but instead drummer Ed Thigpen came aboard. Despite some skepticism, the new grouping carried on, receiving its own high measure of acclaim.

The new trio pursued a grueling schedule over the next six years. In 1964 Peterson recorded his first major extended composition, the Canadiana Suite. Also during that time, the trio traveled to Germany to play and record. By 1965 both Thigpen and Brown had had enough of constant travel and left to pursue their own interests. In the early 1970s Peterson formed another outstanding trio comprised of guitarist Joe Pass and bassist Niels-Henning Orsted Pedersen, whom Peterson had met in Scandinavia. That trio received accolades for its recordings on Granz's new label, Pablo, including such albums as *The Trio.* In 1974 the group toured Russia, cutting the album *In Russia.*

Peterson played in various group combinations, often including Orsted Pedersen and Pass, until the mid-1980s and cut numerous albums. Among the titles were *Porgy and Bess,* on which Peterson plays clavichord exclusively; *Live—Montreux '77; The Paris Concert; The London Concert; Live at the Northsea Jazz Festival;* and *The Oscar Peterson Big 4 in Japan '82.* In 1990 Peterson reunited with Brown and Ellis for a gig at New York's Blue Note, resulting in a Grammy-winning recording. That same year Los Angeles declared July 18 as "Ray Brown and Oscar Peterson Day."

Many honors have been conferred on Peterson, but one that is especially noteworthy came in 1991, when he was installed as Chancellor of York University in Toronto, becoming emeritus chancellor in 1994. From the mid-1980s Peterson had begun soloing more, and he composed his *Easter Suite,* which debuted in 1984. Then the arthritis that troubled him since childhood worsened, causing him to cut back. Still, he continued performing until 1993 when he suffered a stroke. It was feared that Peterson might never perform again, but after two years he was back on tour despite some damage to his left hand. Honors continued to pile up, and in 1997 he received a Lifetime Achievement Grammy and was named to the International Jazz Hall of Fame. In the early 2000s the Oscar Peterson piano continued to be an awesome presence in the jazz scene.

Ray Brown Jr.

Among the Most Influential of Modern Jazz Bassists
1926–2002

When you played with Ray, you felt you were close to the source. To listen to him play was as much about the definition of jazz as it could possibly be.

—Ulf Wakenius, Swedish guitarist, from an obituary by Jon Thurber, *Los Angeles Times*

Ray Brown enjoyed playing the piano, but when he joined the high school orchestra, he discovered he was just one of many pianists auditioning. Realizing that the bass position was open, he decided quickly to take it rather than face the stiff competition at piano. That was a pivotal moment in the history of jazz, for Brown went on to become one of the most influential post–World War II bassists and a significant figure in the development of modern jazz.

Brown had something of a phenomenal rise, emerging from high school, briefly apprenticing with local bands in his hometown of Pittsburgh, then, at nineteen, going to New York City and immediately catching on with elite jazz musicians, including Dizzy Gillespie, Charlie Parker, Bud Powell, and Kenny Clarke. They were playing a new harmonically and rhythmically complex music called bebop. Many of the swing era musicians gave up when they tried to play with the boppers, but Ray Brown fit right in.

A founding member of the Modern Jazz Quartet, Brown further established his bass credentials as a member of the Oscar Peterson Trio, a leader of his own groups, and a manager and accompanist for Ella Fitzgerald. Few would question his place alongside such great jazz bassists as Jimmy Blanton, Oscar Pettiford, Milt Hinton, and Charles Mingus.

Raymond Matthews Brown was born in Pittsburgh, Pennsylvania, on October 13, 1926, into a family with little musical heritage. Ray started out on piano at eight and soon wanted to emulate the famous jazz pianists of the day, among them Duke Ellington, Fats Waller, Earl Hines, and Art Tatum. Preferring to play in the orchestra rather than sit on the sidelines, he took up bass, which he mastered quickly. Professional offers came while he was still in high school, but his parents insisted he graduate first.

After high school Ray Brown soon headed for New York City. Hardly had he arrived when he ran into Hank Jones, a jazz pianist who had played around Pittsburgh. Jones had high regard for Brown's technique, and recommended him to Dizzy Gillespie, then fronting a big band. Gillespie had such faith in Jones's ear that he hired Brown without an audition. When Brown stepped on the bandstand that first night, he stood alongside some of the world's finest jazz musicians. It was enough to freeze a nineteen-year old neophyte, but Brown excelled, and word of the new bass phenomenon spread quickly.

After recording and soloing on such tracks as "One Bass Hit," "Two Bass Hit," and "A Night in Tunisia," Brown left Gillespie in 1947 to form his own trio. Brown's group found the limelight quickly as the backing group for jazz singer Ella Fitzgerald. That year, Brown and Fitzgerald joined the Norman Granz's Jazz at the Philharmonic (JATP) tour. Brown and Fitzgerald struck up a romance in the course of their relationship, and soon they married. Under pressure from their careers, however, the marriage foundered, and in 1952 they divorced. Despite the split, they stayed friends, and Brown remained Fitzgerald's musical director for several years.

While with JATP, Brown accompanied Oscar Peterson as a duo when that remarkable pianist made his U.S. debut at Carnegie Hall. That began a long and fruitful relationship. In 1951 Brown, with other alumni from the Gillespie band, became a member of the Milt Jackson Quartet, later renamed the Modern Jazz Quartet. Leaving after a brief run, he toured with Fitzgerald and then hooked up again with Oscar Peterson. Peterson and Brown worked mostly as a duo before being joined by guitarist Barney Kessel to form the Oscar Peterson Trio.

The trio was hugely successful. Herb Ellis replaced Kessel in 1953, thus forming the group that is often considered the "classic" Oscar Peterson trio. It became internationally famous and influenced other jazz trios. Ellis left the group in 1959 and was replaced by drummer Ed Thigpen, and the trio carried on in that format until 1966. At that point, weary of Peterson's relentless traveling, Brown left the trio, as did Thigpen. During the Peterson years Brown's stature grew as he won numerous polls as top acoustic bassist. Many of Brown's some two thousand recordings were with the trio, including such classics as *The Sound of the Trio, Live at the London House,* and *Night Train.*

Brown relocated in Los Angeles, having in 1954 married his second wife, Cecilia, with whom he had one son. In L.A. Brown found plenty of work in films and on numerous television shows, including the *Steve Allen Show,* for which he wrote the Grammy award-winning theme "Gravy Waltz." Frank Sinatra insisted on Brown for his bassist on his weekly TV show, and in 1974 he recorded with Duke Ellington, *This One's for Blanton,* honoring Ellington's late bassist. That year he formed a quartet that he led until 1983.

In 1990 the Oscar Peterson Trio, with Brown and Ellis, reunited for a gig at the Blue Note in New York City, which resulted in several outstanding albums and more Grammys. Brown continued to perform and record into the 2000s, producing, among others, *Some of My Best Friends Are the Piano Players* and similarly titled recordings for "Sax Players" and "Guitarists." He also cut *Super Bass* and *Live at Scullers* featuring three outstanding acoustic bassists, Brown, John Clayton, and Christian McBride. In 1995 he received the American Jazz Masters award.

Still maintaining a demanding travel schedule, Brown was in Indianapolis, Indiana, when he suddenly died in his sleep on July 2, 2002. In his *Los Angeles Times* obituary, pianist Benny Green was quoted as saying, "Ray had the golden pulse that was infectious. He propelled the music in such a way that it was impossible not to want to play at your best."

John Coltrane

Trane—New Modal Conceptions and Spirituality in Jazz
1926–1967

The most influential jazz musician of the past 40 years.

—Scott Yanow in *The All Music Guide to Jazz*

He is in competition with no one but himself.

—Joe Goldberg,
liner notes to the album *Lush Life*

E very so often in the annals of jazz an artist will gain such stature that he takes on a dietylike presence in the eyes of his followers. John Coltrane goes one better. At Saint John's African Orthodox Church in San Francisco, named for the master reed player, he actually was regarded as a deity, his huge portrait gazing down on the parishioners and his music accompanying the service. It is not surprising that Coltrane is seen in such hallowed light, his music and his persona having grown increasingly spiritual as his career developed. After emerging from a drug hell, he dedicated himself to the glorification of a greater being and the love of mankind. He lived and played accordingly.

Perhaps no one, other than Miles Davis, was more responsible for charting a new course for jazz out of the bebop era than Coltrane. Thelonious Monk, with whom Coltrane played, was a major influence in recasting the saxophonist's musical direction. But Coltrane's experience as part of the Miles Davis quintet took "Trane" to yet another level. In particular, their collaboration on Davis's album *Kind of Blue* became a springboard for the concept of **modal jazz**, in which musicians play within just a few chords, rather than making multiple chord changes as in standard bebop.

As leader of his own quartet, Coltrane extended the modal concept in his 1961 album *My Favorite Things,* which became an all-time jazz classic. He went a step further in 1961, infusing his own spirituality into *A Love Supreme,* ranked among the most highly rated jazz albums ever produced. In those two albums alone Coltrane forever left his imprint and enduring influence on the ever-changing field of jazz.

John William Coltrane was born on September 23, 1926, in Hamlet, North Carolina, the son of a minister's daughter and a tailor. Shortly after he was born, the family moved to High Point, North Carolina, where he grew up. John lived in a musical setting, his father a violin and ukulele player, and his mother a singer and pianist. John enjoyed the big band music he heard on the radio in the 1930s. He learned to play the clarinet when he joined a High Point community band, and when a high school band was formed, he took the first clarinet chair.

John also practiced on alto saxophone and played that instrument with the school band and the dance band. In 1943 John moved to Philadelphia to find work, jobs being plentiful in the wartime years. His real interest was music, however, so he enrolled in a music school to study alto saxophone. He played his first professional gigs before being drafted into the U.S. Navy, which shipped him to Hawaii to play in a navy band. After his discharge in 1946, John returned to Philadelphia, where he worked with Eddie "Cleanhead" Vinson, Jimmy Heath, and others.

Coltrane, intense in his desire to play jazz, practiced every day for hours. He had been intrigued by the tenor saxophone, and because Vinson played alto, Coltrane could play tenor, which became his primary instrument. When Dizzy Gillespie and Charlie Parker came to town, Coltrane met them and was overwhelmed by Parker's playing. He studied Parker intently, and in 1949 he impressed Dizzy Gillespie enough to be hired by the bebop trumpeter. Coltrane played with Gillespie until 1951, and in succeeding years performed with Earl Bostic, Johnny Hodges, and Miles Davis. Coltrane also took classes in theory, harmony, and other musical elements, and came to know the classicists Debussy, Ravel, Bartok, and Hindemith, among others.

The 1950s were trying times for the young Coltrane. He had begun using alcohol and drugs heavily during the late 1940s, and by now the habit was engrained and beginning to affect his work. He was confident that he could succeed in spite of it, but his reliability was questionable. Two things happened in 1955 that began the process of switching Coltrane onto a new life track. One of these was his marriage to Naima Austin, which brought some stability into his life. The other was an invitation to join the new Miles Davis quintet. With Davis, Coltrane received his first major recognition. Coltrane had numerous opportunities to solo on such albums as 'Round About Midnight, Relaxin', Cookin', Workin', and Steamin'. He fit in well with Davis, who was seeking a new post-bebop voice, and Coltrane's sound began to take on a unique shape of its own.

Davis, who had recently shaken his own drug habit, was somewhat tolerant of drug use among his players, but he was a precisionist who could not tolerate unreliability. Subsequently, in early 1957, he could see no recourse other than dropping Coltrane. Coltrane was crushed and depressed by Davis's action; playing was his life. So Coltrane went "cold turkey" (stopped drug usage without tapering off), and after a few weeks of agonizing withdrawal, he picked up his horn again.

Coltrane now decided to lead his own group, and after relocating to New York City, he made his first album under his own name, *First Trane*. Afterward, Coltrane joined the Thelonious Monk quartet for a gig at the Five Spot, which became one of his most rewarding experiences. Coltrane learned a great deal from Monk, who was not only a musical genius, but a teacher willing to share his knowledge. In September 1957, Coltrane made another album under his own name, the acclaimed *Blue Train*.

Davis never doubted Coltrane's talent, and now seeing him clean and on track, invited him to join his new sextet. By now Coltrane's music had been dubbed "sheets of sound," because of his ability to issue cascades of notes rapidly in sort of an unbroken stream. The sextet also featured Cannonball Adderley on alto saxophone. Davis was now looking for an even sharper break with the past, and with Coltrane he explored the modal scale. Coltrane's outstanding solos on two landmark Davis albums, *Milestones* and *Kind of Blue,* exemplify modal playing. His success with Davis, and the success of his own *Giant Steps* in 1961, gave him the impetus to form his own quartet.

For some time Coltrane had been developing ideas about where he wanted to go musically. For one thing, he had opened his mind to music of all kinds, not just American jazz. African music and the music of Asia became influential sources. The philosophies of Eastern and Western religions and the writings of the great philosophers were also changing his perspectives. He took up yoga, and such avant-garde artists as Ornette Coleman and Cecil Taylor advanced his musical conceptions. His quartet did well, but Coltrane was not satisfied. After a few changes he finally attained his classic quartet, consisting of himelf, McCoy Tyner (piano), Elvin Jones (drums) and Steve Davis (bass; later replaced by Jimmy Garrison). This group rocketed to the top in American jazz and achieved international acclaim.

The quartet was propelled by its first album, *My Favorite Things*. Coltrane, ever seeking to expand his universe, had been practicing on the soprano saxophone, an instrument that was not currently popular in jazz. On soprano Coltrane weaves long strands of exotic notes against Tyner's bold chordal background on the album's title song, creating an all-time classic. The album sold fifty thousand copies the first year and eventually received gold certification for selling five hundred thousand copies. Moreover, it served as Coltrane's springboard into a new period of musical creativity.

Coltrane was ahead of his time, and not all of the critics were happy with his new sound, some calling it non-jazz or anti-jazz. Despite those negative comments, *Down Beat* magazine named him Jazzman of the Year for 1961. Coltrane continued his explorations into a new musical world and pursued unique ways to express himself.

After a gig at the Village Vanguard, Coltrane toured Europe, where he was well received except for some critics who took exception to his experimentation. Several albums were made after his death from his European tours. In 1962 he cut an album with Duke Ellington, playing a selection of the Duke's compositions. In a 1963 album, *Live at the Half Note,* Coltrane reflects his interest in free jazz and avant-garde, particularly on his compositions "Brazilia" and "Song of Praise," his solos wandering in an almost abstract way, sometimes crackling and squealing against complex rhythms. As he developed this technique his solos began to take on epic proportions, especially in concert, some lasting forty-five minutes. Occasionally he returned to standard ballads, as on the *John Coltrane and Johnny Hartman* album, Hartman being one of the great jazz ballad singers.

In 1963 Coltrane left Naima and in the same year became companions with a jazz pianist, Alice McLeod, who became his wife and gave birth to his three sons. A year later Coltrane produced what is largely considered his all-time masterpiece and one of the important twentieth-century works of modern music, *A Love Supreme*. This was a culmination of the spirituality he found after his battle with drugs, his musical praising of God. Coltrane wrote the highly reverent liner notes and lyrics to the music. The album achieved gold status in 1970.

Through 1965, Coltrane moved even further from conventional music, becoming increasingly **atonal** and **discordant** on albums such as *Ascension* and *Meditations*. On some sessions he added new members to the quartet, including the soprano/flautist Pharoah Sanders and another tenor, Archie Shepp. In late 1965 Jones finally left, and Tyner did also, unwilling follow Coltrane into a musical unknown. In 1966 Coltrane took his group to Japan, where he was idolized for his music.

After he returned to the United States, Coltrane began to have serious health problems. At first he refused to give in and would not see a doctor. In subsequent weeks, however, his pain became so severe that he went into the hospital for an examination. There was little that could be done for him, and he died of liver cancer on July 17, 1967. A thousand people attended his funeral, among them the cream of jazz society. In 1993 the Bill Clinton White House honored Coltrane, and in 1995 he was commemorated on a U.S. postage stamp.

Miles Davis

Innovator in the Cool Jazz Movement
1926–1991

Miles Davis was a searcher who impelled himself to change, to stake out new territory, to regularly remake himself like a serpent shedding its old skin.

—Don Rose on the Jazz Institute of Chicago Web site

Most jazz artists evolve to a certain individual style that defines them throughout their careers. For Miles Davis, evolution was not a way of achieving a certain kind of musical end, but an end in itself. Davis was first and foremost an innovator who never stopped creating to the end of his life. He started very young, learning from the jazz giants, Charlie Parker, Dizzy Gillespie, and others, who saw his potential. But Davis barely made his name with these titans, whose bebop revolution was still taking hold, when his restless calling began pushing him to another level. Still only twenty-three years old, Davis formed his own group that found a new voice, based in bebop but softer and mellower. It became known over the next few years as "cool jazz."

Most musicians may have been satisfied to be recognized as a main founder of a new musical style, but not Davis. He was quoted in his *New York Times* obituary, September 29, 1991, as saying, "I have to change. It's like a curse." Davis progressed relentlessly to new ground, becoming a catalyst in the formation of emerging jazz movements, hard bop, modal jazz, avant-garde, and fusion. He went from dance bands to small group combos to large ensembles employing strings, French horns, and other orchestral instruments. He was the centerpiece of long classical jazz pieces as part of an enduring collaboration with composer-arranger Gil Evans. All this did not come without controversy. Early, Davis won the hearts and praise of jazz critics and fans, but as he moved from one mode to the next, some of the faithful were lost even as new admirers arrived. His fusion, containing pop, rock, and electronic components, turned away many jazz fans. Davis was undisturbed. By this time he cared little who understood or appreciated his music. His following remained large regardless.

Unlike most trumpeters, Davis played without vibrato, emitting pure brassy tones. Sometimes using a mute, he issued plaintive, almost mournful phrases that seemed to rise from the soul. Through it all one could almost always hear the blues that were embedded in Davis's horn from his youth.

Miles Dewey Davis III was born in Alton, Illinois, on May 25, 1926, the son of a dentist. When he was a year old, his family moved to East St. Louis, Illinois, just across the river from St. Louis, Missouri, with its jazz tradition. There was a musical heritage in Davis's family, but it had been suppressed by racial prejudice. Still, Miles father was determined that his son should have a musical education. Miles began studying trumpet in grade school, and on his thirteenth birthday his father gave him a trumpet. The young Miles progressed rapidly, but struggled for recognition because of racism. Undaunted, his father sought private lessons for Miles, placing him with a trumpeter from the St. Louis Symphony Orchestra.

By the time he was fifteen, Miles was playing in Eddie Randall's big band around St. Louis, and he was influenced by a local trumpet player who went on to jazz fame, Clark Terry. When he was sixteen, Miles could have turned professional, but the eager teenager's mother insisted he finish high school. When the star-studded Billy Eckstine band came to town in 1944, Miles listened night after night to such future jazz icons as Charlie Parker and Dizzy Gillespie. After he sat in with the band one night, his course in music was effectively set.

Davis wanted to go to New York City, the world's jazz center, but his parents objected. After he was accepted at the prestigious Juilliard School, however, they could no longer restrain him. In New York, the eighteen-year-old Davis found the jazz emporiums of Harlem and Fifty-second Street more interesting than his classical studies at Juilliard. Before long he became friendly with Gillespie and Parker, who introduced the young protégé to the new jazz called bebop. Juilliard was forgotten. Davis learned fast, especially from Parker, with whom he roomed for a year. Parker had Davis sitting in at clubs where he was playing, and in 1945 he made his first record with talented reed player Herbie Fields. Later Davis recorded with Parker and Gillespie, and in 1946 he headed for the West Coast with the Benny Carter band.

Gillespie and Parker were already on the coast, and Davis hooked up with them again, but after Parker was busted on a drug charge, Davis joined the Billy Eckstine band in New York. By 1947 Davis had left Eckstine and joined the Charlie Parker quintet, with whom he recorded his own works, "Donna Lee" and "Milestones."

At only twenty-two years of age Davis broke out, and in 1948 he formed his own nine-person unit, which included tuba and French horn. This nonet created a new sound playing the arrangements of Gil Evans and featuring Davis's trumpet. Its members included pianist John Lewis, baritone saxophonist Gerry Mulligan, alto saxophonist Lee Konitz, and drummers Kenny Clarke or Max Roach. Seeking a big-band sound with small-group freedom, their recordings were released after several years as *Birth of the Cool*.

By the time "cool" was born, though, Davis was ready to move on. He had played a jazz festival in Paris in 1949, returned to various recording dates, and was in and out of the Tadd Dameron band. He made the 1950–51 Metronome All-Star band (selected by *Metronome* magazine). Through the early 1950s Davis was, for the most part, drifting. During that period he became addicted to heroin. Miles Davis had an incredibly strong will, however, and after several years of addiction he kicked the habit.

A new, highly productive period of Davis's career began in 1954. He teamed with such outstanding musicians as Percy Heath, Art Blakey, Horace Silver, and Sonny Rollins to produce albums like *Walkin'* and *Blue 'n' Boogie* that accelerated the hard bop movement. A year later Davis appeared at the Newport Jazz Festival, and in the same year he assembled one of his classic quintets, which included the heralded John Coltrane on tenor saxophone. The group cut several acclaimed recordings through 1960. Davis moved to other recording projects as well in 1957, when he and Gil Evans collaborated on their extended piece, *Miles Ahead*.

Davis and Evans produced two more lengthy works, *Porgy and Bess* and *Sketches of Spain*, which won accolades. These large orchestral pieces brought Davis to one of his highest artistic levels. His often muted trumpet and flugelhorn reflected all manner of emotions, from joyful to discordant and agonizing. About the same time, Davis again pushed jazz in a new direction. Employing the quintet plus alto saxophonist Cannonball Adderley, Davis produced *Milestones,* which altered the harmonic and chord structure of bebop. It was followed by *Kind of Blue,* in which the numbers, composed mainly by Davis and pianist Bill Evans, use fewer chords on **modal scales**, rather than **multiple chord** changes. That recording became Davis's best-selling album and one of the top sellers in jazz history.

In this period Davis also recorded the soundtrack for a French film, *Ascenseur Pour L'Echafaud,* but by 1960 he was again looking for new directions. In succeeding years he moved more and more toward avant-garde and free jazz, pulling much of the jazz scene with him. One of his more successful recordings, the 1965 *Live at the Plugged Nickel* (a former Chicago club), reflected new and old trends.

Not everyone could accept the new Davis sound, nor his increasingly aloof attitude toward the audience. Sometimes he even played with his back to the patrons so he could face his musicians. Only his most faithful following stayed with Davis as he wandered far off the mainstream. On the album *Nefertiti* in 1967, Davis showed early signs of his fusion mode, which would define his playing in the late 1960s and early 1970s. He pushed further in that direction in 1968, embracing electronic instruments and utilizing such jazz-rock musicians as George Benson and John McLaughlin.

With *Bitches Brew* in 1969 Davis began his immersion into fusion. It was described in the *New York Times* (September 29, 1991) as "an aggressive, spooky sequel, roiling and churning with improvisations in every register." What Davis lost in jazz followers, however, he more than made up in attracting rockers, who now became his main audience, making the album a best seller. In the early 1970s Davis was experimenting with electric trumpet, and for the album *On the Corner,* he played electric organ as he introduced funk into the mix as well as early hip-hop and **acid jazz**.

Through 1975 Davis produced several more free-form albums that left some listeners confused, but drew praise from those who appreciated their abstract qualities. Davis, in the meantime, had been suffering some health problems, and by the end of 1975 he could no longer work. He went into a temporary retirement that stretched out to 1980 before he picked up the horn again. Upon his return, Davis continued to use electric instruments, reflecting the pop and rock idioms.

Davis, who avoided ever revisiting the past, finally did so when he joined Gil Evans and trumpeter-composer-arranger Quincy Jones at the Montreux Jazz Festival in July 1991. There they "returned in time" to a program of pieces from Davis's cool period and numbers from the Evans–Davis collaborations. It was the last hurrah for the trumpet master. He died just a few months later, on September 28, 1991. Jazz had lost one of its most creative offspring, whose legacy is destined to influence jazz artists for decades to come.

Gerry Mulligan

Jeru—Near Preeminence Among Baritone Saxophonists
1927–1996

He always knew what he wanted musically and he knew how to get it. His ensembles were always the epitome of discipline and musicianship.

—Ken Poston, director of the
California Institute for the Preservation
of Jazz, Long Beach, California

Few jazz musicians have been willing to take on the large and unwieldy baritone saxophone as their primary instrument. Not only is it big but it has not been a very popular instrument in jazz bands. Gerry Mulligan not only took up baritone sax but became the preeminent master of that instrument in jazz, perhaps matched only by Harry Carney of

Duke Ellington's orchestra. Mulligan played some as a sideman, but he largely earned his fame as a composer and arranger who led ensembles of all sizes.

The innovative Mulligan was always eager to advance his musical development. With Miles Davis, Gil Evans, and others he helped usher in the cool jazz era, and his name is almost synonymous with **West Coast jazz**, a close relative to cool jazz. Mulligan played with virtually every major jazz artist and was a regular invitee to major jazz festivals. A Grammy award winner, he consistently won principal jazz polls as best baritone saxophonist.

Gerald Joseph Mulligan was born on April 6, 1927, in New York City, but his family moved about, finally settling in Philadelphia. While growing up he heard all types of music on the radio, but mostly he enjoyed the big swing bands, popular in the 1930s. From an early age he wanted to play music and, rather unusually, he wanted to write arrangements. In high school he asked to play trumpet, but when that instrument wasn't available, he took up clarinet. Mulligan also learned to play alto saxophone, then tenor, and got his first taste of baritone while in high school.

When Mulligan was only seventeen, he was doing arrangements for a Philadelphia radio station. Soon afterward he was hired to arrange for bandleader Tommy Tucker, a job that took him to New York City. Mulligan's charts were bit far out for Tucker, so in 1946 he joined the Gene Krupa band as a player-arranger. By now he wanted to play baritone, but Krupa insisted he play alto. While with Krupa, Mulligan was impressed with bebop, and its influence crept into his work. This continued after he joined the Claude Thornhill Orchestra in 1948, still playing alto.

Finally he got rid of his horns, except for the baritone, which he now really loved. Thus, when he joined the Miles Davis nonet, it was as a baritone player, that instrument being welcomed in a group that also included a tuba and French horn. With the nonet, which started cool jazz, Mulligan also continued as an arranger, contributing charts for "Godchild," "Darn that

Dream," his own "Jeru," "Rocker," and "Venus de Milo." The nonet recorded until 1951, when Mulligan moved to Los Angeles, where he played in jam sessions and arranged for Stan Kenton.

In the jam sessions Mulligan struck up a relationship that propelled his career and instigated a new trend in jazz. His meeting with the trumpet player Chet Baker led to a unique small group concept out of which evolved a new jazz sound. Mulligan and Baker formed the "pianoless quartet," a quite radical notion for the time. The smooth, mellow sounds of the quartet soon influenced a movement that became West Coast jazz. Mulligan and Baker both became stars with the quartet, but it broke up after about a year when Mulligan was arrested on a drug charge.

Mulligan reentered the jazz scene in 1954 and returned to New York where he started working with various groups. One of his main collaborators in this period was valve trombone player and composer Bob Brookmeyer. Brookmeyer replaced Baker in the pianoless quartet, and that group traveled to Europe, becoming a smash hit in Paris. Their live recordings during that period include *Gerry Mulligan in Paris,* volumes 1 and 2. During the 1950s Mulligan also worked with trumpeter Art Farmer, saxophonist Zoot Sims, and drummer Chico Hamilton. At the 1958 Newport Jazz Festival, Mulligan fulfilled a dream, playing a baritone saxophone duet with his idol, Harry Carney. From 1957 to 1960 he recorded with major jazz stars, including Thelonious Monk, Ben Webster, Paul Desmond, Stan Getz, and Johnny Hodges.

In 1960 Mulligan formed the Concert Jazz Band (CJB), a large orchestra that included many previous collaborators as well as such artists as Clark Terry and Mel Lewis. The CJB gave Mulligan an ample forum for his creative ideas with Bob Brookmeyer as his chief collaborator. Mulligan pursued the large group format until 1964, after which he curtailed his activity for a few years. In 1968 he replaced Paul Desmond in the Dave Brubeck Quartet, which then became the Dave Brubeck Trio featuring Gerry Mulligan. Their sensational performance in Berlin was recorded as *Live at the Berlin Philharmonic.* Leaving Brubeck in 1972, Mulligan reunited with Baker for a Carnegie Hall concert in 1974, one of several reunions with the trumpet star.

Mulligan slowed his pace a bit through the 1980s, but his playing and arranging produced several highly rated albums, including *Little Big Horn, Soft Lights and Sweet Music,* and *Symphonic Dreams.* The latter was recorded with the Houston Symphony Orchestra, with whom Mulligan performed a variety of classical and jazz saxophone pieces, including his own *Entente for Baritone Sax and Orchestra.* In the 1990s Mulligan formed another quartet, dubbed the "no-name" quartet, with which he toured Europe. Not averse to revisiting the past, Mulligan in 1991 assembled a group to pay tribute to the Miles Davis cool jazz nonet. His effort resulted in *Re-birth of the Cool,* with Mel Tormé on vocals.

Mulligan continued to perform and record through 1995, producing such outstanding works as *Dream a Little Dream, Paraiso, Lonesome Boulevard,* and, in 1995, his last recording, *Dragonfly,* which hints at fusion. The National Endowment for the Arts presented Mulligan with an award for his musical accomplishments in 1995.

The next year Mulligan had to submit to knee surgery. Sadly, complications from the operation caused his death on January 20, 1996. Tributes to the virtuoso baritone saxophone player rang out from all quarters, including President Bill Clinton, who said, "No one ever played that horn like he did, and no one ever will."

Cannonball Adderley

Evolved Versions of Hard Bop and Soul Jazz
1928–1975

He had that blues thing and I love me some blues.

—Miles Davis
from Davis's autobiography, *Miles*

Cannonball Adderley loved to play his alto saxophone, but he was happy being a high school band director in Florida. So it took some persuading to uproot Adderley in 1955 and get him to move to New York City to try the big-time jazz scene. Adderley's reputation as an alto player was known in Florida, but his name meant little in the Big Apple. That changed one night at the Café Bohemia when Oscar Pettiford's sax player was late and

Adderley sat in. Adderley's solo dazzled Pettiford, who immediately wanted the alto player in his group. With Pettiford, Adderley's reputation soared.

Adderley went on to perform with other outstanding jazz artists and eventually to lead his own groups. His interests went well beyond music, however. He was an avid reader with a keen mind, who used his talent and intelligence to advance artistic and social causes. He was appointed jazz adviser for the National Endowment for the Arts, and he hosted numerous jazz workshops, serving also as Artist-in-Residence for Harvard University. His driving, soulful, sometimes funky sound was captured on numerous recordings, a fitting legacy in the treasury of jazz.

Julian Edwin Adderley was born on September 15, 1928, in Tampa, Florida. Music was prominent in the Adderley family. The father, an educator, played cornet, and Julian's brother Nat also studied cornet, becoming himself a noted jazz musician. By the age of fourteen Julian had taken up brass and reed instruments, before settling on saxophone. He played in the high school band and some swing bands. While in high school Julian earned the name "Cannonball," derived from "Cannibal," which his friends called him because of his huge appetite. After high school he attended Florida A&M University, from which he graduated in 1948 with a music degree.

Adderley, like his father, wanted to teach, and he took a band director's job at a Fort Lauderdale high school, which he held until 1956. He left education temporarily when the army drafted him in 1950, and eventually he directed the 36th Army Dance Band. After his 1952 discharge Adderley played in and led groups, directed the high school band, and continued his musical studies. In time, though, Adderley's performing talent outshone everything else, and in 1955 his friends persuaded him to take his talent to New York City.

Adderley was an almost immediate success after his sensational debut with Pettiford, but in a few months he returned to his high school teaching job. The demand for his playing, however, caused him to return to New York in 1956. Some admirers even hailed him as the next Charlie Parker, and, indeed, his early sound did resemble Parker's. Initially he formed his own quintet, featuring his brother Nat, but financial problems beset the group and it disbanded. Adderley was not free for long, as Miles Davis quickly added him to the Davis quintet, which became a sextet featuring Adderley with Davis and John Coltrane. Their albums *Milestones* and *Kind of Blue* are classics.

Adderley formed another quintet in 1959, which again included brother Nat. With Davis, Adderley had blended into the cool jazz and West Coast jazz sound, a smoother, mellower bebop. In his quintet Adderley established a new style that largely followed the tenets of the emerging hard bop school. Hard bop discarded some of the subtleties of cool jazz, while employing some funk and **soul** with hard-driving rhythms. Elements of the new trend appeared in Adderley's 1958 album *Somethin' Else,* which also included Miles Davis in a rare sideman's role.

Over the next few years, Adderley's hard bop became increasingly soulful, until it was dubbed "soul jazz." It started with the recording *The Cannonball Adderley Quintet in San Francisco,* which included such swinging, funky items as "This Here." The new Adderley sound had great appeal, and the alto player enjoyed commercial success with such albums as *Dirty Blues, What Is This Thing Called Soul?, Paris 1960,* and *The Quintet Plus.* The latter employed Adderley's sextet format, and by 1962 he fronted what is widely considered his finest group, consisting of his brother Nat, Yusef Lateef (tenor and flute; later replaced by Charles Lloyd), Sam Jones (bass), Louis Hayes (drums), and Joe Zawinul (keyboards). One of their biggest hits was the 1966 *Mercy, Mercy, Mercy,* by Zawinul.

Adderley's success did not come without paying a price, for some jazz critics assailed him for commercialism, claiming he was appealing to pop trends. But most jazz followers felt that Adderly's music held to its jazz integrity. In fact, Adderley, with his teaching background, later became an articulate spokesperson for jazz on television and in university settings.

In the late 1960s and 1970s Adderley's work reflected his social consciousness, even as it moved from soul into progressive jazz. His album *Country Preacher,* a live benefit performance for the Reverend Jesse Jackson's Operation Breadbasket, was still substantially soul jazz. The title "The Price You Got to Pay to Be Free" strongly reflects the album's message. By the early to mid-1970s, Adderley had picked up on Davis's progressive electronic and fusion sounds and Coltrane's adventures with new sounds. Those trends appear in Adderley's *Pyramid and Phenix.*

Adderley's health had been questionable in the 1970s, his weight and diabetes being contributing factors. Still, the jazz world was shocked when he died of a stroke on August 8, 1975 at age forty-seven. During his lifetime Adderley had accrued most of the honors available to a career jazzman. He had won major polls, been honored by numerous institutions, and in 1975 was elected to *Down Beat*'s Hall of Fame. Uniquely, the Florida legislature had proclaimed Cannonball Adderley musical ambassador of the state.

Bill Evans

A Major Influence in Modern Jazz
1929–1980

The sixties were the period when Evans . . . became the most influential jazz pianist since Bud Powell.

—Bob Blumenthal
from *The Oxford Companion to Jazz*

Jazz writers have a bounty of expressive words to describe the playing of Bill Evans. Some of them include "exquisite," "delicate," "lyrical," "mystical," and "Zen-like." All of them apply. Evans could swing with anybody, but his touch was light. Perhaps his most impressive work is contained in the melodic, sensitive, almost meditative pieces that that exude peace and calm. Maybe Miles Davis described Evans's playing best of all: "Bill had

this quiet fire that I loved on the piano . . . the sound he got was like crystal notes or sparkling water cascading down from some clear waterfall" (from *Dick Hyman's Century of Jazz Piano*).

Bill Evans was influenced by Lennie Tristano and Bud Powell, and he is often considered the successor to Powell. But Evans did not always play with the speed and power of Powell. He used notes more sparingly, making each count significantly. Evans attributed his piano voicing more to the phrasing of such horn players as John Coltrane and Miles Davis. Not everyone "digs" Evans, despite his album *Everybody Digs Bill Evans*. For some his playing was too laid back, too reserved. Nevertheless, Bill Evans stature and his influence as a jazz innovator, a composer, and arranger has continued to grow.

Bill Evans was born in Plainfield, New Jersey, on August 16, 1929. His father, of Welsh origin, and his Russian Orthodox mother were both musically inclined. Bill and his older brother Harry had early musical exposure in their mother's church. Something of a prodigy, Bill took up piano at six, violin a year later, and flute when he was thirteen. He was adept in these years at playing boogie woogie, popular in the early 1940s. He hated playing scales, instead practicing on Bach and Schubert and modernists such as Debussy, Stravinsky, and Milhaud.

In 1946 Evans received a music scholarship to Southeastern Louisiana College (now University). During college Evans was impressed by jazz pianists, including Tristano, Powell, Nat King Cole, and Horace Silver. Evans graduated from college in 1950, then joined Herbie Fields before being drafted into the army in 1951. After his discharge in 1954 he headed for New York City to pursue a jazz career, finding jobs with the Jerry Wald dance band, with whom he made his record debut, and progressive reed player Tony Scott. He backed Lucy Reed in a 1955 recording, and a year later hooked up with George Russell, who was pursuing advanced musical concepts. Meanwhile, Evans continued his studies at the Mannes College of Music in New York.

Evans had a breakthrough in 1956 when Riverside Records signed him to do an album under his own name. Despite his obvious talent, Evans felt he wasn't ready and had to be coaxed into the studio. He chose a trio format for the recording *New Jazz Conceptions,* which included his own signature piece "Waltz for Debbie." The album won critical acclaim but had little commercial success.

In 1958 Evans got a career-turning break. In that year Miles Davis beckoned Evans to join his sextet, which, with a front line of Davis, Coltrane, and Cannonball Adderley, was one of the most acclaimed jazz groups ever. Evans stayed with Davis until late that year, participating in several albums, and returned in 1959 to record *Kind of Blue,* an all-time classic that brought modal jazz to the forefront of modern music. Evans was a key player in establishing this new direction in jazz.

After Davis, Evans formed his own trio, seeking to develop original musical concepts. Despite his success with Davis, Evans still had to be talked into the studio for his second album as a leader, *Everybody Digs Bill Evans,* which became a classic. On it Evans swings in delightful, although complex, patterns, but two slow mood pieces became defining pieces for Evans. One is the Leonard Bernstein composition, "Some Other Time," with a Debussy-like quality, while the other is his own quietly eloquent "Peace Piece."

In 1959 Evans formed what is probably his classic trio, including drummer Paul Motian and bassist Scott LaFaro. The three fit together like the works of a fine watch. LaFaro, in particular, became Evans virtual alter ego. The trio made two highly regarded albums in the studio, and then they were recorded live at the Village Vanguard on June 25, 1961. The music recorded that day has taken on an almost cultlike status, with Evans's devotees marking that gig as an almost transcendental moment for Evans. Forty years later Adam Gopnik wrote a piece for the *New Yorker* reminiscing on the music created that day. It is captured on the albums *Sunday at the Village Vanguard* and *Waltz for Debby.*

Unfortunately, only two weeks later LaFaro was killed in an automobile accident. The news devastated Evans, and he withdrew from public life for several months. By this time, Evans was using heroin, a habit that shook his career and personal life. In 1962, however, he cut several albums, including *How My Heart Sings* and *Interplay,* the latter with a quintet. In 1963 Evans experimented with overdubbing, in which he recorded three separate piano lines dubbed together as a single piece. Aptly entitled *Conversations With Myself,* the acclaimed album won a Grammy. Over the next few years Evans formed several trios, performed with outstanding jazz artists, and was recorded live at the Montreux Jazz Festival.

Tragedy struck again in 1970 when Evans's wife, also an addict, committed suicide. Evans had been attempting to kick his habit, but regressed briefly in his sorrow. He recovered to resume his career and even married a second time. Through the 1970s Evans performed memorable concerts in Japan and Europe that were recorded live. Also noteworthy from the 1970s are his albums *But Beautiful* and *Blue In Green.*

Evans's drug habit caught up to him, and he died on September 15, 1980. His memory and art are kept alive by his timeless recordings and continuing interest in his work. An archive of Evans's life and work is housed at Southeastern Louisiana University.

Joe Pass

The Art Tatum of the Guitar
1929–1994

Truly a master of the Guitar.
—Jazzhall Web site

Joe Pass had to endure some detours early in his career that set back his progress as a professional jazz guitarist. He was just out of high school and working some gigs when the first interruption occurred: military service. After serving in the navy in the early 1950s, he started playing again, but drug use caused a second detour. For about ten years Pass's remarkable talent was largely untapped as he dealt with addiction. Finally he entered a California self-help institution called Synanon, from which he emerged in 1962 with his habit left behind.

Pass did not entirely waste his time at Synanon. There were many good musicians at the institution, some of whom recorded an album entitled *Sounds of Synanon*. Pass's work on selected numbers drew particular praise and helped him make a fresh start as he picked up gigs with some emerging West Coast jazz stars. The mastery of the guitar he developed thereafter has been equated with Art Tatum's talent on piano, often conceded to be the greatest in jazz history.

Joe Pass was born Joseph Anthony Jacobi Passalaqua on January 13, 1929, in New Brunswick, New Jersey. He showed early talent with the guitar, and in high school he played local gigs and even toured with the Tony Pastor dance band. In 1947 he hooked up with Charlie Barnet, who led one of the nation's top swing bands, and his future looked promising until he went into the U.S. Navy. After his discharge Pass spent years in a drug haze before being rehabilitated and getting his career on track. From 1962 Pass's reputation on the West Coast spread quickly, and he found work with such jazz stars as Bud Shank, Gerald Wilson, Bobby Troup, Julie London, Earl Bostic, and Les McCann. His work in this period was largely in the studio, and *Down Beat* magazine heard enough to make Pass their 1963 New Star awardee.

Pass was working mainly as a sideman, although his own 1964 album *For Django* with a quartet received some acclaim. That album honored the French guitarist Django Reinhardt, although Pass's more direct influence was Charlie Christian. Pass received wide recognition in the mid-1960s when he toured with the internationally known pianist George Shearing, and in the early 1970s he played guitar duets with the renowned Herb Ellis. In 1973 jazz impresario Norman Granz signed Pass to a record contract. It was the breakout move that made Pass a headline act. Granz had Pass cut a solo album, *Virtuoso,* that was an immediate hit. On it Pass displayed his "finger-picking" technique, which allowed him to literally accompany himself on such bop numbers as "How High the Moon" and "Cherokee."

Pass recorded three more solo *Virtuoso* albums during the 1970s, and Granz teamed the guitarist with top recording jazz stars, including Oscar Peterson, Ella Fitzgerald, Sarah Vaughan, Benny Carter, Dizzy Gillespie, Zoot Sims, and the Duke Ellington and Count Basie orchestras.

As Pass's fame grew, so did the demand for him to appear at festivals and concerts, and he increasingly toured overseas. He traveled to Australia with Benny Goodman in 1973 and was recorded live at the Montreux Jazz Festival in 1975 and 1977. In Germany he became particularly fond of Hamburg, marrying a native of that city and establishing a home there in 1989. In 1992 he dedicated an album to his wife, *Songs for Ellen*.

Pass was active in music virtually to the end of his life, even when he was weakened by cancer. After his death on May 23, 1994, he was heralded as one of the all-time great jazz guitarists, recognized for having greatly advanced methods of playing solo on both the acoustic and electric guitar.

Clifford Brown

"Brownie"—Successor to Jazz Trumpet Masters
1930–1956

His was one of the fullest and most beautiful sounds in jazz . . . above all his music exuded warmth and joy . . . qualities which gave his brilliance such human eloquence.

—Ian Carr, from *Jazz, the Rough Guide*

The story of gifted trumpet player Clifford Brown is among the most joyous and most tragic in jazz. He was one of those musicians whose star burned brilliantly, then all too quickly was snuffed out. Clifford Brown was being hailed as heir apparent to the throne that had been held by the masters of the instrument, including Louis Armstrong, Dizzy Gillespie, and Miles

Davis. Then with startling suddenness his life ended in an automobile accident, leaving a void that some say may never be filled. He was not yet twenty-six years old, and his professional life had lasted a mere five years.

In those few years Brown rose cometlike in his profession. Still a teenager, he arrived on the jazz scene in the late 1940s and almost immediately was playing alongside the elite of jazz. Despite his brief career, his contributions to jazz art were great. He made a substantial number of recordings in his few years, and young jazz musicians still listen to his eloquent solos and learn.

Clifford Brown was born in Wilmington, Delaware, on October 30, 1930, the son of a multi-instrumental father who played trumpet, violin, and piano. Brown was fascinated by the trumpet even as toddler, and at thirteen his father bought him his first instrument. Brown studied trumpet in high school and mastered it quickly. He soon began playing jazz locally, amazing the area's professionals.

When Dizzy Gillespie came to Wilmington, he heard of the local trumpet phenom, and invited Brown to sit in with the band. Brown dazzled Gillespie with his power, speed, and tone, and the master told Brown he could turn professional. But Brown chose to finish his schooling, having come from a family that valued education. After high school he enrolled at Delaware State College with a music scholarship, but later transferred to Maryland State College because of its superior music program.

While still in school Brown played gigs in Philadelphia, where he came into contact with rising jazz stars such as Fats Navarro and drummer Max Roach. Trumpeter Navarro became Brown's idol, and Roach would later become important in his career. In 1950 an automobile accident brought Brown's career to a screeching halt, and sidelined him for a year. In 1952 he made his first recordings with Chris Powell's Blue Flames, a rhythm and blues group. A year later Brown played with the Tadd Dameron band in Atlantic City, and then joined Lionel Hampton's all-star trumpet section.

While on a European tour with Hampton, Brown made several recordings, including one with Art Farmer and the Swedish All Stars, and another released as *The Clifford Brown Quartet in Paris,* which became a classic. Back in the United States, Brown joined Art Blakey for an historic gig at Birdland, February 1954, which was recorded live and released as *A Night at Birdland.* That recording became a model of hard bop, combining the talents of drummer Blakey and Brown with pianist Horace Silver, alto saxophonist Lou Donaldson, and bassist Curly Russell. Brown's solos on such tunes as "Wee-Dot" and "Quicksilver" exemplified his rich tone, his sensitivity, and his high speed improvising, hitting every note pure and clean.

Brown won the *Down Beat* Critics New Star Award in 1954, and that spring Max Roach, now a top bebop drummer, invited Brown to join him in a new quintet. After he accepted, Roach insisted that Brown share equal billing on their bookings. The collaboration with Roach began the finest hour of Brown's career, as the quintet played top clubs and festivals.

Brown not only performed with the quintet but composed much of its repertoire, including "Jacqui," "Swingin'," "Sandu" and "Daahoud." Among the leading albums they cut were *Jordu, Jam Session, A Study in Brown,* and *At Basin Street,* the last of these being Brown's final official recording. The quintet was playing on the East Coast and was scheduled to open at Chicago's Blue Note. Brown sent his wife and child ahead by plane, but decided he would drive with the pianist Richie Powell (brother of Bud) and his wife. When Powell's wife fell asleep at the wheel, the car veered off the road, killing all three passengers.

When Clifford Brown died on June 30, 1966, he was just twenty-five years old. Many jazzmen have died at an early age because they burned themselves out, living on the edge with drugs and alcohol. Brown avoided that pitfall. He lived an orderly, disciplined life, remaining close to his wife and child. Affectionately called "Brownie," by his colleagues, his loss was mourned by jazz devotees everywhere.

Betty Carter

Distinctive Modern Jazz Vocal Stylist
1930–1998

She . . . could improvise with as much harmonic and rhythmic sophistication and surprise as any horn player."

—Mark Stryker, Music Writer,
Detroit Free Press

Betty Carter was a late bloomer as a jazz singer. Her talent was recognized early by critics, but she was over forty years old before she established herself as a bona fide jazz star. Perhaps the most significant reason the spotlight eluded her was that she would not compromise her principles. She began as a fairly mainstream jazz singer who showed much promise. But Carter wanted to establish her own individual voice, and as that individuality drifted from the mainstream so did her popularity.

Despite growing indifference to her work, Betty Carter did not give up, stubbornly pursuing her dream. After all, wasn't this what jazz was all about: taking risks, experimenting with musical ideas, striving to establish your originality? Carter stuck to her guns, and by the late twentieth century was among the most acclaimed jazz singers. The honors she accumulated in her lifetime, however, did not just reflect her singing. She was also a leader in discovering new jazz talent and in educating children in the art of jazz. Perpetuating the jazz art form became a major pursuit.

Betty Carter was born Lillie Mae Jones on May 16, 1930, in Flint, Michigan. With work scarce during the Depression, her family moved to Detroit, where her father became a choir director. At an early age Betty studied piano at the Detroit Conservatory of Music, and, as a teenager at Northwestern High School, she became interested in jazz, which was being infused by bebop. The young Betty Carter lied about her age to get into jazz clubs, and before long she was entering local talent contests. Still in her teens, she sang with local jazz bands, even once sitting in with alto saxophonist Charlie Parker.

When the Lionel Hampton band came to town in 1948, word of the promising vocalist reached the leader, who hired Carter on the spot. At eighteen she was traveling with the Hampton band, but before long Carter's modern jazz style became a problem. Hampton had not yet embraced bebop, while Carter eagerly joined the new trend with swinging scat vocals. Hampton even billed her as Betty "BeBop" Carter. She left Hampton after they reached New York City in 1951, making her home in Brooklyn. Carter appeared at the famed Apollo Theater, sharing the stage with Dizzy Gillespie, Max Roach, and other stars. She made her first recordings in the mid-1950s, cutting one album with pianist Ray Bryant.

During 1958 and 1959 she sang a few times with Miles Davis, one of the more progressive jazz musicians. In the late 1950s she cut two more albums,

I Can't Help It and *Out There,* neither of which did well despite their critical success. In 1960 *The Modern Sound of Betty Carter* debuted, but the public was apparently not ready. Help came from an unexpected source: Ray Charles. The very popular Charles was an R&B and soul singer, but he loved Carter's voice and asked her to join him. The ensuing *Ray Charles and Betty Carter* album was her first real commercial success. Her rendition of "Baby It's Cold Outside" caused President Bill Clinton (in 1997) to comment, "It makes you want to curl up in front of the fire, even in the summertime."

Just as success was at her door, the unpredictable Carter, who was now married, decided to stay home and raise her two sons. She was largely dormant musically until her return in the late 1960s. After struggling with record companies, Carter established her own company, Bet-Car, in 1971. Carter's career was on the upswing from that point on. Her albums *At the Village Vanguard* and *The Audience with Betty Carter* were acclaimed and sold well. Audiences were now receptive to her distinctive style.

In the 1980s Verve signed Carter to a recording contract and reissued many of her earlier works. She won a Grammy award for her 1988 release of *Look What I've Got,* which includes two of her own compositions. Carter had taken an interest in developing jazz talent, and in 1993 she founded Jazz Ahead, an educational program, to pursue that aim. The White House called for a Carter command performance in 1994, and in 1997 the National Endowment for the Arts awarded her the National Medal of the Arts.

In the meantime Carter had assumed a role of leadership in promoting jazz education and black culture. She was especially interested in conducting school workshops, and she made one of her last appearances at such a session in Detroit. Carter had become ill with pancreatic cancer, and she died on September 26, 1998. Carter had spent much of her later life teaching jazz to young people. In one interview she reflected, "I am not going to live forever . . . I don't want it to die with me. I want it to live on."

Ornette Coleman

Pioneer of Free Jazz
1930–

Rarely does one person change the way we listen to music, but such a man was Ornette Coleman.

—Eyeneer New Jazz Profiles Web site

Duke Ellington liked to label special talent "beyond category." There could be no more apt candidate for the term than Ornette Coleman, because he could not—would not—be categorized. Hardly anyone was neutral about the music that Coleman played, either hating it or rendering it high praise. He may be one of the few, if not the only, person in jazz who literally took a beating for not playing what pleased the crowd. That was in 1949 when he gave a Louisiana rhythm and blues swing dancing crowd a lesson in modern New York style bebop. For his trouble, he was beaten and his tenor saxophone trashed. Undeterred, Coleman kept on pursuing his musical dream until he found his own niche in jazz.

Coleman refused to be restricted even by the advanced jazz modes of the 1940s and 1950s. He found new ways to put harmony and melody together based on what he termed his "harmolodic theory." For some listeners, his music comes across as orchestrated noise, but over time others have come to support Coleman's music, finding within it a unique brilliance and beauty. Striving to shed the musical structure of the past, he became a primal figure in the development of "free jazz."

Ornette Coleman was born in Fort Worth, Texas, on March 19, 1930, the son of a cook-mechanic father and seamstress mother. He was influenced in music by his cousin, a music teacher, and by the time he was fourteen he was teaching himself the alto saxophone. He began playing rhythm and blues, and in a few years switched to tenor saxophone, the more popular R&B instrument. After being introduced to the bebop of Charlie Parker, the teenager adopted that style. He discovered, however, that it was little appreciated in the Fort Worth area, and in 1949 he went on tour, ending up in Los Angeles, where he remained for much of the next ten years.

Even in Los Angeles there was little interest in his music, and he had to work in menial jobs while studying music theory and harmony. Eventually he managed some small gigs while developing his unorthodox style, which departed from conventional jazz. Playing sharp or flat, he believed, did not matter because you could still be in tune. Established musicians often refused to play with Coleman, because they feared his unorthodox anti-music would drive audiences away, which sometimes it did.

Coleman had to search for musicians who believed in his radical jazz, almost as though he were establishing a new religion. But by the late 1950s he had established a quartet, consisting of Don Cherry (trumpet), Billy Higgins (drums), and Charlie Haden (bass). Gigs were infrequent, but in 1958 Contemporary Records agreed to let him cut two albums. For the first, *Something Else!!!!,* Coleman, then playing an inexpensive white plastic alto sax, added a piano (seldom used thereafter) and bass. The second, *Tomorrow Is the Question,* included Shelly Mann on drums and Percy Heath on bass. The albums sent shock waves through the jazz community and left many scratching their heads. But it was an opening wedge for free jazz.

Interest mounted as such respected music people as critic Nat Hentoff, pianist John Lewis, and classical conductors Gunthar Schuller and Leonard Bernstein encouraged Coleman. With such support, in 1959 he opened with a quartet at the Five Spot in New York City. The new sounds drew curious crowds, including many musicians, and the cries of "fake" and "genius" were alternately heard. But free jazz was now out of the box, never to return. Coleman recorded seven albums for Atlantic during 1959–1962, and his music aroused such interest that he was invited to the Newport and Monterey jazz festivals and New York City's Town Hall. The flap over Coleman's music took many forms, but it was generally agreed that it was blues-based and had an innate swing, clearly elements of jazz.

Coleman, in 1963, decided to temporarily retire. During a reflective period he took up trumpet and violin, instruments that he would later employ in performances. Returning in 1965, he played some New York gigs, then took a trio on a European tour, recording his two-volume *At the "Golden Circle" in Stockholm.* In the late 1960s Coleman made another unorthodox move, adding his ten-year-old son, Denardo, as a drummer to his quartet. Coleman had received the first Guggenheim Fellowship for jazz composition in 1967.

Perhaps tired of the resistance of club owners, Coleman opened his Artist House in Manhattan in 1972, a space for exhibitions and performances. That year Coleman unveiled his full-length symphony, *Skies in America,* recorded by the London Symphony Orchestra, and later performed at Newport and at Lincoln Center by the New York Philharmonic. The experimental work allowed improvisation by all members of the orchestra.

In the mid- to late 1970s Coleman infused his performances with rock music powered by electronic instruments and played by his double quartet, Prime Time. In 1985 the **double quartet** played a Hartford, Connecticut, festival in which Coleman received the keys to the city. He recorded more albums in the late 1980s, and then withdrew again from 1989 until the mid-1990s, except for composing music for the film *Naked Lunch*. He reemerged to record with acclaimed pianist Geri Allen and make a duo album with German pianist Joachim Kuhn.

By the turn of the twenty-first century, Coleman had eliminated many detractors, his work having gained wide recognition. He still finds ways to arouse controversy, but he has influenced a large body of modern musicians, and few would argue that he ever wavered from his musical principles.

Cecil Taylor

Far Beyond the Mainstream
1933–

Since the 1960s, Taylor's music had become totally abstract—non-tonal and without any kind of conventional jazz rhythm.

—Ian Carr, from the *Rough Guide to Jazz*

Cecil Taylor has been called about everything in the book, from "genius" and "brilliant" to "charlatan" and "fake." Some jazz writers have loved and adored him, positively gushing over his unorthodox, atonal, unpredictable piano patterns. Others scorn his total disregard of any traditional harmonic, rhythmic, and tonal standards. Sometimes a house would virtually empty during one of Taylor's furious hour-long musical tirades, in which he sometimes pounded the piano as if it were a percussion instrument. Many, even by the broadest definition, hesitated to call his music jazz.

Taylor has won over some critics, his music of the 1980s and 1990s having found an increasingly appreciative audience. He has won polls for best jazz pianist, including Down Beat Critic Poll, and is credited for helping institute and perpetuate free jazz, and beyond. Taylor's followers admire his sheer will to plunge, undaunted, into outer musical space, but despite such gains, he remains controversial, and some jazz devotees still renounce his music.

Cecil Percival Taylor was born on March 15, 1933 (some sources say 1929), in New York City. His mother was a dancer who played violin and piano, and his uncle also played violin and piano, as well as drums. Cecil started piano lessons at age five, and was first influenced by Duke Ellington, Louis Armstrong, Billie Holiday, Erroll Garner, and Fats Waller. As a young man, he admired the modern jazz artists, among them Bud Powell, Charles Mingus, and Thelonious Monk.

Taylor enrolled in the New England Conservatory of Music in 1951, and over the next four years studied classical music, including Bartók, Stravinsky, and Schoenberg. At the same time, he was being inspired by jazz, and determined that it would be the path he would follow. Taylor began as a sideman, performing with such established jazz musicians, as Lawrence Brown, Johnny Hodges, and Hot Lips Page, who played mainstream jazz. But Taylor even then had other ideas, and it became quickly apparent that he was straying from current jazz trends. His technique was scorned by some top musicians, and Taylor realized he must lead his own group. By the mid-1950s he had a quartet.

Taylor's quartet cut its first record, *Jazz Advance,* in 1955, and in 1956 they went into the Five Spot Café. At that time Taylor's playing still adhered to a conventional chord structure. A year later, when the quartet appeared at the

Newport Jazz Festival, much of the structure had been stripped away, and by the early 1960s, he had evolved into abstract forms. His following was small in the late 1950s–early 1960s but he cut some albums, including *Jumpin' Punkins* and *New York R and B.*

Although work was scarce, Taylor managed some gigs and a six-month European tour. After returning in 1962, he did not work for about a year, but helped establish the Jazz Composers Guild in 1964. In the late 1960s and early 1970s Taylor supplemented his meager earnings by working as a cook and dishwasher. He also taught occasionally at such institutions as the University of Wisconsin and Antioch College (Ohio). Reportedly, he lost the Wisconsin job for flunking too many students. By the mid-1970s Taylor began to receive recognition but mostly from Europe and Japan.

Taylor wanted to compose for dance, despite his music's unrhythmic quality, and in the late 1970s he wrote music for dancer Dianne McIntyre and for the ballet *Tetra Stomp: Eatin' Rain,* which featured Mikhail Baryshnikov. Taylor was invited to play at a White House jazz presentation for President Jimmy Carter in 1979, and he received acclaim for duets with drummer Max Roach. The pianist played regularly with his Cecil Taylor Unit, and his prestige grew steadily. Recording dates produced *The Cecil Taylor Unit* (1979) and a 1980 solo album, *Fly! Fly! Fly! Fly! Fly!*

Perhaps Taylor's foremost recognition came in 1988 when a festival in Berlin, Germany, was held in his honor. During the festivities Taylor collaborated with some of Europe's exponents of free jazz, resulting in the multi-album *Cecil Taylor in Berlin '88.* In the 1990s and into the new century, Taylor sought new ways to challenge his audience, sometimes chanting, reading poetry, dancing, and wearing flamboyant costumes. Musically, it seems, Taylor will always go his own way.

Ron Carter

Leading Bassist-Cellist in Jazz and Classical Genres
1937–

Ron Carter is one of the most original, prolific, and influential bassists in jazz.

—From the NEA American Jazz Master
Fellowship Awards Web site

Jazz and classical music have come together in many places, one of the most glorious being in the acclaimed bass of Ron Carter. As a young student, Carter coveted a classical career playing the cello, but as an African American he saw racial barriers and switched to the double bass and a career in jazz. Carter did not forget his classical roots, however, bringing such masters as Rachmaninoff, Chopin, and Bach into his work. That hardly qualifies Carter as uncool. His credentials as a swinging musician were set from the time he became Miles Davis's bassist in one of the most heralded rhythm sections in jazz. Over the years Carter has performed continuously with world-class musicians, becoming one of the most recorded bassists of all time.

Ronald Levin Carter was born in Ferndale, Michigan, on May 4, 1937, one of eight children in a musically oriented family. All of the siblings received musical training. Ron began studying cello at ten and developed an interest in classical music. After Ron entered high school in Detroit, he felt that he had a better chance of success in jazz with the bass than with the cello in classical music. Later, the cello would become an important part of Carter's professional life, along with other instruments he came to master, including bass guitar, violin, clarinet, trombone, and tuba. His precocious talent led to a scholarship at the Eastman School of Music in Rochester, New York, where he earned a bachelor's degree in 1959.

At Eastman, Carter pursued his classical interests with the Eastman Philharmonic Orchestra, while leading his own groups in Rochester. After Eastman he moved to New York City, where he took his first professional job, as a bassist in Chico Hamilton's band. He was a good fit with Hamilton, who utilized classical instruments such as cello and flute. He enrolled in the Manhattan School of Music, where he earned his master's degree in 1961. Carter left Hamilton in 1960 to freelance with New York's elite jazz players, cutting his first recordings with Eric Dolphy and Don Ellis. He also performed with Herbie Mann and Betty Carter and went on a European tour with Cannonball Adderley.

Carter played with Art Farmer in 1963, before joining Miles Davis and his groundbreaking quintet. The Davis rhythm section of Carter, Herbie Hancock (piano), and Tony Williams (drums) set new standards for the post-bop era, allowing far more freedom for rhythm instruments. Carter's recordings with Davis brought him recognition, and he was named best jazz bassist in the top polls. Carter also freelanced during his Davis years, in particular going to Europe to play in Friedrich Gulda's Euro-jazz orchestra. Carter left Davis in 1968 just as Davis was going into his fusion period. Afterward, he performed with such headliners as Lena Horne and Lionel Hampton.

In the early 1970s Carter toured Europe and Japan with other jazz artists and in 1976 formed his first quartet. In order to make his solos more prominent, Carter took up the piccolo bass, which has a higher sound and better projection than double bass. He also began using the bow for solos, in addition to playing pizzicato (plucking the strings). His recordings through the 1970s included such albums as *Piccolo* (1977) and *Parade* (1979). He continued to freelance and in 1977 toured worldwide with a group that included several Miles Davis alumni.

In the 1980s and 1990s Carter returned to his love of classical music, bringing classical composers into his compositions and recordings. These include *Friends* and the Bach-based albums, *Brandenburg Concerto* and *Ron Carter Meets Bach*. On the latter Carter accompanies himself with ensemble bass lines through multitracking. His album of the *Bach Cello Suites* received gold certification.

Carter's intellectual interests led him into education, and he has lectured at numerous institutions, including the universities of North Carolina, Rutgers, Howard, and the Harlem School for the Arts. At the City College of New York, his primary teaching appointment, he has taught both the art and business of playing jazz. Among his books are *Ron Carter Bass Lines, Ron Carter Comprehensive Bass Method,* and *The Music Bass Lines.* In 1988 Carter's composition "Call Sheet Blues" for the film *'Round Midnight* won a Grammy. He has enjoyed nonjazz dates, including those with the New World Symphony, the Brooklyn Philharmonic, the Black Composers Orchestra, and the rap group A Tribe Called Quest. In 1998 Carter received the American Jazz Masters award from the National Endowment for the Arts.

Charlie Haden

Bassist Used Artistry to Improve Society
1937–

We're here to bring beauty to the world, and make a difference in this planet. That's what art forms are about.

—Charlie Haden, quoted on *NPR Jazz Profiles*

The odds against Charlie Haden becoming a jazz bass player seemed high. He was born in a tiny Midwestern town and raised on folk and country music. Also, he was brought up to be a singer, belting out homey songs that appealed to the local folk. Sadly, Haden lost his singing voice to the effects of polio while in his teens. But Haden did not give up. Rather than sing he would play an instrument, which turned out to be the bass. He was drawn to jazz, the idiom in which he became world famous.

Some jazz bassists have great technical skills, plucking the strings with blinding speed. Haden was more noted for the deep, rich, sonorous tone that he coaxed from his instrument. The hallmark of his playing, however, was his versatility. Haden could adapt to any jazz style, from swing to bebop to the unstructured forms of free jazz. Haden also felt music should make a statement, social or political. Art, he believed, should help make the world a better place.

Charles Edward Haden was born in Shenandoah, Iowa, on August 6, 1937, the youngest of four children, born into a country-western-music-performing family. The Hadens were popular within the range of the local radio station that broadcast their music. Charlie's mother had him in the family act before his second birthday, and he performed with the family until his bout with polio curtailed his singing. The bass then became his focus, and by 1955 he was playing on a network TV show, *Ozark Jubilee,* out of Springfield, Missouri.

Haden studied music at the Westlake College of Modern Music in Los Angeles. Jazz had already attracted him, and he moved quickly into performing. In 1957–59 he played variously with saxophonist Art Pepper, pianist Hampton Hawes, and pianist Paul Bley, all of whom embraced modern jazz. One night Haden happened into a club where an alto saxophonist was sitting in with the band and playing extremely unusual music. Haden was impressed, however, and sought out the altoist, whose name was Ornette Coleman. They eventually played together with Paul Bley.

In 1959 Haden went to New York City with Coleman and became part of Coleman's quartet, whose brand of jazz was a radical departure from what most people were used to hearing. When Coleman opened at the Five Spot, he helped usher in a new era in jazz, to which Haden was an accomplice. Their music was called free jazz. Haden played periodically in Coleman groups through the 1960s. In the early 1960s Haden had problems with drug dependency, which he overcame.

Haden also worked with other progressive musicians during the 1960s, including saxophonists Archie Shepp and John Coltrane, and in 1966 he toured with pianist Keith Jarrett. In 1969 Haden formed a highly controversial group, the Liberation Music Orchestra (LMO) in association with composer Carla Bley, wife of Paul. The orchestra's initial recording, *Liberation Music Orchestra,* released in 1970, included themes from the Spanish Civil War, a rendition of "We Shall Overcome," and Haden's "Song for Che," which commemorated Che Guevara, the communist Cuban rebel hero. Attempts to ban the album failed, and it received major awards as well as a Grammy nomination. The recording brought free jazz into a large orchestral context.

In 1976 Haden joined a group called Old and New Dreams, dedicated to Coleman's music, which he stayed with through the late 1970s. In 1984 Haden cut *Ballad of the Fallen,* his second album with LMO, which won the Down Beat Critic Poll for Record of the Year. In 1987 Haden participated in a reunion of the Coleman quartet to cut the album *In All Languages.* That year he formed his first group, Quartet West.

While it seemed Haden was strictly into heavy social music and far-out jazz, his Quartet West proved otherwise. This group reflected Haden's interest in the film noir style of 1940s Hollywood detective movies, employing the music themes of those old films. Some of the original sound tracks were dubbed into their progressive recordings. Their albums include *In Angel City, Haunted Heart,* and *The Art of Song.*

Haden has also focused on music education, and in 1982 he initiated a jazz studies program at the California Institute of the Arts in Valencia, of which he became artistic director. Perhaps Haden's greatest honor came at the 1989 Montreal Jazz Festival, which dedicated eight concerts to the artist, each having him appear with one of his noted collaborators. Haden's musical explorations continued unabated into the new century.

McCoy Tyner

Groundbreaking Pianist with Coltrane and More
1938–

To me living and music are all the same thing.

—McCoy Tyner, quote from the WNUR People in Jazz Web site

By the time McCoy Tyner was sixteen, he was already playing jazz piano around his hometown of Philadelphia. One job was with a band that had a steady gig at the Red Rooster club. On one occasion the club owner asked the band to back the featured act, and that was Tyner's lucky day. The pianist was privileged to play with saxophonist John Coltrane, and their meeting grew into a bond that helped change the course of modern music.

Years later, when Coltrane formed his famous quartet, he selected Tyner to take the piano bench. That quartet became one of the most highly acclaimed in jazz history. Had Tyner done nothing more in his career, his Coltrane years would have guaranteed an enduring legacy. Tyner, however, wanted to find his niche under his own name, so he formed a group. Progress was slow, but eventually Tyner's groups ranked among the top jazz ensembles. Whether with Coltrane or on his own, his signature style of rich, melodious harmonies established him among the most influential pianists in jazz.

Alfred McCoy Tyner was born in Philadelphia, Pennsylvania, on December 11, 1938, the oldest of three siblings. His mother, a beautician, played piano, and when he was thirteen his mother started him studying piano. After his mother bought him his own piano, he had to practice at her beauty parlor because his father would not allow the piano in the house. Tyner enrolled at the Granoff School of Music at about the same time as he started a rhythm and blues band, and he began playing professionally when he was fifteen. While still in his teens, Tyner converted to Islam and took the name Sulaimon Saud, although continuing to perform under his given name. His conversion profoundly influenced his life and work.

Philadelphia had a renowned jazz community, and Tyner met and played with many future jazz stars, such as trumpeter Lee Morgan and saxophonist Benny Golson. Among his neighbors were the Powell boys, Bud and Richie, both of whom became star jazz pianists. Other major influences were pianists Art Tatum and Thelonious Monk. After graduating from high school, Tyner was snapped up by saxophonist Benny Golson for a gig at the San Francisco jazz workshop. In 1959 he joined the Benny Golson–Art Farmer Jazztet in New York City, spending six months with that group.

The next year John Coltrane formed his classic quartet consisting of himself, Tyner, Elvin Jones (drums), and (at first) Steve Davis (bass). Success came almost immediately as the group's first recording, *My Favorite Things,* signaled a new wave in jazz. On this record Tyner set a style that became his musical signature. He used his piano to create a rhythmic musical pattern against which Coltrane weaved intricate saxophone solos. Tyner's own solos spun out of the same pattern. On that recording Middle Eastern and African musical influences are clearly evident, as they were in much of the later work of Coltrane and Tyner.

Tyner spent five glorious years with Coltrane, during which the quartet reached the pinnacle of jazz art. It is widely considered one of the most significant jazz groups ever to perform, recognized for its innovations in modal jazz. In 1965 Tyner left Coltrane to form his own group. There may have been disagreements between the two because of Coltrane's musical direction, but Tyner never confirmed this. Tyner formed a trio and found some gigs, but for the most part it was tough going. But in 1967 he produced a landmark recording, *The Real McCoy,* with a quartet that included saxophonist Joe Henderson, bassist Ron Carter, and Elvin Jones. He made other recordings that received praise, but Tyner's career as a leader did not take off until 1972 when he signed with Milestone Records.

Tyner's debut album for Milestone, *Sahara,* brought new recognition, the Down Beat Critics Poll naming it Album of the Year. Tyner led mostly quartets through the 1970s, formed the McCoy Tyner Big Band in 1984, but frequently reverted to a trio during the 1980s and 1990s. In 1989 Tyner's *A Tribute to John Coltrane* (one of several tributes to Trane) won his first Grammy award, but it was not the last. He received more Grammys in 1992, 1994, 1995, and 1996.

In the late 1990s Tyner worked with a trio, but sought an occasional change of pace, going so far as to make a tribute album to pop composer Burt Bacharach, which included a big string background. But he countered in 1997 with another outstanding tribute to John Coltrane. Tyner's work continued to receive acclaim in the new century, and in 2002 he accepted the National Endowment for the Arts Jazz Masters award.

Chick Corea

Keyboardist Ranged from Classic to Experimental Jazz
1941–

Chick Corea has been one of the most significant jazzmen since the '60s.

—Scott Yanow,
from the *All Music Guide to Jazz*

There is just about no place that Chick Corea has not been in music. His boundless energy and intellectual curiosity have led the pianist in explorations all over the musical map, from straight-ahead jazz to free jazz to electronic fusion to symphonic works. His extensive recordings testify to his excellence. He has been comfortable in the musical traditions of Europe and Latin America as well as the United States and is accomplished on acoustic piano as well as keyboards. Through it all Corea has stated that his single purpose is to create and communicate the music that he loves.

Armando Anthony Corea was born on June 12, 1941, in Chelsea, Massachusetts, and was raised in a house where music was ever present. His father, a Latin jazz trumpet player, encouraged his son's musical leanings, and by the age of four he was studying piano. Growing up, he was exposed to the modern jazz offerings of such bebop pioneers as Dizzy Gillespie and Charlie Parker, and especially pianists Horace Silver and Bud Powell. But Chick, as he came to be called, also heard and played the music of Bach, Beethoven, Mozart, Chopin, and other classical composers. He eventually traveled to New York City, where he enrolled for short periods at the Juilliard School and Columbia University. Now living in the world center of jazz, Corea soon stepped into the city's music scene.

Corea's first noteworthy professional job was recording with Latin jazz percussionist Mongo Santamaria, which accelerated his interest in Latin music. From 1962 to 1966 he was a sideman with various groups, including the Blue Mitchell band, with which he recorded his first composition. After playing with such elite jazz artists as Herbie Mann, Elvin Jones, and Stan Getz, he formed his own group. In 1966 he recorded his first album under his own name, *Tones for Joan's Bones,* which was largely of Corea's compositions, as would be true of most of his work. He accompanied vocalist Sarah Vaughan, and in 1968 recorded the influential advanced hard bop album *Now He Sings, Now He Sobs* with a trio. That year he joined the internationally renowned Miles Davis band.

Corea played electric piano with Davis, who was then reaching fusion. During his two years with Davis, Corea participated in some of the trumpeter's most significant recordings, including *Bitches Brew.* Corea toured internationally with Davis, then in 1969 formed his own avant-garde group, Circle. The new band, influenced by the free jazz exponent Ornette Coleman, explored to the outer edge of music. Their albums *Early Circle* and *Circulus* exemplified atonal, discordant music. Corea left Circle in 1971, and, looking for new directions, he cut his reflective solo two-volume *Piano Improvisations*. He then organized his classic group, Return to Forever.

Return to Forever (RTF) continued much as the piano improvisations, the quartet being sometimes accompanied by a vocalist, as on *Light as a Feather*. Although the group emphasized electronic instrumentation, the music tended to be toned down. They drew lightly at first, but by the time of their 1972 Tokyo tour, crowds were huge. Their popularity surged as the band evolved more and more into fusion, with its heavy use of rock rhythms. Corea's success with RTF continued until the group disbanded in the late 1970s.

During the 1970s and early 1980s Corea also freelanced, and his duets with pianist Herbie Hancock and vibraphonist Gary Burton were particularly praiseworthy. Playing acoustic piano, the Corea-Hancock work sometimes resembles modern classical music. In the mid-1980s Corea formed the Elektric Band, which became another top-ranked fusion group. He also continued to foster classical leanings, recording a Mozart piano concerto and premiering his own piano concerto. The Elektric Band produced several outstanding albums, including the Grammy-winning *Light Years* and *Eye of the Beholder*. Simultaneously, he formed the Akoustic Band.

In the 1990s and into the new century Corea continued to cover the broad musical spectrum that included fusion, electronic and acoustic playing, straight-ahead jazz, and classical music. In his 1997 release, *Remembering Bud Powell,* he pays tribute to his jazz inspiration. The Powell release was the first with his own record company, Stretch Records. In the late 1990s he led a new sextet, Origin, and in 1999 he performed and recorded his piano concerto with the London Philharmonic. His *Spain for Sextet and Orchestra* from the same album won the 2001 Grammy for Best Instrumental Arrangement. Over several decades Corea won major polls as best jazz pianist and/or keyboardist.

Gary Burton

Master Vibraphonist and Jazz Educator
1943–

Gary is a complete and magnificent musician.

—Chick Corea,
quoted on the Concord Record Web site

Gary Burton's instrument, the vibraphone, was a kind of late addition to the jazz orchestra. It got started in the 1930s and 1940s with Lionel Hampton and Red Norvo leading the way. From the 1960s Gary Burton has been widely regarded as a leading voice on vibraphone. Burton has great respect for his instrumental forebears, but he sought his own technique. His main departure came with the use of four mallets instead of two. With two mallets in each hand he could effect broad, mellow chords, sounding at times as if he is accompanying himself. His style is pianolike, and he has stated that the acclaimed jazz pianist Bill Evans inspired him as much as any of the great vibraphonists.

The versatile Burton moved from country music to jazz to fusion, rock and roll, and pop. His primary instrument is the vibraphone, but he has also played piano and organ and done vocals. Burton's interests go beyond playing. Few jazz musicians have gone further in music education than Burton, who moved up the ranks to become Executive Vice President at Boston's Berklee College of Music. As an educator, he has exerted a strong influence on young musicians and is noted for his discovery and development of new talent.

Gary Burton was born on January 23, 1943, in Anderson, Indiana. He started learning piano at the age of six and studied piano and composition in high school. He also played marimba in high school, and taught himself to play the similar vibraphone. He started out playing jazz-oriented instrumental country music with such stars as Hank Garland and Chet Atkins, making his record debut in Nashville, Tennessee, when he was seventeen. Afterward, he enrolled at Berklee, where his interest in jazz blossomed. While still in college, in 1961, Burton produced his first album as a leader, appropriately entitled *New Vibes Man in Town.*

After about two years at the college he joined renowned pianist George Shearing for a tour of the United States and Japan, and in 1964 Burton joined another jazz titan, saxophonist Stan Getz. While with Getz, Burton won the 1965 *Down Beat* award for Talent Deserving of Wider Recognition.

Burton left Getz in 1966 and formed his own quartet in 1967. It was a time of experimentation, and Burton joined the trend of mostly younger musicians, who were broadening the scope of jazz to include elements of rock, pop, and country music. This widened his audience, and *Down Beat* made him its 1968 Jazzman of the Year. During the late 1960s Burton recorded some Carla Bley compositions and worked with her material thereafter. In 1971 Burton began teaching at Berklee.

In the 1970s Burton began a trend of playing solo and in duets, collaborating with such outstanding modernists as pianists Chick Corea and Keith Jarrett. Noteworthy are some of the albums with Corea, including *Crystal Silence, Duet,* and *Chick Corea and Gary Burton in Concert,* the latter two winning Grammys. Among the outstanding solo albums is *Alone at Last,* which includes material from his appearance at the Montreux Jazz Festival. That album also garnered a Grammy. In the mid-1970s the Burton group added a young guitarist, Pat Metheny, who went on to his own stardom. In the late 1970s and early 1980s Burton toured worldwide with Corea.

Burton also immersed himself in an ambitious educational agenda with a broad schedule of lectures and seminars. In 1985 he was appointed Dean of Curriculum at Berklee, and in 1989 that institution awarded him an honorary doctorate. In the 1990s, Burton continued collaborations with Corea, their duet album *Native Sense* winning another Grammy. Latin music had also attracted Burton, and in the 1990s he produced two albums of tango music featuring leading Argentine tango artists. Also in the 1990s, Burton returned to conventional jazz, producing concerts honoring Lionel Hampton and Benny Goodman and cutting several mainstream jazz albums. These included *For Hamp, Red, Bags, and Cal,* which pays homage to historic jazz masters of the vibraphone.

Burton accumulated numerous honors over his career. The U.S. State Department chose Burton as a jazz ambassador to several countries, including Russia. He won the Down Beat Readers' poll consecutively from 1969 to 1974 for best vibraphonist, and in 1998 he won a fifth Grammy for the all-star album, *Like Minds.* In the new century Burton continues to advance his multiple careers of instrumentalist, leader, composer-arranger, musical ambassador, and educator.

Keith Jarrett

Piano Genius Reminiscent of Mozart
1945–

Keith Jarrett is one of the most influential pianists to emerge after Thelonious Monk.

—Jazz Profiles from
National Public Radio

Keith Jarrett was not just another precocious child. He was a true child prodigy, something along the lines of Mozart. He started piano lessons before the age of three and began improvising and composing shortly thereafter. At seven he played his first classical concert, which included some of his own work. A brilliant student, he entered the third grade when he was just six years old. He played Madison Square Garden in New York City at nine and had acquired professional experience by twelve. Jarrett, a veteran of touring by this time, was touted as a coming genius of the classical piano, to which he had devoted most of his childhood.

In addition to piano, Jarrett was also able to play almost any instrument placed in front of him. That included drums, vibraphone, organ, harpsichord, and saxophone, all of which he learned to play at a professional level. Early in high school Jarrett became interested in jazz, but it was not the classical field's loss. Jarrett never wavered in his love of classical music, and he periodically returned to the classical stage.

One trait that sets Jarrett aside is that he sometimes plays whole concerts of improvised piano without any preparation, feeling that this involves the audience in the creative process. Another characteristic is that he occasionally accompanies his playing with wordless vocal sounds, a not uncommon trait among pianists.

Keith Jarrett was born on May 8, 1945, in Allentown, Pennsylvania, the oldest of five musically talented brothers. Keith's abilities stood out, however, and by the time he finished elementary school he had played in numerous recitals and was composing classical pieces. Interest in jazz came in high school, and he attended big band leader Stan Kenton's summer camp. Early inspiration came from such celebrated jazz pianists as Art Tatum, Oscar Peterson, and especially Bill Evans. At seventeen Jarrett performed a solo concert of his own works, and a year later he enrolled on a scholarship at Boston's Berklee College of Music, with its acclaimed jazz program.

While at Berklee, Jarrett played around Boston, but in 1965 he headed for New York City. He found occasional small gigs until he joined the esteemed Art Blakey and his Jazz Messengers. Although he only stayed with Blakey several months, he made an impression, particularly on the album *Buttercorn Lady*. In 1966 Jarrett hooked up with the Charles Lloyd quartet for his first extended group experience. Lloyd's jazz was progressive but more melodic and mellow than some of the period's avant-garde groups. Jarrett also composed and arranged for Lloyd.

With Lloyd, Jarrett visited Europe, including the (then) Soviet Union, and East Asia. Jarrett left Lloyd in 1969, and shortly thereafter, his playing caught the attention of Miles Davis, then into his electronic fusion stage. Jarrett joined Davis as one of his two electric piano-organist players. The other was Chick Corea. In this bizarre arrangement the two ended up in high-pitched keyboard battles that rattled the walls. 1n 1971 Jarrett decided to move on, forswearing the use of electronic instruments. His solo album *Facing You* kicked off a series of solo concerts and recordings, among them *Solo Concerts: Bremen and Lausanne, The Köln Concert,* and *Sun Bear Concerts,* the latter from a Japan tour.

During the 1970s Jarrett successfully led two quartets, the American Group and a European contingent, the Belonging Group. In the early 1970s he won a Guggenheim Fellowship from which he composed the classical-jazz album *In the Light.* In the early 1980s Jarrett went extensively into classical music, and by 1984 his work was exclusively classical. In 1980 he completed *The Celestial Hawk,* a classical piece that he performed with the Syracuse Symphony Orchestra.

In 1983, Jarrett formed the Standards Trio, including bassist Gary Peacock and drummer Jack De Johnette, but they did little while Jarrett focused on classical music. In 1985 Jarrett worked again in classical and jazz forms, and apparently the strain of doing both caused a breakdown. He briefly withdrew from music, then did some homemade, folk-type recordings in which he played all of the instruments by overdubbing. The resulting album, *Spirits,* seemed to rejuvenate Jarrett. He reformed his Standards Trio, playing in a largely mainstream jazz format. Several highly touted albums resulted, including *Standards I and II, Standards Live,* and *Tribute.*

In 1995 Jarrett played the La Scala Opera House in Milan, Italy, performing mostly his own music. It was the first time nonclassical music had been performed there. In 1996 Jarrett developed chronic fatigue syndrome, and became largely inactive for two years. He finally returned in 1998, slowly increasing his activity into the new century. By this time Jarrett had become one of the most prodigiously honored musicians to play in both the jazz and classical mediums.

Paquito D'Rivera

Reed Virtuoso of Latin Jazz and Classical Works
1948–

Whether playing Bach or post-bop, D'Rivera's mastery of the instruments . . . is unquestionable.

—From the Barnes and Noble Web site biography by Craig Harris, quoted from *Classical New Jersey*

Paquito D'Rivera had already achieved worldwide fame as a virtuoso reed player by 1981 when he went on tour in Spain. He was acclaimed in the fields of jazz and **Latin jazz**, as well as classical music. He could have been satisfied with his musical career as it was, but he felt something was not right. D'Rivera was a Cuban, and he believed that his country's state-run cultural programs restricted him. He longed for complete artistic freedom.

While in Spain, D'Rivera presented himself at the American embassy and requested asylum, which was granted. In the United States, D'Rivera's career thrived. He found work with leading jazz musicians and orchestral groups, and established himself as a major proponent of Latin jazz. D'Rivera did not emphasize the familiar percussion of Latin American music, such as conga drums, bongos, and tom-toms. Rather, his music related more to modern American jazz with Latin influence. Whatever his musical ethnicity, his role as a leading exponent of modern music is well founded.

Paquito D'Rivera was born in Havana, Cuba, on June 4, 1948, and his musical talent was recognized early. His father, a classical conductor and saxophone player, started his musical training when he was five years old. A year later he made his professional debut, and at seven he became possibly the youngest musician to endorse a musical instrument, the Selmer saxophone. At age ten his performance at Havana's National Theater brought raves. Two years later the prodigy enrolled at the Havana Conservatory.

In 1965 D'Rivera performed as a saxophone and clarinet soloist with the Cuban National Symphony Orchestra. After a stint with the Cuban Army Band, D'Rivera, with pianist Chucho (Chu Chu) Valdes, formed the Orquesta Cubana de Música Moderna, a progression into Latin jazz. After two years with the orchestra eight of its members, including D'Rivera, Valdes, trumpeter Arturo Sandoval, and others formed the group Irakere. Irakere created a unique form, combining jazz, rock, Afro-Cuban, and classical music. The ensemble traveled worldwide, becoming the first Castro-era group to sign with a U.S. record company. They performed at a 1979 Havana music festival, recorded on two *Havana Jam* albums, and that year won the Best Latin Jazz Ensemble Grammy.

After D'Rivera defected, Dizzy Gillespie and others took him in hand, and he was soon playing and recording, releasing two solo albums, *Paquito*

Blowin' (1981) and *Mariel* (1982). For several years D'Rivera played New York jazz clubs, and was featured in *Time* magazine and the *Jazz Times*. In 1988 he became a founding member of the United Nations Orchestra, led by Dizzy Gillespie and devoted to blending Latin and U.S. jazz. After Gillespie's death in 1993 D'Rivera led the orchestra. In the meantime D'Rivera had appeared with the National Symphony Orchestra for a 1988 classical performance at the Kennedy Center in Washington, D.C.

In the 1980s and 1990s D'Rivera toured worldwide and recorded with several of his own groups. They included the chamber ensemble, Tríangulo; his Paquito D'Rivera Big Band; his quintet; and the Caribbean Jazz Project. In 1991 D'Rivera received the Lifetime Achievement Award from Latin Jazz U.S.A. Numerous jazz recordings in the 1990s and afterward are represented by such outstanding albums as *Portraits of Cuba, Live at the Blue Note,* and *Habanera*.

D'Rivera regularly receives commissions to compose for classical music organizations. The Gerald Danovich Saxophone Quartet commissioned and recorded his *New York Suite* in 1989. In 1994 the Aspen Wind Quintet premiered his *Aires Tropicales,* which it had commissioned, and his *Panamericana Suite* was commissioned by Jazz at Lincoln Center. In addition, D'Rivera has performed with the Brooklyn Philharmonic, The London Philharmonic, and the Costa Rican National Symphony. In 1999 D'Rivera went to Germany to participate in a *D'Rivera Meets Mozart* program.

D'Rivera is also an accomplished writer, having produced the autobiographical *My Saxual Life,* and a novel, *En Tus Brazos Morenos*. In 1999 the Universidad de Alcalá de Henares honored him for his artistic and humanitarian contributions to society and his promotion of greater rights for artists.

Jon Faddis

Trumpet Protégé of Dizzy Gillespie
1953–

His resurgent jazz work exhibits his brilliant combination of exuberance and discipline.
—Brian Priestley from *Jazz—The Rough Guide*

Maybe it all happened too quickly for high-register trumpeter Jon Faddis. By the time he was eighteen he had already played with Lionel Hampton, moved on to the Thad Jones-Mel Lewis Big Band, filled in for Roy Eldridge at Carnegie Hall, and had gigs with Dizzy Gillespie and Sarah Vaughan. He was the toast of the town. But in his early twenties Faddis chose to withdraw from the pressure and take refuge in the recording studio.

For several years Faddis hung out in the studio, bringing his soaring trumpet work to recordings covering the whole spectrum of nonclassical modern music from jazz to pop to rock to commercials. He was well suited to such work because he could play like anybody—Louis Armstrong, Roy Eldridge, Dizzy Gillespie—but having his own distinctive style as well. In the early 1980s Faddis broke out and began performing in public again. From that point, he became one of the young lions of jazz, carrying on the pioneering traditions of the jazz trumpet legends.

Jonathan Faddis was born in Oakland, California, on July 24, 1953. He and his siblings were encouraged in music, and Jon took up trumpet when he was eight, after being awed by a Louis Armstrong performance on television. Focusing on jazz, Jon took lessons from a former Stan Kenton trumpet player who introduced him to the artistry of Dizzy Gillespie. He was wowed by Gillespie, who was already a bebop legend. Jon had a thrill in his mid-teens when he sat in with Gillespie's group at the San Franciso Jazz Workshop.

During high school Faddis played with local rhythm and blues groups, and in 1971, after graduating, became a full-time professional with the Lionel Hampton band. At only eighteen he was a soloist with Hampton's power-house trumpet section. In 1972 he joined the Thad Jones-Mel Lewis Big Band, which had a Monday night gig at New York's Village Vanguard. Before long Faddis was performing and recording with top-ranked New York jazz artists. He toured with bassist Charles Mingus and recorded with Gillespie and pianist Oscar Peterson.

Perhaps Faddis was burned out, or maybe he thought he could do better financially, but whatever the reason, in the mid-1970s he rejected the lime-light to concentrate on studio work. The diversity of recording jobs helped Faddis find his own style in music. During his studio era he accompanied such artists as Duke Ellington, Quincy Jones, Frank Sinatra, Aretha Franklin, Paul Simon, and the Rolling Stones. He also recorded movie soundtracks, including *Bird* (about Charlie Parker), *The Gauntlet,* and *The Wiz.* In 1982 Dizzy Gillespie invited him to a White House showcase for young talent. That live appearance apparently inspired Faddis, who soon was playing with his own quintet.

Faddis was active in and out of the studio the next few years, recording several notable albums, including *Jon and Billy* and *Legacy.* On the latter he paid respects to virtuoso trumpeters of the past, blowing outstanding imitations of Armstrong, Eldridge, and Gillespie. That Faddis' style has often been compared to Gillespie's is not surprising. The old master was Faddis's hero and groomed Faddis, probably so he could carry on the traditions Gillespie wanted to preserve. In 1987 Faddis became musical director of Gillespie's big band, which toured internationally in celebration of Dizzy's seventieth birthday. A year later Gillespie organized the United Nations Orchestra, and Faddis took a leader role in it as well.

Having demonstrated such leadership qualities, Faddis in 1991 was appointed musical director of the Carnegie Hall Jazz Band, showcasing prominent jazz artists. The band specialized in programs dedicated to jazz legends until it broke up in 2003. Faddis also led the Lincoln Center Orchestra's Louis Armstrong tour and the Newport Jazz Festival Fortieth Anniversary Tour. Among Faddis's longer works is *Lulu Noire,* a jazz opera that had a 1997 premiere in Philadelphia. His significant albums of the late twentieth century include *Into the Faddisphere, Hornucopia,* and *Remembrances.*

Geri Allen

Progressive Jazz Pianist Remembers the Masters
1957–

Geri Allen has been called the most promising and versatile pianist that has emerged in the field of jazz within the last decade.

—From the JAZZPAR Web site, statement
upon presentation of the prestigious
international JAZZPAR Prize to Geri Allen

Geri Allen has taken the jazz trail about as far as it goes, from the mainstream to the far reaches of modern progressive music. Wherever her musical journey takes her, however, Allen remembers to honor great jazz artists of the past. While going forward with avant-garde, she periodically returns to the music of such icons as Bud Powell, Bill Evans, Thelonious

Monk, Miles Davis, and particularly, Mary Lou Williams. In October 2000 she performed Williams's lengthy *Zodiac Suite,* the first time in decades it had been done in its entirety.

Allen went even further in preserving Williams's musical image. She actually portrayed the legendary pianist in the 1996 Robert Altman film *Kansas City.* At the other extreme Allen has learned from such contemporary progressives as Ornette Coleman, Charlie Haden, Ron Carter, Eric Dolphy, and Cecil Taylor. In 1993 and 1994 Allen received the *Down Beat* magazine award for Talent Deserving Wider Recognition. By the turn of the century that recognition had been achieved.

Geri Antoinette Allen was born on June 12, 1957, in Pontiac, Michigan, but was raised in Detroit. Her father, an amateur pianist, had her studying piano at age seven. After elementary school she qualified to attend the Cass Technical High School, noted for its musical program. At Cass she encountered Marcus Belgrave, a trumpet player who became her mentor and, later, a collaborator. She had concentrated on classical studies, but in high school Belgrave helped stir her interest in jazz. She attended Detroit's Jazz Development Workshop before going on to Howard University in Washington, D.C., where she earned her bachelor's degree in jazz studies. Moving to New York City, Allen studied under modern jazz pianist Kenny Barron, then took a master's degree in ethnomusicology from the University of Pittsburgh.

Returning to New York in 1982, Allen became involved with the free jazz movement and took up with M-Base, a loosely organized coalition supporting jazz, funk, soul, and hip-hop, headed by saxophonist Steve Coleman. Allen appeared on Coleman recordings. In 1984 she cut her first recording as a leader, *The Printmakers.*

By the late 1980s Allen had formed a collaboration with bassist Charlie Haden and drummer Paul Motian. One of their early efforts, *Etudes,* enhanced Allen's stature, and in 1989 they produced *In the Year of the Dragon,* a mix of progressive and traditional jazz with original material by Allen. The trio's gig at the Village Vanguard in New York was recorded live, resulting in one of their most successful albums.

In 1990 Allen had collaborated with Marcus Belgrave to record *The Nurturer,* with original treatments of traditional jazz pieces. Allen worked again with Belgrave on a 1992 album, *Maroons,* dedicated to African American slaves. That work featured her trumpeter husband, Wallace Roney. In the early 1990s Allen teamed also with vocalist Betty Carter.

In 1991 Philadelphia's American Music Theater commissioned Allen's *Fur on the Belly,* a musical play about the environment and the homeless. Jazz at Lincoln Center commissioned her 1993 suite *Sister Leola: An American Portrait.* Allen toured with Ornette Coleman in 1994, and she recorded with Coleman on his two *Sound Museum* albums. Allen went to Copenhagen, Denmark, in 1996 to receive the Danish JAZZPAR Prize award—sometimes called the jazz Nobel Prize. While there she produced the album *Some Aspects of Water,* a tribute to the occasion.

Allen had put together a trio in 1994 that included bassist Ron Carter and drummer Tony Williams and produced some of her best work. Their album *Twenty One* is a tribute to jazz piano traditions of the past.

Allen also devotes herself to jazz education. She has served as assistant professor of music at Howard University and taught at the New England Conservatory of Music. Howard honored Geri Allen with its Distinguished Alumni Award.

Branford Marsalis

Virtuoso in Jazz, Classical, and Rock
1960–

I don't care who likes it or buys it. Because if you use that criterion, Mozart would have never written Don Giovanni, Charlie Parker never would have played anything but swing music. There comes a point at which you have to say, this is what I have to do.

—Branford Marsalis, quoted in *Zen Guitar* on the Music Thoughts Web page

Saxophonist Branford Marsalis, at forty-two, had been around music a long while before forming his own record company, Marsalis Music. He had been professional since his teens and commercially successful at the highest levels of both jazz and rock. His label, however, would focus primarily on artistic development rather than commercial gain. It would promote young artists who could not find outlets for their creative work through the major record companies.

Marsalis urges individuality in jazz, but he feels this is best achieved by learning first what the masters had to say. Through his father, Ellis, also a jazz musician and teacher, he learned from Ellington, Armstrong, Gillespie, Parker, and Davis, as well as such contemporaries as Ornette Coleman. He would say on his own Web page, "The best way to get an original sound is by researching the greats. You can't circumvent the mountain. You've got to climb it." Marsalis's very first release on his new label in 2002, his own *Footsteps of our Fathers,* salutes some of the founders of jazz tradition.

Branford Marsalis was born in Breaux Bridge, Louisiana, on August 26, 1960, the oldest of six sons, four of whom would become prominent musicians. Their father, a pianist, is perhaps most significant as a jazz educator who taught such musicians as Terence Blanchard, Harry Connick Jr., and Nicholas Payton. Add to that list his own sons, saxophonist Branford; trumpeter Wynton, probably the best-known active U.S. jazz artist at the turn of the century; trombonist Delfeayo; and drummer Jason. In this environment, Branford's career was taken for granted. He started piano lessons at age four, but at fifteen, after trying clarinet, switched to saxophone. While growing up, Branford was influenced by John Coltrane and Sonny Rollins.

Branford played in his brother Wynton's band as a teenager while studying with his father, then went to Southern University where he studied with noted teacher Alvin Batiste. Batiste convinced him that he should attend the Berklee College of Music in Boston for jazz studies. While still at Berklee, Marsalis joined the Art Blakey big band, playing baritone saxophone on a summer tour of Europe, switching to tenor for a stint with Lionel Hampton. He left Berklee in 1981 to play with trumpeter Clark Terry's band, but after three months he rejoined Blakey and the Jazz Messengers.

About five months later Blakey joined Wynton's quintet.

In 1983 Marsalis recorded *Scenes of the City,* his debut album as a leader and also went on a worldwide tour with Herbie Hancock's band. In 1985 he made a decision that stunned his family and followers. He suddenly joined a start-up English rock band led by the singer Sting, which became world famous. Marsalis had a good time with Sting, but it was a temporary diversion. He left in 1986, seldom engaging in pop thereafter. While in London he made his first classical record, *Romances for Saxophone.*

Returning to jazz, Marsalis formed a quartet and toured Europe and Japan. In the late1980s he played on the sound track for the Spike Lee film *Do the Right Thing,* and in 1990 followed with another soundtrack for Lee's *Mo'Better Blues.* Film provided yet another facet for Marsalis's career as he took on straight acting roles in several movies, including *Bring on the Night, Throw Momma From the Train,* and Lee's *School Daze.* With such Hollywood connections it is perhaps not surprising that in 1992 Marsalis landed the music director's job on *The Tonight Show* with Jay Leno. This was an extremely high profile job, but not particularly fulfilling for Marsalis. Nevertheless, he hung on until 1995, then returned to developing his musical concepts.

During his tenure with Leno, Marsalis had formed a recording fusion group, Buckshot LeFonque, which combined pop, rock, reggae, jazz, and African nuances. He won a Grammy for his 1992 recording of *I Heard You Twice the First Time,* and he received a Grammy nomination for his rendition of the "Star Spangled Banner" on the PBS documentary *Baseball.* In 2000 he produced another Grammy winner, *Contemporary Jazz,* often considered his finest work. His second classical album, *Creation,* was released in 2001.

The multitalented Marsalis also teaches music. In May 2000 he joined the faculty of the San Francisco University music school to instruct master classes and workshops. Previously he had worked in music education with

Michigan State University. Marsalis has also used the airwaves in the cause of jazz, hosting the Jazzset show for PBS (1992–2001).

Branford Marsalis's career has taken many directions, but whether playing, teaching, or discovering talent, it is clear that he is dedicated to the perpetuation of jazz as an art form.

Wynton Marsalis

The Modern-Day Face of Jazz
1961–

Wynton Marsalis is the most accomplished and acclaimed jazz artist and composer of his generation.

—Jazz at Lincoln Center Web site biography
of Wynton Marsalis

At the outset of the twenty-first century the virtuoso trumpet player Wynton Marsalis was clearly the most prominent figure in jazz. There are many good reasons for this, not the least of which is that Marsalis, a brilliant musician and composer, is also a masterful jazz educator. He may be without peer in the United States in spreading the word of jazz, and through electronic media he has virtually become its face. In the

early 1990s he was credited by sources, including a *Time* cover story, as being the savior of jazz, which had seemingly lost its way after the 1960s.

By the time Marsalis began recording in the early 1980s, he determined not to go with the current trend: fusion (mixing jazz with pop and rock), electronic instruments, and the avant-garde and free jazz tangents. Marsalis did not want to go backward, but he felt that jazz musicians should understand the past before taking on the future. So Marsalis shook jazz society by going back to playing entirely with acoustic (nonelectric) instruments and honoring the work of the jazz masters.

As famous as Marsalis is in jazz, he is almost equally as well known as a soloist in classical music. He has played with symphony orchestras and composed numerous classical works, including music for ballet, theater, and film. In his dual role he won 1984 Grammy awards for recordings in both classical music and jazz, which had never been done before. Then he repeated the feat the next year. He is said to have as great a mastery over his trumpet as anyone. An occasional criticism is that he does not play with the passion of a Louis Armstrong or a Clifford Brown. True or not, Marsalis remained the foremost figure of American jazz at the turn of the century.

Wynton Marsalis was born on October 18, 1961, near New Orleans, Louisiana, into what would later be called "America's first family of music." Rarely has a family produced as many successful musicians as the Marsalis family. Ellis, the father, was a professional pianist and jazz educator by the time the first of the six Marsalis brothers came along, Wynton being the second. Next in fame to Wynton is his oldest brother Branford, a noted jazz saxophone player, composer, and leader. Two other brothers, Delfeayo (trombone) and Jason (drums), have played with top musicians, including their brothers. No wonder that Wynton began his music education early, receiving his first trumpet at age six and beginning classical lessons at twelve.

As a teenager Wynton played in marching bands, jazz and funk bands, and took a trumpet chair in the New Orleans Philharmonic Orchestra. He performed the Haydn trumpet concerto when he was fourteen. At seventeen he studied at the Berkshire Music Center in Tanglewood, Massachusetts, and in 1979 he enrolled in the famed Juilliard School in New York City. He studied at Juilliard until 1981, but at the same time played in a Broadway musical, **salsa** bands, and the Brooklyn Philharmonic. In 1980, with his brother Branford, he joined the Art Blakey Jazz Messengers, a performing training ground for jazz artists. Marsalis stayed with Blakey until 1981, then toured the United States and Japan with pianist Herbie Hancock's V.S.O.P. quartet.

In 1981 Marsalis formed his own quintet with Branford. His first album as a leader, *Wynton Marsalis,* was voted the best jazz record by *Down Beat* magazine in 1982. Afterward Marsalis traveled the United States, Europe, and Japan. His acoustic style in the tradition of the jazz legends caught on, and he became the rage. Recordings by the quintet included *Hot House Flowers* and *Black Codes (From the Underground),* both of which won Grammy awards. He also played and recorded with symphonies, gaining recognition as one of the great classical trumpet players. His first classical album, made in London, won a Grammy too, and in 1984 he made a classical tour.

The quintet broke up in 1985 when Branford left to play with the British rock musician Sting, causing a temporary rift in the Marsalis family. In 1987 Wynton moved to a another level when he became artistic director of Jazz at Lincoln Center (JLC) and assembled the Lincoln Center Jazz Orchestra. The JLC became enormously successful under Marsalis. He continued to play with small groups, making some significant records, including the three-volume *Soul Gestures in Southern Blue* and *The Majesty of the Blues,* the latter extending the work of Mingus and Ellington.

Marsalis debuted his septet in recording the soundtrack for the film *Tune in Tomorrow.* The larger group allowed more versatility for Marsalis's composing skills, which in the 1990s began to focus on more extended pieces. Among these are *In This House, on This Morning,* a suite that depicts a church service and acknowledges the Ellington influence, and *Citi Movement,* part of which became the score for the ballet *Griot New York.*

In 1994 Marsalis disbanded the septet, needing more time for Jazz at Lincoln Center, jazz education, and composing. In that year he completed work on his jazz oratorio *Blood on the Fields,* which follows the lives of a slave couple. Commissioned by Jazz at Lincoln Center, the work likely represented his highest accomplishment. The piece brought Marsalis yet another honor: in 1997 he became the first jazz musician to win the Pulitzer Prize for music.

In the late 1990s Marsalis began composing a massive eight-volume work entitled *Swinging into the 21st Century,* that runs the gamut of American music. It includes jazz and classical themes, and music for dance, and is based on original works and standards from the early jazz of Jelly Roll Morton to the modern work of Thelonious Monk. One of the dance pieces was *Sweet Release,* choreographed by Judith Jamison and premiered by the Alvin Ailey American Dance Theater. Another dance score came from his 1997 *Jump Start & Jazz,* adopted by ballet artists Peter Martins and Twyla Tharp. Marsalis also continued with small group jazz, and his 1998 release *The Midnight Blues: Standard Time Vol. V* debuted at number one on the *Billboard Magazine* jazz chart, staying twenty-five weeks in the top ten. In 1999 Marsalis took the Jazz Orchestra on a yearlong tour celebrating the hundreth anniversary of Duke Ellington's birth.

Somehow Marsalis kept up with his educational commitments. Through Jazz at Lincoln Center he created *Jazz for Young People,* an introductory series, which spawned a four-part PBS television program, *Marsalis on Music.* Another educational venture was Marsalis's multipart program for National Public Radio, *Making the Music,* which won a 1996 Peabody Award. Additionally, he conducted numerous workshops in schools and colleges.

Marsalis also uses the written word to promote jazz. His 1994 book *Sweet Swing Blues on the Road,* traces Marsalis's life on tour.

Few musicians have accumulated more honors and awards than Wynton Marsalis. By the end of the century he had received eight Grammy awards, and he was only thirty-nine years old. His honorary degrees come from, among other, Rutgers, Amherst, Yale, Princeton, Brown, Columbia, Johns Hopkins, and Brandeis. In 1997 he was named to the New York State Council on the Arts and the previous year, *Time* magazine listed him among America's twenty-five most influential people. Perhaps his most significant award came in 2001, when Secretary-General of the United Nations presented him with the Messenger of Peace award. The next year the U.S. Congress honored him with its Horizon Award. He has received the Grand Prix du Disque from France, and he is an honorary member of England's Royal Academy of Music. Most importantly, Marsalis ranks among the world leaders in seeking to preserve the great jazz heritage passed on by the masters of the art.

Diana Krall

Sings the Standards with Her Own Dazzle
1964–

Diana Krall possesses an extraordinary talent for creating music that speaks personally to every individual who hears her perform.

—CanEHdian Web site
biography of Diana Krall

Diana Krall does not consider herself a jazz singer. That self-assessment notwithstanding, she has already won a considerable number of awards in the jazz field in her young career. No matter how Krall sees herself, others rank her as an outstanding jazz vocalist. That's not surprising, considering the singers who inspired her: Peggy Lee, Dinah Washington, Carmen McRae, and, especially, Nat King Cole.

Like Cole, her career began as a pianist-vocalist playing with a trio, but she advanced to singing with large backings, including strings. Despite such grandiose accompaniment, Krall has maintained the voice quality and delivery of a jazz singer. She works largely with American songbook standards, vocalizing in a husky, warm, sometimes smoldering voice that is reminiscent of such classic stylists as Anita O'Day, Chris Connor, and Julie London. Some modern jazz singers break stylistically from the past, often composing their own material. Krall performs standards, but in a fresh and original way. As the old jazz saying goes: it's not what you do, it's the way that you do it.

Diana Jean Krall was born on November 16, 1964, in Nanaimo, on Vancouver Island, in British Columbia. Music was a part of her life from the beginning, with piano-playing parents and a singing grandmother. Much of the music being played at home was jazz, and among the early pianists she heard were Fats Waller, James P. Johnson, and Earl "Fatha" Hines. Later she came onto Nat King Cole and Bill Evans. Krall started piano lessons when she was only four, concentrating on classics while growing up but eventually focusing on jazz.

In 1981 Krall won a local jazz festival contest, and her prize was a scholarship to the Berklee College of Music in Boston, noted for its jazz tradition. She returned to her hometown in 1983, where she continued to perform while also attending Bud Shank's jazz workshop in nearby Washington state. Krall impressed a workshop staff member, drummer Jeff Hamilton, who invited famed bassist Ray Brown to hear her perform. Brown saw promise in Krall and suggested she go to Los Angeles to study, which she did with the aid of a Canada Arts Council grant. In Los Angeles, from 1985 to 1987, Krall studied with Jimmy Rowles, a jazz piano legend and vocalist. During this time she developed her singing, although remaining primarily a pianist.

Brown encouraged and supported Krall as she traveled extensively before settling in New York City in 1990. Her prestige grew over the next couple of years as she put together a trio, playing and singing mainly in Boston. Her first record break came in 1993 with *Stepping Out,* which did well considering it was released only in Canada and Europe. A year later her second album, *Only Trust Your Heart,* included such elite jazzmen as Ray Brown, bassist Christian McBride, and saxophonist Stanley Turrentine. That recording's success led to two more albums, *All for You* in 1996 and *Love Scenes* in 1997, which brought Krall's first and second Grammy nominations.

Krall now stood at the brink of stardom. The final push came with the June 1999 release of her album *When I Look in Your Eyes,* which lifted Krall to the top rung of jazz artists. It held number one on the *Billboard* jazz chart for an astounding fifty-two weeks, winning two Grammy awards, including one for Best Jazz Vocal Performance. Perhaps even more stunning was its nomination for Album of the Year, the first such honor for a jazz recording in twenty-five years. The demand for Krall was now huge, and she performed frequently at concerts as well as on television and in films. Her popularity had grown beyond jazz, and in 1998 she wowed the crowd at the Lilith Fair, a pop and rock festival.

Krall followed her success with another smash hit, *The Look of Love,* released in 2001. That album garnered prestigious Juno awards in Canada for Best Artist, Best Vocal Jazz Album, and Best Album. On this recording Krall's singing was up to expectations, but some jazz critics found the big string background and bossa nova rhythms a distraction. Such accompaniment was designed to widen her audience, but it reduced its appeal to some jazz devotees. Afterward Krall traveled to Europe for a concert performance, resulting in another hit album, *Live in Paris.* Diana Krall's artistic and popular success appears well on its way in the new century.

Brad Mehldau

Young Lion of Progressive Jazz
1970–

When he plays, embers glow, then burst into flame.

—The European Jazz Network,
quoted from *Stereophile*

Brad Mehldau's piano styling seems to follow a line out of Oscar Peterson, into Bill Evans, and through Keith Jarrett and probably others. As much as any of those musicians, Mehldau's playing is a marriage of classical music and jazz. Listing his major influences Mehldau cites classicists Brahms, Schubert, Beethoven, and Schumann along with Peterson, Evans, and Jarrett, Wynton Kelly, McCoy Tyner, and Herbie Hancock. Non-pianist influences include

Miles Davis and John Coltrane. Whatever his influences, the jazz style he evolved is distinctly his own.

Mehldau performs with intense mood and emotion whatever he is playing. On some arrangements, his exquisitely light and melodic touch has been called hypnotic. Generally, his recordings are combinations of his own compositions and standard melodies, although he is not averse to bringing in themes from rock and other musical forms. The youthful Mehldau already has a considerable jazz following. He is one of the leaders of the budding group of jazz musicians sometimes referred to as the young lions, who are breaking new ground in jazz.

Brad Mehldau was born on August 23, 1970, in Jacksonville, Florida. Showing early talent in music, he began on piano at age four and started classical lessons at six. His family moved about, finally settling in Connecticut when he was ten. As a youngster, he was typically drawn to rock, but was soon impressed by the jazz fusion of Miles Davis. He played in his high school jazz band and won the Best All-Around Musician award in the Berklee College of Music's high school competition. After high school he enrolled in a jazz studies course at New York's New School for Social Research. One of Mehldau's instructors there was drummer Jimmy Cobb.

Mehldau so impressed Cobb that the drummer hired him for his own group, Cobb's Mob. After Cobb, Mehldau played and recorded with some local groups and had his own trio for a while before joining the fast-rising Joshua Redman quartet. Redman combined some of the finest young talent in jazz, the quartet also including bass prodigy Christian McBride and highflying drummer Brian Blade. Mehldau toured with the quartet, and was recorded on their album *MoodSwing*.

After the tour Mehldau formed his own trio with Larry Grenadier on bass and Jorge Rossy on drums, and in 1995 they cut their first record, *Introducing Brad Mehldau*. Mehldau composed several pieces for the album, which won critical acclaim. A series of albums followed, starting in 1997 with the *The Art of the Trio, Vol. 1.* Gathering momentum, the trio toured and played top festivals and clubs, including the Village Vanguard in New York City. In the next year Mehldau and the trio recorded two more albums, *Live at the Village Vanguard: The Art of the Trio, Vol. 2* and *Songs: The Art of the Trio, Vol. 3.*

Mehldau also began making solo appearances, including one at the Lincoln Center Piano Masters solo program. In 1999 his first solo album *Elegiac Cycle* was released, and was regarded by some as his best work to date. Its mood-invoking pieces, composed by Mehldau, prompted *Time* to state that "Mehldau achieves an almost spiritual resonance" with his echoing chords. Also in 1999 Mehldau produced *Art of the Trio, Vol. 4: Back at the Village Vanguard.* On this album Mehldau does a jazz rendition of Radiohead's "Exit Music (For a Film)," a treatment he used on such other pieces as the McCartney-Lennon "Blackbird" and McCartney's "Junk."

In 2000 Mehldau produced *Places,* an album of originals that recounts musically places the trio had visited. The next year Mehldau cut another of his continuing series, *The Art of the Trio, Vol. 5: Progression,* in which the group combines swinging bebop with mood pieces. Mehldau had a change of pace in 2002 with the album *Largo,* which involved such classical orchestra instruments as oboes and French horns, and electronic instrumentation.

Mehldau rarely if ever plays a piece the same way twice, referring to his playing as "a work in progress." His improvisational ability has amazed audiences and reviewers alike. Having already created an impressive body of music, and still early in his career, most authorities believe his best work is still to come.

Christian McBride

Fast-Rising Star of Jazz Bass and Composition
1972–

Just make the music that's in your heart.
—Christian McBride
from an All About Jazz online interview

It would be difficult to find many musicians who have gone as far in jazz as quickly as bassist Christian McBride. Of course he had a good start, being descended from a line of bass players. He had his first professional job when he was thirteen, played with name musicians in New York City at seventeen, performed at Lincoln Center when he was nineteen, and led his own recording group in his early twenties. McBride was writing commissioned works and teaching by his mid-twenties. At thirty

McBride had achieved a preeminent position in jazz bass playing, carrying on the traditions of Milt Hinton, Charles Mingus, Ray Brown, and others.

McBride plays mostly mainstream jazz, but he has engaged in everything from classical to rock. He has played with fusion groups, but he has stated that his favorite music is rhythm and blues and traditional jazz. McBride has mastered both the electric and the acoustic bass, but the acoustic is his primary instrument. Plucking with fingers or bowing, McBride produces richly varnished melodious tones that have distinguished his playing among contemporary jazz artists.

Christian Lee McBride was born on May 31, 1972, in Philadelphia, Pennsylvania. His father and his great-uncle were both accomplished bassists. His father was a sideman with Philadelphia soul groups and Latin jazz bands, including Mongo Santamaria. His great uncle played progressive jazz, and he encouraged Christian's jazz studies. Christian started on electric bass at nine, and acoustic bass at eleven. His musical studies were mainly classical, but at thirteen he was playing local Philadelphia clubs. McBride qualified to attend Philadelphia's High School for the Creative and Performing Arts.

In high school McBride studied classical music and took lessons with a bassist from the Philadelphia Orchestra. He attended jazz workshops, at one of which he made a connection that became his springboard into professional jazz. That workshop was conducted by influential trumpeter Wynton Marsalis, who recognized McBride's potential. After graduation McBride toured Europe with the Philadelphia Youth Orchestra and played with a fusion group before heading for New York City and a scholarship with the Juilliard School.

At Juilliard, McBride studied classical music, but he was drawn into the jazz scene, Marsalis paving the way for the seventeen-year-old bassist. McBride was too good and the lure of jazz too strong for him to concentrate on classical studies, and within a year he left Juilliard. His first significant job was with saxophonist Bobby Watson's group, which featured trumpeter Roy

Hargrove. When Hargrove formed his own unit, he beckoned McBride. McBride spent brief periods with Hargrove and legendary trumpeter Freddie Hubbard, before the reigning master of jazz bass, Ray Brown, contacted him in 1991. Brown was forming a group called SuperBass and wanted McBride to be one of his several bassists. McBride joined Brown, and the next year *Rolling Stone* named McBride "Hot Jazz Artist" for 1992.

McBride played with guitarist Pat Metheny in 1993 before joining popular saxophonist Joshua Redman. A year later McBride made his first album as a leader, *Gettin' to It*, featuring both Hargrove and Redman. On one piece McBride engaged in a battle of basses with Milt Hinton and Ray Brown. About then Wynton Marsalis, artistic director of Jazz at Lincoln Center, offered McBride a commission, resulting in *Blues in Alphabet City*, premiered by McBride and the Lincoln Center Jazz Orchestra.

From the mid-1990s, McBride's production included *Number Two Express*, featuring pianist Chick Corea, and his 1997 release, *Fingerpainting: The Music of Herbie Hancock*. The next year McBride received a great challenge: a commission to write an extended piece for orchestra and a large gospel choir depicting the 1960 civil rights movement. McBride's work resulted in *The Movement Revisited*, which was presented at several concerts.

McBride's next work took a new turn with his 1998 release, *A Family Affair*, which found him returning partly to electric bass for a session of soul, funk, and rock mixed with jazz elements. Some of McBride's jazz audience were disappointed, but he felt the need to expand creatively. His next album, *Sci-Fi*, released in 2000, headed toward fusion.

Like many jazz artists, McBride became involved in jazz education. He has presided over jazz workshops and is involved with music programs at Aspen, Colorado, the University of Richmond, and the University of the Pacific. In playing, composing, and education Christian McBride has risen to a leadership role in finding new directions for jazz.

More Extraordinary People in Jazz

As with the main text of this book, the names included in this addendum are not exhaustive. They are meant to be a representation of the large body of outstanding musicians who have contributed to jazz. Space limitations cut short our listing of the hundreds of significant jazz artists that might well have been included, even as main entries.

Chet (Chesney Henry) Baker, a trumpet player with movie-star good looks, had a James Dean-like charisma that attracted audiences. He was a leader in developing the West Coast "cool" style of jazz, first becoming prominent in the 1950s as a part of Gerry Mulligan's "pianoless" quartet. His soft, romantic trumpet sound combined with a very high, sensitive singing voice made him a rage. Baker fell prey to drug use and lost some of his teeth in a drug-related incident, causing him to be out of music for a couple of years. Remarkably, he regained prominence, but on a trip to Europe he mysteriously fell from a hotel room window in Amsterdam and was killed. Chet Baker was born in Yale, Oklahoma, December 23, 1929, and died May 13, 1988.

Sidney Joseph Bechet was one of the early masters of jazz who, among other things, brought the soprano saxophone to prominence as a jazz instrument. He was, with Louis Armstrong, one of the first great soloists. He began on clarinet in New Orleans, before traveling to Chicago and joining a tour. In London in 1919 he bought a soprano saxophone, and it became his primary instrument. During the 1920s he played with major bands, including Duke Ellington, but the 1930s were tough years as swing became the craze. In 1949 Paris greeted him like a national hero, and he made his home there. Born, New Orleans, May 14, 1897; died, Paris, France, 1950 on his birthday.

Bix (Leon) Beiderbecke is largely regarded as the foremost white cornetist of the Roaring Twenties. Born and raised in Davenport, Iowa, he began playing piano at age three, but switched to cornet at fifteen. His parents sent him to Lake Forest Military Academy near Chicago in 1921, but young Beiderbecke sneaked off to play in local Chicago bands until he was expelled. His first important gig was with the Wolverines. In the mid-1920s Beiderbecke made some impressive recordings with Jean Goldkette and Frankie Trumbauer, then joined Paul Whiteman's famous orchestra in 1928. Beiderbecke's career was cut short due to alcoholism. Born March 10, 1903; died August 6, 1931.

Jimmy (James) Blanton broke the mold for bass players in the 1930s, combining a driving pulse rhythm for the band with an innovative solo technique. The standard he set influenced the elite bass players that followed. Blanton started out on violin while growing up in Chattanooga, Tennessee. He took up bass in college, and after moving to St. Louis in 1937 he played in Mississippi riverboat bands before joining Duke Ellington in 1939. Ellington allowed him to develop his bass style. Their bass-piano duets are acclaimed. Blanton also participated in some of the sessions at Minton's Playhouse in Harlem that evolved into bebop. He contracted tuberculosis in 1941 and died in 1942. Born, Chattanooga, Tennessee, October 5, 1918.

Dee Dee Bridgewater (Denise Garrett) has been a leading jazz singer since the 1970s despite career diversions. The daughter of a trumpet player, she sang with her father's band in Flint, Michigan. In 1970 she married trumpet player Cecil Bridgewater, but the marriage lasted only a few years. Bridgewater sang with the Thad Jones-Mel Lewis Orchestra (1972–74), and in 1975 won a Tony for her performance in the musical play *The Wiz*. She toured Europe with a review, *Sophisticated Ladies* in 1984, and in the 1980s appeared in *Lady Day*. She was acclaimed in the 1990s for her Horace Silver and Duke Ellington tributes. Born, Memphis, Tennessee, May 27, 1950.

Dave (David Warren) Brubeck, despite coming from a classical background, became one of the most popular jazz musicians of all time. He played a refined, cool type of jazz that often reflected classical influences. Raised in California, Brubeck graduated from the College of the Pacific in 1942. After serving in World War II, he studied with classical composer Darius Milhaud, and in 1951 he put together his classic jazz quartet with Johnny Desmond on alto saxophone. The quartet became the rage of college campuses, and two of their pieces, "Blue Rondo á La Turk" and "Take Five" became jazz classics. Desmond left in 1967 and was replaced by baritone saxophone player Gerry Mulligan. Brubeck worked his three sons into his group in 1972–74 before briefly retiring, but returned to perform and record into the twenty-first century. Born, Concord, California, December 6, 1920.

Big Sid (Sidney) Catlett was a drummer's drummer, not flashy, but with outstanding technical skills. He was a favorite of elite jazz bandleaders, including Louis Armstrong, who called Catlett his favorite drummer. He could play any style, moving effortlessly from traditional to swing to bebop. Catlett had his first professional gig in Chicago in 1928. He moved to New York City in 1930 and joined Louis Armstrong in 1938, staying until 1942, except for a stint with Benny Goodman. He rejoined the Armstrong All-Stars from 1947 to 1949. He played in the Chicago area until his death. Born, Evansville, Indiana, January 17, 1910; died, Chicago, March 25, 1951.

Roy "Little Jazz" (David) Eldridge, perhaps the preeminent swing trumpet player, is considered the stylistic link between traditional Louis Armstrong and bebopper Dizzy Gillespie. Eldridge played with top swing bands in the 1930s and 1940s and often led his own bands from the 1950s. He was acclaimed for his power, speed, and piercing high notes and was also accomplished on vocals, drums, and piano. Eldridge left his hometown, Pittsburgh, in 1930 and headed for New York, joining Fletcher Henderson in 1935. Some of his biggest hits came in 1941–42 while with the Gene Krupa band. In the 1950s Eldridge became a regular with Jazz at the Philharmonic. A stroke slowed him in 1980. Born January 30, 1911; died February 26, 1989.

Stan (Stanley) Getz was a premier tenor saxophonist of the pre-bop through post-bop periods, who created a distinctively light and delicate saxophone style. Getz was born in Philadelphia, but grew up in New York City, playing with Stan Kenton, Benny Goodman, and others before he was twenty. He gained fame with Woody Herman in 1947 on recordings of "Four Brothers" and "Early Autumn." His popularity soared in the early 1960s when he joined with guitarist Charlie Byrd and Brazilian stars to bring in the jazz-bossa nova era. His 1963 album *Getz/Gilberto* yielded "The Girl from Epanema" an all-time hit sung by his guitarist João Gilberto's wife, vocalist Astrid Gilberto. Getz taught at Stanford University from 1986, and played until contracting cancer. Born, Philadelphia, February 2, 1927; died June 6, 1991.

Dexter Keith Gordon was one of the foremost tenor saxophonists of the swing and bop eras. He had a powerful, rich tonal quality whether playing ballads or hot solos. Gordon joined the Lionel Hampton band in 1940, staying for three years. In 1944, he played with the Louis Armstrong and the Fletcher Henderson groups before joining Billy Eckstine's band in New York City. During the 1950s drug problems hampered him. He performed in Europe from 1962 until 1976. In 1986 he played the lead in a film, *'Round Midnight,* receiving an Academy Award nomination. Afterward his health deteriorated. Born, Los Angeles, February 27, 1923; died, Philadelphia, April 25, 1990.

Herbie (Herbert Jeffrey) Hancock, a diverse and successful composer-pianist-leader, who has divided his talent between acoustic jazz and electronic jazz and rock. Something of a prodigy, he played a Mozart piano concerto with the Chicago Symphony Orchestra at eleven. A Grinnell College (Iowa) music major, Hancock went to New York City in 1961 and in 1962 released his first album, *Takin' Off,* with its hit single "Watermelon Man." The next year he joined Miles Davis, and stayed for five years. In the 1970s, Hancock focused on funk, rock, and pop. In the late 1970s he toured with his V.S.O.P. all stars. Hancock composed the film score for *'Round Midnight,* winning a 1987 Oscar. Born, Chicago, April 12, 1940.

Fletcher Hamilton Henderson is largely recognized as a leader of big jazz bands whose arrangements inspired the swing era. A superb organizer, he led some of the top bands of the 1920s and 1930s. He studied classical piano in Georgia before traveling to New York City in 1920, where he produced records before forming his first jazz orchestra in 1924. By the late 1920s it was the country's foremost jazz band. In the 1930s Henderson sold arrangements of "King Porter Stomp," Blue Skies," and others to Benny Goodman, helping make him "King of Swing." He worked for Goodman in the 1930s and led groups in the 1940s, but a stroke in 1950 ended his career. Born, Cuthbert, Georgia, December 18, 1897; died, New York City, December 29, 1952.

Woody (Woodrow Charles) Herman, a successful big-band leader and clarinetist of the swing and bop eras, was noted for stocking ensembles with outstanding talent. Many of the top jazz names came through the Herman Herds, as his bands were called. His Herds from the 1940s played with great power, heat, and drive. His first unit in 1936 scored a solid hit with "Woodchopper's Ball." That group evolved into the (First) Herd in the mid-1940s and produced such spirited numbers as "Apple Honey" and "Caldonia." The Second Herd in 1947 was also called the Four Brothers band for its bebopping saxophone quartet. Herman formed one Herd after another, with continued success. He never did retire. Born, Milwaukee, May 16, 1913; died, Los Angeles, October 29, 1987.

Fatha (Earl Kenneth) Hines, who led star-studded bands from the 1920s to the 1960s, was renowned for his distinctive piano style, sometimes called "trumpet piano." Hines, in 1927, managed a Chicago nightclub and played in Louis Armstrong's band. In 1928 Hines formed a big band and moved into Chicago's

Grand Terrace Hotel for a twelve-year residency. He led big bands into the late 1940s. One of his groups, touted as the first bebop big band, included seminal boppers Charlie Parker and Dizzy Gillespie. Hines's career declined in the 1950s, but he made a comeback in 1964 with a series of concerts in New York. Born, Duquesne, Pennsylvania, December 28, 1903; died, Oakland, California, April 22, 1983.

J. J. (James Louis) Johnson, often called the best jazz trombone player ever, is thought to be the first to adapt the slide trombone to bebop. Johnson left Indiana and toured before joining the Benny Carter big band in 1942. He played the first Jazz at the Philharmonic concert in 1944, then joined Count Basie for 1945–46. He recorded with Miles Davis in the early 1950s, and in 1954–56 he co-led a quintet with trombonist peer Kai Winding. In 1959 his extended composition *El Camino Real* debuted. In the 1960s he toured with Miles Davis. By the 1970s Johnson was mostly composing. He retired from performing in 1997. Born, Indianapolis, January 22, 1924; died February 4, 2001.

Stan (Stanley Newcombe) Kenton was an innovative pianist leader who created distinctive large-ensemble music he called progressive jazz. His loud and rich sound often featured high screaming trumpets and solid, driving reeds playing original compositions. Kenton's 1941 gig at California's Balboa Beach Rendezvous Ballroom initiated his progressive mode with numbers like "Artistry in Rhythm" and "Intermission Riff." Through the 1940s his band mixed in swing numbers and vocals by singers, including Anita O'Day and June Christy. In the 1950s his Innovations in Modern Music Orchestra swelled to about forty pieces with strings, offering such extended works as *City of Glass.* Later he focused on workshops, spreading his musical gospel. Born, Wichita, Kansas, December 15, 1911; died, Los Angeles, August 25, 1979.

Lee Konitz, a distinguished alto and tenor saxophonist, plays a highly individual, cool bop style that sets him apart from Charlie Parker followers after the1940s. Konitz studied with pianist Lennie Tristano, and in the late 1940s played with the Claude Thornhill band. Around 1950 he joined the Miles Davis nonet that initiated cool jazz. Konitz played with Tristano and tenor man Warne Marsh in the 1950s, and periodically thereafter. In 1952–54 Konitz worked with the Stan Kenton orchestra. After that he led his own groups and toured Europe. In the 1970s he led his own nonet, and in 1992 won the Danish Jazzpar Prize. Born, Chicago, October 13, 1927.

Bobby McFerrin is a singer who takes jazz vocalizing in a new and original direction. Often without accompaniment, he sings in high and low keys, can vocalize breathing in or out, keeps time beating his chest, and sounds like multiple voices. McFerrin studied piano at the Juilliard School. After college he worked with vocalist Jon Hendricks. In the 1970s and early 1980s he toured with various artists, including Wynton Marsalis and Dizzy Gillespie. In the 1980s he started singing unaccompanied, and in the 1990s he formed an unaccompanied ensemble called Voicestra. McFerrin has conducted classical orchestras and recorded with cellist Yo-Yo Ma. Born, New York City, March 11, 1950.

Carmen McRae was inspired by Billie Holiday, but had her own distinctive vocal style. Like Holiday, however, she sounded as if she had lived every word she ever sang. In her prime she had a deep, rich voice and was an adept scat singer. During the 1940s she was married for a time to drummer Kenny Clarke, and began a long recording career. Her 1980s tribute albums to Billie Holiday and Thelonious Monk, *For Lady Day* and *Carmen Sings Monk,* are memorable, as is her duet album with Betty Carter, *Carmen McRae–Betty Carter Duets.* Health problems forced her to retire in the early 1990s. Born, New York City April 8, 1920; died, Beverly Hills, November 10, 1994.

Lee Morgan was a brilliant hard bop trumpet player who helped fill the void left by the death of Clifford Brown, until he was killed while in his prime. His big, rich tone, intricate phrasing, and blazing improvisations distinguished his work. Dizzy Gillespie hired him at eighteen, and two years later he joined Art Blakey and the Jazz Messengers. Morgan reached stardom with Blakey, cutting a number of albums including *1958-Paris Olympia*. Leaving Blakey in 1961, he recorded under his own name, producing several albums, including his top seller *The Sidewinder* (1963). His life ended abruptly when he was shot by a girlfriend. Born, Philadelphia, July 10, 1938; died, New York City, February 19, 1972.

Jelly Roll Morton (Ferdinand Joseph Lamothe) was a founding father of jazz, although he bragged that he alone invented jazz in 1902. Morton was a gifted pianist, composer, vocalist, and leader. He started piano at ten and in his teens was playing New Orleans' bordellos. He hit it big with recordings under the name Jelly Roll and his Red Hot Peppers in 1926–27. Among his famed numbers are "King Porter Stomp" and "Mr. Jelly Roll." When the 1930s big band craze took off, his fame faded. He performed in Washington, D.C., briefly, making oral history and solo piano recordings for the Library of Congress. In 1939 he became ill, but continued to record. Born, New Orleans, October 20, 1885 or 1890; died, Los Angeles, July 10, 1941.

Fats (Theodore) Navarro was a vital link in the modern trumpet heritage that passed from Roy Eldridge and Dizzy Gillespie to Clifford Brown, Lee Morgan, and others. Navarro had a big, brassy sound, was remarkably inventive, and played complex bop phrasings flawlessly. Navarro replaced Dizzy Gillespie in the Billy Eckstine big band in 1945. He later played with Kenny Clarke, Coleman Hawkins, Lionel Hampton, Benny Goodman, and others. He joined Tadd Dameron, 1947–1949, making acclaimed recordings for Blue Note. His drug habit, complicated by tuberculosis, ended his life. Born, Key West, Florida, September 24, 1923; died, New York City, July 7, 1950.

Joshua Redman, an outstanding saxophonist and one of the leading young lions of jazz, has honored current trends while keeping up with the past traditions. The son of distinguished jazz saxophonist Dewey Redman, he embraces bebop, funk, and avant-garde. A Harvard graduate, he was headed for Yale Law School when music won out. He won the saxophone award at the 1992 Thelonious Monk competition, and by 1993 he had his first recording as a leader. He has teamed with such top young jazzmen as bassist Christian McBride and drummer Brian Blade. Born, Berkeley, California, February 1, 1969.

Sonny (Theodore Walter) Rollins, a giant of the tenor saxophone, reflects the influence of Coleman Hawkins, Charlie Parker, and Dexter Gordon while advancing modern jazz. He is considered the major tenor between Parker and John Coltrane. At seventeen he made his first record, and by the early 1950s he had played with Thelonious Monk, Bud Powell, Art Blakey, and Miles Davis. He joined the Max Roach-Clifford Brown quintet in 1955–57, and began recording under his name. His *Saxophone Colossus* of 1956 was acclaimed. During the 1960s he toured Europe, delved into avant-garde jazz, and composed music for the film *Alfie*. From 1972 he explored a pop-oriented style, but remains a master of jazz saxophone. Born, New York City, September 7, 1930.

Horace Martin Tavares Silver, a hard-driving pianist, was a force in the creation of hard bop, which includes elements of funk, gospel, and rhythm and blues. His Portuguese father's folk music from the Cape Verde Islands was an early influence. He joined Stan Getz 1950–1951, and in 1953 he and Art Blakey created the Jazz Messengers. Silver left the Messengers in the mid-1950s to form his own quintet and recorded for Blue Note for over twenty-eight years. His albums include *Blowin' the Blues Away* and *Song for My Father*. His other major works include "The Preacher," "Doodlin'," and "Opus de Funk." Born, Norwalk, Connecticut, September 2, 1928.

Bessie Smith, "The Empress of the Blues," was one of the earliest significant blues singers, and the prototype of those who followed. With her bell-like, slightly raspy voice she belted out the blues lyrics of pain, suffering, and joy. Raised in poverty in Tennessee, Smith learned to sing blues from an earlier master, Ma Rainey, and by 1920 had her own show in Atlanta. She settled in New York City in 1923 with a record contract and a soaring career. Touted as the country's top-earning black entertainer, she toured in a custom-made railroad car. Her hits included "St. Louis Blues," "Jail-House Blues," and "After

You've Gone." Smith's career declined in the 1930s, and she died in a car accident in 1937. Born, Chattanooga, Tennessee, April 15, 1894; died, Clarksdale, Mississippi, September 26, 1937.

Billy (William) Strayhorn, a pianist, composer, and arranger, spent almost his entire career as a collaborator and close associate of Duke Ellington. It was difficult to tell one's work from the other. Ellington hired Strayhorn in 1939. Strayhorn composed "Lush Life," "Take the 'A' Train," "Chelsea Bridge," "Passion Flower," and "Rain Check." Strayhorn also collaborated with Ellington on longer works, including *A Drum Is a Woman, The Perfume Suite, Such Sweet Thunder,* and *The Far East Suite.* Strayhorn, nicknamed "Swee' pea" by Ellington, was diagnosed with cancer in the late 1950s. Born, Dayton, Ohio, November 29, 1915; died, New York City, May 31, 1967.

Mel (Melvin Howard) Tormé, a multitalented musician, was famous as a singer, but was also a composer, arranger, pianist, and drummer. In the 1940s he was a romantic ballad singer dubbed the "Velvet Fog," for his smooth, husky-voiced vocals. Later he was an award-winning jazz singer noted for scat. By 1944 Tormé led his own vocal group the Mel-Tones. After military service he was mostly a solo act, going strong as jazz singer until his stroke in 1996. Among Tormé's hit compositions are "The Christmas Song," "Stranger in Town," and "Mountain Greenery." He acted in films and wrote an autobiography, *It Wasn't All Velvet,* and other books. Born, Chicago, September 13, 1925; died, Los Angeles, June 5, 1999.

Chucho Valdes, son of the famed Cuban jazz pianist Bebo Valdes, ranks among the leaders in Afro-Cuban and Latin Jazz. A composer, leader, and pianist, he is noted for his spectacular, high-speed rhythmic flights on the keyboard. In 1967 he helped form the Orquesta Cubana de Musica Moderna, and in 1973 the jazz group Irakere. Valdes remains based in Cuba, but exports his music through tours and recordings for Blue Note Records. In 1980 he organized the Havana International Jazz Festival, which has grown steadily. He appeared with his father in the 2000 film *Calle 54.* Born, Quivicán, Cuba, October 9, 1941.

Fats (Thomas Wright) Waller was one of the all-time great jazz pianists, composers, and leaders. His influence resonates in jazz to the present day. Waller's skill as a stride school pianist and serious musician was masked by his clowning, but he truly loved the limelight. Waller was playing clubs and recording in the 1920s, during which he wrote jazz standards, including "Ain't Misbehavin'," "Honeysuckle Rose," and "Black and Blue." His 1930s hits included "Your Feet's Too Big." Waller wrote for Broadway reviews and acted in films. In London he recorded his extensive *London Suite*. In 1943 Waller became ill and died in Kansas City while on a train to New York. Born, New York City, May 21, 1904; died, Kansas City, Missouri, December 14, 1943.

Dinah Washington (Ruth Lee Jones) is among the great jazz singers who also became a pop star. When she sang jazz in her blues-gospel voice, few could surpass her. In 1943 she joined the Lionel Hampton band, and her recording of "Evil Gal Blues" became a hit. By 1946 she was a single act, and her career accelerated through the mid-1950s. Her hits included "Look to the Rainbow" and "Love for Sale," and jazz stars often backed her. Then in 1959 her "What a Diffirence a Day Makes" became a pop hit, and she became a pop star. Her personal life was tragic, however, and she died at thirty-nine from a drug overdose. Born, Tuscaloosa, Alabama, August 29, 1924; died, Detroit, December 14, 1963.

Chick (William Henry) Webb, a drummer whose big band was a fixture at Harlem's Savoy Ballroom in the 1930s, helped lead the way into the swing era. Chick Webb succeeded despite a hunch-backed, dwarflike body. His drum sets had to be custom made to fit his small size. At the Savoy, Webb was famous for challenging big bands to "battles of the bands." Most famous was his encounter with Benny Goodman's band. Webb gave young Ella Fitzgerald her big break and with Fitzgerald had his only hit record, "A-Tisket A-Tasket." In the late 1930s, Webb's health began to fail, and he died after surgery. Born, Baltimore, February 10, 1909; died June 16, 1939.

Glossary

acid jazz—A jazz offshoot that evolved in Britain in the 1980s. It includes a mixture of fusion, funk, and soul that was introduced by electronically oriented jazz groups of the 1960s and 1970s.

Afro–Cuban—Musical style that mixed Cuban rhythms with jazz. Largely popularized after World War II by Dizzy Gillespie, Manchito, and others.

atonal—Music that lacks a tonal center, and thus may sound harsh and discordant to listeners.

avant-garde—Generally any music that is leading the change from what has become standardized. In jazz also refers to groups that progressed from standard bebop into less-structured forms beginning in the late 1950s and 1960s. Overlaps with free jazz. (See also *free jazz*.)

bebop or bop—Now considered a classic jazz form from which all other more advanced forms emerged. In the early to mid-1940s it broke from big band swing to establish a small group style emphasizing improvisation based on chords rather than melody and more complex polyrhythms. Early proponents were Dizzy Gillespie, Charlie Parker, Thelonious Monk, and Kenny Clarke, among others.

Big band—Closely associated with the swing movement, big bands evolved out of the 1920s and reigned as the popular music standard until replaced by small bebop groups in the mid to late-1940s. Big bands, sometimes called orchestras, largely played dance music and usually included around sixteen to eighteen pieces (four or five reeds, five or more brass, four or more rhythm, and often a male and/or female singer).

blues—A musical form that evolved from early African American folk songs that gave rise to jazz. It exists today as a separate musical style emphasizing vocal music.

boogie woogie—Largely a piano style that began in the 1920s and is characterized by a repetitive left-hand bass (often eight beats to the bar), while the right hand plays melodies or improvises. It was adapted to big band and voice, but lost popularity in the 1940s.

changes—Also, chord progressions or chord changes. The pattern or changes serve as the structure for improvisation.

charts—Music that is written down by an arranger for the different band pieces and sections.

chord—A fundamental part of harmony, usually comprised of three or more notes played together.

classic—In jazz, the term often applied to the music that became popular in the 1920s, such as New Orleans or Dixieland jazz. Broadly, it is refers to the original or standard of any style, such as bebop, or the most typical work of an artist. Someone might refer to a work by Dizzy Gillespie as "that's classic Diz."

cool jazz—A style of jazz directly descended from bebop. It is softer toned, less hot, and has an understated and sometimes a rather detached quality. Popularized in the 1950s mainly by Miles Davis. (See also *West Coast Jazz*.)

cut—Has several meanings. One is simply: to make a recording. Or it can mean a section of a recording. Another refers to the practice of "cutting" or trying to outplay, or "cut," another musician.

discordant—Is sound that is out of harmony, generally caused by a clashing of tones that are played together and produce a harsher, perhaps grating music.

double quartet—Two quartets, each playing the same instruments.

dub and overdub—Dubbing is usually the process of inserting a new sound into recorded material. Overdubbing is adding material, like a trumpet solo over a previously recorded rhythm section or a solo voice over a string background.

free jazz—Is sometimes used synonymously with avant-garde, although authorities commonly distinguish between the two, allowing that avant-garde embraces some structure, while free jazz may be totally unstructured.

funk—In jazz, a bluesy kind of music that blends in the heavy beat and soulfulness of gospel. Evolved in the early 1950s and is reflected in the rock music of James Brown and others.

fusion—Basically the adaptation of rock rhythms and electric and electronic instruments to jazz. Popularized by Miles Davis beginning in the late 1960s. Sometimes called jazz-rock, although that term can be defined as jazz-tinged rock music.

gig—Generally, a job. Musicians refer to any kind of playing date as a gig, but a day gig may mean a nonplaying job.

hard bop—Often described as a reaction to the cool jazz school, hard bop is more energetic and heavily rhythmic. Incorporating elements of blues, soul, and funk with bebop, it took off in the mid-1950s, led by Art Blakey, Horace Silver, and others.

harmonics—Has various meanings but in jazz often means producing sounds at a higher or lower pitch by techniques such as (in reeds) overblowing. Creates unusual effects.

harmony—A combination of notes played together to form a chord. Commonly, harmony is a combination of sounds blended together in a pleasing way.

hot—Refers most often to loud, lively playing with a heavy rhythmic beat. More commonly used in the early days of jazz.

improvisation—Making up the music, usually during a solo, without following written music. Written arrangements usually allow for improvised solos.

Improvisation is said to be the very essence of jazz, although much jazz is also written down.

jam/jam session—Jamming is when musicians get together informally and play for themselves. Historically, this happened in clubs where musicians gathered after regular gigs to play for fun and camaraderie. Such jam sessions are less common today.

jive—Once referred to a kind of swing-type dance and music, but now more commonly refers to untruthful or exaggerated statements. A person who is jivin' is not to be trusted. Also a type of humorous jazz talk or lyrics laced with catchy made-up words.

jump/jump band—A type of swinging blues music that preceded rhythm and blues. Becoming popular in the 1940s, was usually played in small groups (Louis Jordan and his Tympany Five) that included driving rhythm behind a honking horn and often comical lyrics. Saw a revival in the late 1990s.

Latin jazz—Any of the Latin American popular musical styles that are jazz-based or include jazz elements, such as the Brazilian bossa nova and Afro-Cuban, a term sometimes used for Latin jazz. The term sometimes refers to jazz with Latin rhythms or themes played by American bands.

LP—A phonograph record designed to be played at $33\frac{1}{3}$ revolutions per minute.

mainstream—In jazz, originally referred to swing musicians playing in small groups in the 1950s, who stuck basically to their swing style while resisting the strong influence of bebop. Later, bebop and its offshoots became mainstream relative to avant-garde and free jazz.

modal jazz—Indicates improvisation on the modal scales (derived from ancient seven-note scales). Allows the musician to improvise on a few or even one chord as opposed to the many chord improvisations of bebop and the melodic improvisations of swing. Exemplified by the work of Miles Davis and John Coltrane in the 1960s.

modern jazz—Came into popular use in the late 1940s and 1950s to cover the breakaway jazz styles of bebop and its offshoots and such jazz orchestrations as those of Stan Kenton.

New Orleans jazz—The music originating in New Orleans that gave rise to the entire jazz movement. Groups can be roughly six to eight pieces and usually includes cornet, trombone, clarinet, and rhythm section of piano, drums, banjo, and a tuba or bass.

orchestra—See *big band*.

polyrhythm—Is the use of two or more rhythms playing simultaneously. Polyrhythms in jazz date back to the early days of New Orleans jazz and evolved widely, especially with the introduction of Latin jazz and the more rhythmically complex bebop, progressive, and free jazz.

overdub—See *dub*.

progressive jazz—A term used by Stan Kenton in the late 1940s to describe his advanced large orchestra jazz, which featured longer, largely composed pieces. The term came to cover various aspects of cool jazz and West Coast jazz as exemplified by Dave Bruebeck and the Modern Jazz Quartet.

ragtime—an early jazz root that was popular from around 1900 to the mid-teens. Characterized by a syncopated, bouncy rhythm, it was often played on solo piano, but also could have rhythmic accompaniment. Ragtime tunes were often called rags, such as "Maple Leaf Rag" or "Harlem Rag."

rhythm and blues (R&B)—An outgrowth of jump music, which was an outgrowth of swing. R&B is heavily black-oriented with strong emphasis on horns and vocals, including group vocals.

riff—A repeated instrumental phrase that forms the basis of a musical piece and presents a take-off point for improvising soloists. They can be two to four bars in length.

salsa—A type of Latin dance music that developed in the 1970s, which is tinged with jazz and elements of Afro-Cuban rhythms. The term has come to be generally used to cover all forms of Latin music.

scat—A style of jazz singing in which the vocalist improvises like a jazz instrumentalist, using a vocabulary of nonwords (e.g., shuby doo duby du bah) to imitate the notes that would be played on an instrument.

soul—A type of jazz that evolved from hard bop. Mixing doses of gospel, blues, and funk, it became a popular jazz form of the 1960s and evolved into black popular music. Gave rise to such organ-based combos as that of Jimmy Smith.

standards—Usually songs written by the great composers of American popular music, such as Irving Berlin, George and Ira Gershwin, Cole Porter, Duke Ellington, and Richard Rogers, that have endured as favorites of the American public. Those songs are a permanent part of jazz repertoire.

studio bands or musicians—Are hired to play for studio recordings and do not necessarily play together in clubs or concerts. Similar to session musicians, who play in theaters, on radio and TV, and on film soundtracks.

swing—Is the name given the era of big-band music that lasted from the 1930s through the mid to late-1940s. It is exemplified by such bands as Benny Goodman, Count Basie, Woody Herman, Glen Miller, Chick Webb, and others. Musicians playing exceptionally well in an upbeat tempo are said to be swinging. Swing dancing is performed to the music.

third stream—Essentially refers to a fusion of jazz and classical music. A chief proponent and inventor of the term was classical composer Gunther Schuller. The movement never took off, but continues to have a niche in jazz.

vibrato—The vibrating or pulsing of a single note by an instrumentalist or a singer. Also called a tremolo.

West Coast jazz—The West Coast has a long history of jazz, but West Coast jazz is commonly the term applied to the extension of the cool jazz movement centered on the coast and led by Chet Baker, Gerry Mulligan, Dave Brubeck, and others

To Find Out More

There are hundreds more jazz musicians who might have been included in this book except for the space limitations. The sources that follow detail their contributions to jazz and provide a guide for further explorations into the world of jazz.

GENERAL REFERENCE BOOKS

Carr, Ian; Fairweather, Digby; and Priestley, Brian. *Jazz: The Rough Guide,* 2nd ed. London: Rough Guides Ltd., 2000.

Eriewine, Michael, executive editor. *All Music Guide to Jazz,* 3rd ed. San Francisco: Miller Freeman Books, 1998.

Feather, Leonard and Gitler, Ira. *The Biographical Encyclopedia of Jazz.* New York: Oxford University Press, 1998.

Kirchner, Bill, ed. *The Oxford Companion to Jazz.* New York: Oxford University Press, 2000.

Lee, Jeanne. *Jam! The Story of Jazz.* New York: Rosen, 1999.

Weatherford, Carole, Boston. *The Sound that Jazz Makes.* New York: Wilkes and Co., 2000.

OTHER JAZZ READING (SELECTED BIOGRAPHICAL WORKS)

Louis Armstrong
Armstrong, Louis. *Louis Armstrong: A Self Portrait.* New York: Eakins Press, 1971.
Travis, Dempsey. *The Louis Armstrong Odyssey.* Chicago: Urban Research Press, 1997.

Count Basie
Basie, Count. *Good Morning Blues: The Autobiography of Count Basie.* New York: Da Capo Press, 1995.

John Coltrane

Kofsky, Frank. *John Coltrane and the Jazz Revolution of the 1960s.* New York: Pathfinder, 1998.

Selfridge, John. *John Coltrane: A Sound Supreme.* New York: Franklin Watts, 1999.

Miles Davis

Davis, Miles. *Miles: The Autobiography.* New York: Simon and Schuster, 1990.

Szwed, John F. *So What: The Life of Miles Davis.* New York: Simon and Schuster, 2002.

Duke Ellington

Ellington, Edward Kennedy. *Music is My Mistress.* New York: Da Capo Press, 1976.

Nicholson, Stuart. *Reminiscing in Tempo: A Portrait of Duke Ellington.* Boston: Northeastern University Press, 1999.

Ella Fitzgerald

Nicholson, Stuart. *Ella Fitzgerald: A Biography of the First Lady of Jazz.* New York: Da Capo Press, 1995.

Dizzy Gillespie

Gillespie, Dizzy. *Dizzy: To Be or Not to Bop.* New York: Oxford University Press, 1980.

Benny Goodman

Collier, James Lincoln. *Benny Goodman and the Swing Era.* New York: Oxford University Press, 1989.

Wynton Marsalis

Marsalis, Wynton. *Jazz in the Bittersweet Blues of Life.* Cambridge, Ma.: Da Capo Press.

Charles Mingus

Mingus, Charles. *Beneath the Underdog: His World as Composed by Mingus.* New York: Vintage Books, 1991.

Thelonious Monk

De Wilde, Laurent. *Monk.* New York: Marlowe and Co., 1997.

Charlie Parker

Parker, Charlie. *My Life in E Flat.* Columbia: University of South Carolina Press, 1999.

THE JAZZ STORY ON VIDEOCASETTE, DVD, COMPACT DISC

Blues and Swing. New York: CMV Enterprises and Wynton Marsalis, 1988. (video-casette)

Jazz. Washington D.C.: PBS DVD (produced by Ken Burns), 2000. (DVD and videotape)

Ken Burns Jazz: The Story of America's Music. New York: Sony Music Entertainment, 2000. (compact disc)

Sound of Jazz. Music Video Distribution. (1957 live TV show), 2003 (DVD)

The Story of Jazz. BMG Video, 1991 and 2002 (DVD and videotape)

ONLINE SITES FOR JAZZ

All About Jazz
www.allaboutjazz.com
Extensive profile list and links to all phases of jazz; good material for beginners.

British Broadcasting Company
www.bbc.co.uk/music/profiles
Concise profiles of prominent jazz artists, some with sound clips.

Down Beat
www.downbeat.com
Coverage of the jazz score of today and yesterday; extensive biographical and historical coverage with many links.

Jazz at Lincoln Center
www.jazzatlincolncenter.org/jazz
Educational coverage of traditional and modern jazz; extensive sound components.

National Public Radio
www.nprjazz.org/programs/
In-depth interviews of artists with sound clips, tapes, and transcripts available.

Smithsonian Jazz
www.smithsonianjazz.org
Emphasis on the roots of jazz and interactive jazz instruction.

JAZZ ORGANIZATIONS

International Association for Jazz Education
PO Box 724, Manhattan, Ks 66505
(785) 776-8744
E-mail: info@iaje.org
www.iaje.org/default.asp

Jazz Institute of Chicago
410 S. Michigan Ave., Chicago, Il 60605
(312) 427-1684
www.jazzintituteofchicago.org

Los Angeles Jazz Society
PMB 176, PO Box 4172, Woodland Hills, Ca 91365-4172
E-mail: information@lajazzsociety.org

SELECTED DISCOGRAPHY

This listing is a sampling of classic jazz albums by leading jazz musicians of the past and present. These albums were chosen, for the most part, because they represent the artists and music that reflect turning points in the history of jazz, resulting in movements into new styles and forms.

Louis Armstrong
100 Years of Louis Armstrong (Delta)

Art Blakey
A Night at Birdland, Volumes 1–2 (Blue Note)

Clifford Brown and Max Roach
In Concert-Clifford Brown/Max Roach (GNP/Crescendo)

John Coltrane
My Favorite Things (Atlantic)
A Love Supreme (Impulse)

Charlie Christian
The Genius of the Electric Guitar (Columbia)

Ornette Coleman
The Shape of Jazz to Come (Atlantic)

Miles Davis
Birth of the Cool (Capitol)
Kind of Blue (Columbia)

Duke Ellington
The Carnegie Hall Concerts (January 1943) (Prestige)
Ellington at Newport (Columbia)

Bill Evans
Sunday at the Village Vanguard (Original Jazz Classics)

Dizzy Gillespie
Groovin' High (Savoy)

Benny Goodman
Benny Goodman Carnegie Hall Concert (Columbia)

Billie Holiday
Lady Day—The Best of Billie Holiday (Columbia)

Charles Mingus
Mingus Ah Um (Columbia)

Charlie Parker
Yardbird Suite: The Ultimate Collection (Rhino)
Jazz at Massey Hall (Original Jazz Classics)

Bud Powell
The Amazing Bud Powell, Volumes 1–3 (Blue Note)

Art Tatum
Piano Starts Here (Columbia)

Index

Numbers in *italics* represent illustrations.

Photo Credits

Photographs © 2004: AP/Wide World Photos: back cover bottom left, 254 (Jim Cooper), cover bottom left, back cover bottom right, back cover left center, 12, 25, 30, 35, 40, 44, 80, 103, 187 (Bettmann), cover top left, 1, 65, 85 (Terry Cryer), cover center, 177, 220, 243 (Lynn Goldsmith), 58 (Hulton-Deutsch Collection), 201 (Craig Lovell), back cover top right, 95, 141, 143, 148, 153, 171, 204, 208, 211 (Mosaic Images), 214 (Roger Ressmeyer), 61 (Derick A. Thomas; Dat's Jazz), 162 (Underwood & Underwood), 119 (Ted Williams); Getty Images: 54 (Agence France Presse), 73 (Frank Driggs Collection), back cover right center, 248 (Gary Hershorn/Reuters), cover bottom right, 109 (Herman Leonard), 198 (Metronome), 99, 106, 115 (Bob Parent), 50 (Charles Peterson), 157 (Pictorial Parade); Hulton|Archive/Getty Images: 127, 135; Redferns Music Picture Library: 236 (Stuart Nicholson), 123, 191 (Andrew Putler), cover right center, back cover top left, 130, 138, 144, 167, 195, 217, 223, 226, 230, 233, 239, 251 (David Redfern); William P. Gottlieb/From the Library of Congress Collection: cover top right, 18, 68, 76, 90, 18.

Copyright extends to corresponding image on Contents page.

About the Author

Marvin Martin was born in South Bend, Indiana, but did most of his growing up in Chicago during the Great Depression and World War II. The airwaves then were saturated with the swing, jazz, and blues that shaped his musical interests. After graduation from a public high school, he spent two years in the military. He received a B.A. in English from Roosevelt University.

Martin then went on to work in an editorial position for World Book Encyclopedia and Encyclopedia Britannica. After retiring, he began a writing career, contributing education articles to the *Chicago Tribune* and other publications. He is also the publications co-editor for the Rochelle Lee Fund, a non-profit educational organization in Chicago. In 1996 Franklin Watts published his first book, *The Beatles: Music Was Never The Same.* That company also published his second book, *Arthur Ashe: Of Tennis and the Human Spirit* in 1999.